NEVER ANSWER
TO A WHISTLE

Published by Griffin Publishing UK Limited

Paperback ISBN-13: 978-1-9162053-0-7
Hardback ISBN-13: 978-1-9162053-1-4
.epub eBook ISBN-13: 978-1-9162053-2-1
.mobi eBook ISBN-13: 978-1-9162053-3-8

This book is memoir. It reflects the author's present recollections of experiences over time. Some names and characteristics have been changed, some events have been compressed, and some dialogue has been recreated.

For permission requests, please contact: mike.h@griffinpublishinguk.co.uk

Find out more about the author and upcoming books online at:

www.griffinpublishinguk.co.uk

Facebook: /mike.howard.777158
Instagram: /michael_thepilot
Twitter: @Mike_ThePilot

Produced in the United Kingdom

Editorial services by www.bookeditingservices.co.uk

Cover and layout design by www.spiffingcovers.com

NEVER ANSWER
TO A WHISTLE

MICHAEL HOWARD

GRIFFIN
PUBLISHING

CONTENTS

DEDICATION

This book is dedicated to my Mum, Lynn and my Father, Roy. I wish they could be here to see this story in print.

I also dedicate this to Heather, my lovely wife. Heather persuaded me to leave the story that I was working on and write the true story. This was on the basis that it was a fascinating, incredible true story that would make an amazing read (and be a bit easier to sell as it is a true story and I am an unknown author).

Also, my wonderful sister Jenny, for her help with the editing/ proofreading and also helping with the cost of self-publishing (not a cheap exercise!). Jenny, Heather and I funded this between the three of us.

Also, a huge thankyou to all my 'Test Readers' who have read the manuscript during the writing process and given honest feedback as to whether or not it is any good!! John, Lorna, Carole, Bob, Rob and Kim – thank you all for your huge support and encouragement.

Lastly, my lovely daughter Victoria who has faced some very tough challenges and shown great fortitude and strength of mind to overcome them all – chip off the old block?? Victoria now has a degree and started a career. I am immensely proud of her.

PROLOGUE

Lagos Airport, Nigeria
Saturday, 19 May 1984 – 17:45 hrs

I noticed the veins on my hands standing out as I advanced the thrust levers on the Hawker Siddeley 125 executive jet. It moved forward slowly from its parking spot in Ikeja, Lagos, Nigeria. I felt remarkably calm, considering what I was about to do: break just about every rule and regulation in the aviation rule book.

Ikeja is the 'general aviation' part of Lagos International Airport in Nigeria officially known as Murtala Muhammed International Airport but as this is a bit of a mouthful, we will stick to Lagos International! Lagos airport is around the size of Gatwick and just as busy, both with domestic and international flights.

It was early evening, the orangey red sun still visible and shimmering in the dusty heat on the African horizon. The area around me was filled with a wide range of aircraft, from Hawker Siddeley 125 executive jets to small twin-engined, turboprop aircraft involved in oil support operations further down the coast.

This Hawker Siddeley 125 (from now on I'll refer to as H125) was registered as 'G-LORI'.

The HS125 executive jet was designed by the British company de Havilland. It could carry up to nine passengers in armchair comfort, with two pilots flying the aeroplane.

Powered by two Rolls-Royce 'Viper' engines producing 3,500 lbs of thrust per engine, it could fly to an altitude of 41,000 feet and had a range of around 2,000 nautical miles. The HS125 was 'a pilot's aeroplane'; an absolute delight to fly. It could be flown by just resting your fingers on its 'ram's horn', upside down V-shaped control column that sat in front of the captain and first officer.

The HS125. This one was registered G-FFLT. It was the '600 series'. It was converted into an "Air Ambulance" by Fairflight Charters of Biggin Hill.

I had a 'Double Engine Failure' in this one and glided it into Gatwick on way back from Kos Island in Greece.

Photo courtesy of Pedro Aragão. Taken in Faro, 1991

As G-LORI moved forward, pushed by the thrust of the two jet engines bolted on the rear, I lifted my hand and waved to Ken Clark and Angus Patterson. Ken and Angus were my engineer friends; they had helped to prepare the aircraft for this flight. Ken and Angus moved back to allow the aircraft to turn as it headed towards Runway 19L (pronounced 'One Nine Left' in aviation lingo), one of the two main runways at Lagos International Airport. The main airport terminal was visible in the haze with floodlights flickering in the blistering heat of the late African afternoon.

The terminal buildings sit between the two main runways, rather like Terminals 1, 2 and 3 sit between the main runways at Heathrow Airport.

I had selected both VHF comms (communications) radios into my headphones, so I could hear both Lagos tower and Lagos approach radar air traffic controllers, which allowed me to assess the inbound air traffic. I was looking for a decent gap, large enough between the landing aircraft to line up and take off safely. This was because what I was about to do was pretty well *the most* illegal thing you could do as a professional pilot, let alone at an international airport, with a jet aeroplane: namely, taking off without permission or filing any sort of flight plan! How the hell did this guy get himself into this situation, you might be wondering. I will endeavour to fully explain, but first I'm a bit busy getting this aeroplane into the air safely.

I stopped the aeroplane about 50 yards from Runway 19L and set the parking brake. This position allowed me to look up the approach to see the aircraft on 'final approach' to land on runway 19L.

As I said, Lagos airport was nearly as busy as Gatwick, and as I looked up the approach I could see the landing lights of a number of aircraft flying down towards the runway. Waiting patiently, listening to both the tower and approach frequencies, I was assessing and analysing the gap between the approaching aircraft. After a period of time, a gap appeared as a slower aircraft joined the queue to land. The adrenaline in my system was high and I was sweating in the near 30 degrees – the aircraft's air conditioning was struggling to control the cabin temperature. All of this added to the high level of anticipation, but strangely I felt very, very calm.

I looked to my right. Sitting in the co-pilot seat was my girlfriend, Catriona Spalding.

Catriona had never flown an aeroplane, nor had she a pilot's licence. In fact, this was the first time she had sat in a pilots seat. What I had done was to get her a Flight Radiotelephony Operators Licence – an RT Licence. This was obtained after calling in a big favour from a good friend, Ivan Palmer. Ivan 'owed me' for a lot of help acquiring his pilot's licence years before. The RT Licence was the minimum qualification to sit in the co-pilot's seat of a jet such as the HS125. Catriona looked at me with nervous anticipation.

'We are going to take off very shortly, Catriona.' I sounded calm and reassuring. 'We will be okay, don't worry.' I might have spoken a bit soon about that!

Why had I taken my girlfriend on a flight such as this? A lot of my pilot friends were rather pissed off that it was Catriona and not one of them on this trip, but I will explain everything a little later.

As a jet airline aircraft, a Boeing 737 landed ahead of the slower aircraft, I inched the HS125 out onto the runway and lined up on the centre line and waited the short time needed for the aircraft to move off the runway. I watched the 737 begin to follow the curved line, which marked the way off the runway onto the adjacent taxiway, leaving the runway clear for the next landing aircraft.

The runway was more than 200 feet wide and made of black tarmac with a patchwork of dark grey squares where it had been repaired from time to time. There was a dotted line of white paint down the runway centreline just to the side of white flush lights that marked the middle of the runway for night flying. The white line and the runway perspective narrowing into the hazy distance, formed an arrow that pointed towards the anti-aircraft guns sited at the end. The guns were always a mystery to me. The army manned these guns, presumably to shoot down any airliner that had not paid their landing fees.

I listened as air traffic control cleared the slower aircraft to land as the preceding aircraft left the runway.

A moment later, the landing aircraft's pilot, who could now see G-LORI on the runway ahead of him, began squawking in a deep, resonating African lilt 'There is an aircraft on the runway! There is an aircraft on the runway! How can you clear me to land? What are you doin'? What is goin' on?'

At that stage, I slid the thrust levers forward, advancing them to full take-off power. The HS125 leapt forward with massive acceleration. Two Rolls-Royce Viper jet engines screamed as they reached maximum power. With only fuel and two people on board, the acceleration was breathtaking.

In my periphery vision, the lights at the edge of the runway flashed into a blur as the speed increased to 60 mph in a few seconds.

I could still hear the captain of the landing aircraft protesting away, accusing the air traffic controller of all sorts of incompetence and stupidity.

A few more seconds passed and G-LORI reached 100 miles an hours. At this point it was not possible to stop; I was just reaching 'V1 speed'. This is the speed after which, if you close the thrust levers and apply the brakes, you cannot stop on the runway and will go off the end – 'going gardening' as it is colloquially known. In aviation, V1 is the 'decision speed'. In other words, it is the 'go' speed if you have an engine failure or similar. Some of us who had worked in Nigeria for a long time had some T-shirts made with the words 'Happiness is V1 Lagos!' printed on them.

It was around that V1 speed that I heard the radar controller transmit:

'Tiger One Two, Tiger One Two, *your target* is taking off from Runway One Nine Left. Intercept immediately!'

When I heard this, I uttered the most common word that is heard on a cockpit voice recorder just before an impact: 'SHIT!'

Your target? Your fucking target? I had no idea what was behind this completely unexpected turn of events, but those words by the radar controller brought an instant realisation that somehow I had been duped.

This was Saturday night in Africa. Even in Europe, if you started a major war on a Saturday morning nothing much would happen until the army and air force got back to work on Monday morning!

The fact that a fighter (I guessed probably an Alpha Jet) was airborne *waiting for me* was an indication of some sort of major Nigerian skulduggery.

The Nigerian Air Force had things like Hercules transport aircraft, some MIG Russian fighters (a bit too powerful for your average

Nigerian Air Force pilot) and some Alpha Jets – two-seater, ground attack/air combat training aircraft. These were still formidable equipment and the training pilots were 'shit-hot'.

The calmness that I felt at the beginning of the flight was still there. I did not react to what was happening other than to begin applying (my very limited) strategies to counter the threat. I was surprised at my lack of anxious reaction to what was occurring.

I glanced over towards Catriona, who had her head firmly between her knees. I rather wished I could do the same!

Having flown from Lagos for many years, I was well aware that there were anti-aircraft guns at the end of both runways. Lagos was, as well as being an international airport, also the main base of the Nigerian Air Force. As I said earlier, previously I had regarded these as a bit of a joke. In past whilst taking off from Lagos, I had seen the gun crew lying about sleeping in the sun.

However, the fact that there was an interceptor airborne waiting to (presumably) shoot me down, meant these anti-aircraft guns and crew immediately became a serious potential risk. Today they could not be regarded as a bit of fun, I had to assume they were on a state of high alert.

Whilst steering the aircraft down the centre of the runway, I began making an assessment in those few seconds. G-LORI was a civilian executive jet capable of around 450 mph; the Alpha Jet however, is a military fighter capable of speeds up to 620 mph. I thought all this through very, very quickly and had to make major changes to the original plan. The Alpha Jet had presumably been holding to the north-east of Lagos, 15 miles away, and could catch me up within minutes.

The fighter pilot would also have to see me to fire at me (again, presumably) with cannon or air-to-air missiles. I had two options: fly high, but radar would steer him towards me or fly very low, below radar, leaving the fighter pilot the only option of locating me by basic visual contact before engaging me with his weapons.

As I gently pulled back on the ram's horn, V-shaped control column, lifting G-LORI's nose wheel, I felt the main wheels behind me leave the bumpy runway surface. I pushed the control wheel forward slightly to stop the aircraft climbing. G-LORI was only at a height of just a few feet.

G-LORI was not climbing but sliding on a cushion of air under the wings, which is called 'ground effect'. This ground effect enabled G-LORI to accelerate even more rapidly.

Flying with one hand, with my other hand I reached over to the middle/right of the instrument panel and grabbed the wheel-shaped undercarriage lever, moving it to the 'up' position. This was normally the job of the first officer, but I did not think Catriona was going to be much help today – her shiny, black hair fell over her legs as her head was still firmly thrust between her thighs.

"Ooooh God!" she uttered in a muffled voice.

The wheels of the undercarriage made a reassuring *clunk* as the wheels locked into the 'up' position. This removed the air resistance from those big lumps of metal and rubber hanging down below the nose and wings helping the acceleration.

Without having to look, I then reached down to my right, between the two pilot seats, and closed my fingers on the flap lever, selecting the take-off flap to 'up', just before G-LORI reached the flap-limiting speed during the rapid acceleration. The aircraft sank slightly as the wing flaps retracted to the 'up' position. My hand moved the control column backwards, automatically, to counteract the effect of the flaps retracting and at the same time, keeping G-LORI from gaining any height.

G-LORI continued its rapid acceleration through 250 mph, maintaining about 10 feet off the ground.

As correctly guessed, the normally sleeping anti-aircraft gun crew where definitely not sleeping at the moment. The crew were moving the gun around on its pivot frame to line up with the approaching HS125. Visible beyond them there was a sea of corrugated iron hut roofs. The roofs were covered in red dust that coated everything in this area of the world.

My best chance of distracting the gunnery crew was to point the aircraft straight at their guns. I could see them now, beginning to move around in a panic as they realised the aircraft was coming straight at them.

G-LORI passed only a few feet above the guns. The jet thrust of the Rolls-Royce Vipers and general turbulence created by the wings threw up a massive amount of dust and debris as we passed over the heads of the hapless gunners, not giving the crew any chance of pulling a trigger.

Leaving the gun position behind, the corrugated dusty iron roofs now rushed towards me. The red dust covering the roofs of the huts is blown off the Sahara by a wind called the 'Harmattan'. Most of the population of Lagos live in these shanty town huts outside the perimeter of the airfield towards the main city. These makeshift homes packed almost every foot of available space, forming a sort of red sea in front of me extending towards the main part of the city.

The best course of action was to gather speed rather than height at this stage; we passed no more than 50 feet over the roofs of these huts. Ahead of us to the left was Lagos city with its archetypal high-rise towers reaching up, punctuating the skyline like most modern cities.

I headed towards the city, and picked up the Ikeja Highway. The Ikeja Highway was a four-lane motorway carving a line from the airport towards the main city and its tower buildings. I followed the line of this road, allowing me to dip a bit lower. The road gave me the assurance of no obstacles to bump into along its route. I just had to look out for electricity and telephone cables – tangling with them would seriously fuck up my already unpredictable day!

In the midst of what was a very challenging piece of flying, a bizarre thought came to my mind: this road was a place where I had often seen bodies just dumped at the side on Sunday mornings, left to bloat in the sun; the result of some accident, contract killing or gang murder.

In Nigeria at that time, if you reported a body, even a family member who had passed away, you were immediately arrested for murder. After suitable negotiation, usually involving payment of cash to the police, 'dash' (the local term for this sort of transaction), you would be let off. However, you would still be responsible for the burial, and you may not be related to the body in any way other than reporting it! Hence, these poor unfortunates were just left at the side of the road. The Christian community, normally (and very discreetly) attended to the removal and burial in the quiet of night.

I followed the Ikeja Highway, streaking low along the road as it drew a guiding line towards the centre of the city through the tall buildings and on to the harbour where I was heading.

The HS125 rocketed towards the city. Still following the road, I started to weave the aircraft between the tall buildings on each side of us. A warning started to sound loudly in the cockpit. *BEEP, BEEP, BEEP, BEEP* – this was the 'maximum speed warning horn', it indicated the aircraft was approaching its maximum safe speed of 420 mph.

Catriona lifted her head from between her knees and looked out of the co-pilot's window. It took a moment for her to appreciate the picture in front of her. We were very low to the road with tall buildings on either side of us. She took a sharp intake of breath at the view that confronted her.

'Mike, what is that noise? Are we going to crash?'

'It's the maximum speed warning horn. We're going faster than the normal maximum – but no, we are *not* going to crash, just yet,' I stated matter-of-factly, but with a hint of ironic humour.

At this stage, I thought it best not to mention that we were being pursued by a fighter trying to shoot us down: that knowledge would not have helped her at this stage.

Moving my left hand from the control column to behind and above my left ear, my thumb and forefinger touched one of the many circuit breakers in the bank of breakers on the bulkhead behind my head. I pulled the circuit breaker; the noise stopped.

The adrenaline was pumping and my brain was working at a very high level. You hear people say after they've had a dramatic car accident that everything was like a slow-motion film. On reflection, it seemed that at a time of massive processing demands on the brain, it goes into a higher level of processing power. This was happening to me. I was so familiar with the HS125 that operating the aeroplane was instinctive, hence knowing the exact position of that circuit breaker without looking.

As I passed through the northern boundary of the city the larger buildings fell behind. I descended further, dropping down into the 'Lagos Lagoon', aiming G-LORI for the gap between the harbour walls. The Lagos Lagoon is a wide area of water that formed a deepwater harbour for the container ships. This led to the harbour gates and out to the Atlantic Ocean beyond. Lagos Harbour was very similar to the size of Dover and it handled many ships. There were container ships and huge oil tankers docked there. Also, I was aware that many very large oil tankers waited beyond the harbour out in the Gulf of Guinea, ready for the uplift of 'black gold'. These tankers were going to be my next defensive strategy. I was now rocketing down the Lagos Lagoon, heading for those huge concrete walls of the harbour entrance and the shimmering open sea beyond. I could only imagine the spray and noise my passing was creating.

The walls of the harbour rapidly appeared. They were as high as those at Dover and I passed below the level of the walls at around 420mph. As I passed between the waves and the top of the walls, I could see figures running away, clearly thinking that the very fast-moving jet was going to crash into the concrete wall. *Not quite yet*, I thought. Now, my focus moved beyond the walls towards the tankers out in the Gulf of Guinea beyond.

From take-off until now, I was thinking about what the interceptor would be doing somewhere behind me. It would have been impossible for him to get any sort of radar steer. He would have had to acquire G-LORI by 'Mark 1 Eyeball' (in other words, using his own eyes). If he did see us, there was no way he would have risked a shot with me staying so close to buildings and people.

Now, as I passed out to sea, I had to use the 'cover' of the tankers. It would have been a massive, colourful pyrotechnic display if he shot me and I crashed into an oil tanker or, indeed hitting the tanker by accident, with the whole lot exploding.

My earlier 'guestimate' that the fighter had been holding somewhere to the north-east of Lagos Airport, meant it would have had approximately 15 miles distance to catch up with us. To catch me, with the Alpha Jet's higher speed capability, combined with the accelerating HS125, the time for it to be close enough to take a shot or fire a missile would have been approximately four to five minutes. This was the approximate time that we had now been airborne; so I guessed we were reaching a critical part of the flight.

Of course, to take a shot, the pilot of the Alpha Jet would have to be able to *see* me!

The harbour walls disappeared behind. Now, ahead of me, I could clearly see the undulating swell of the South Atlantic Ocean.

The focus now was to stay as low as possible, remaining between 20 and 30 feet, a height and speed normally only experienced by operational military pilots. This would be creating a maelstrom behind G-LORI.

The jet wake, combined with the turbulence created by the wings, would be throwing up a massive amount of spray behind the aircraft. Rather like the dust I had used to distract the gunnery crew at the end of the runway, the spray would add a problem for any pursuing fighter. At this height, the spray would probably be thrown up some half a mile behind G-LORI. Any aircraft behind would get covered in saltwater. This saltwater would make a mess of the interceptor's nice clean canopy, making it almost impossible to see out and making visual contact by the fighter pilot almost impossible.

Also, in order to take a shot at me, the fighter pilot would normally have to lower the nose to get me in his sights. If he did that, the pilot would be swimming home.

Ahead of me were numerous huge oil tankers waiting in the gulf to be replenished with oil. I began heading towards the first tanker.

I knew that the Alpha Jet could be equipped with heat-seeking missiles. The maximum height that I was flying was approximately 50 feet. At that height, I was hoping that the spray would mix with the jet efflux to mix up any infrared signal. It was only a minor hope, but any port in a storm, as they say!

I had adjusted G-LORI's pitch trim controls slightly nose-up. Sorry to be a bit 'technical' on this, but basically, if I relaxed on the controls at all, the aircraft would start to climb rather than splashing into the ocean – which obviously was not part of my plan.

At 400 mph, it would only take half a second to hit the water if my concentration was to lapse. With the aircraft trimmed this way, I had to continuously press forward on the control wheel to stay at this exceptionally low height. All the time, the twin Viper jet engines would be throwing up that lovely spray!

As I zeroed in on my first 'target' tanker, I turned slightly, adjusting G-LORI's direction, aiming for the bow (front) of the ship.

My plan with these ships was to pass close, banking very steeply and pulling hard on the controls to stay as near as possible to the front. Doing this meant that my position in the captain's seat put me physically very close to the hull but with the ability to adjust the closeness. Also, because I was putting the hull on the inside of the turn, inertia was tending to take me away from the bulk of the ship. By pulling on the control column, I could safely (in this situation 'Safely' is a relative term!!) get much closer to the ship, almost underneath the curve of the bow. The laws of physics helped me not to actually hit it, which was obviously also not part of my plan.

The size of these tankers became apparent as I got closer. They were huge. The orangey brown rust on the steel came into focus as I got closer, along with the massive horn shape of the ship's anchor, the size of a small house, sticking out towards me. The bow flashed past in the blink of an eye.

Once I was clear of that hull, I would rapidly bank in the other direction to zero in on my next tanker. I was so low that I had to climb slightly to avoid the wing tip hitting the dark green, foaming waves of the Atlantic a few feet below me.

I began to weave between the tankers, well below deck level heading roughly south out into the Atlantic. There was a really bizarre moment as I flashed past the bow of one of the tankers. A crew member, a large black guy, was leaning on the rails over the edge of the deck, looking down at me sitting in the captain's seat. The look of total shock, surprise and horror on the man's face was recorded in an instant – rather like the shutter of a camera recording a picture – as I dashed past. I can still clearly see the man's face some 30 years later.

These events would prove to be the beginning of a massive international and political storm in which Catriona and I were at the centre – involving abduction, theft and the real risk of death.

When you read this true story, you will probably conclude that this was a great example of naivety (or stupidity) on my part!

I need to rewind and take you back a few weeks to provide some background, but I will let events unfold so I don't leave this current part of the story for too long.

So, before moving on, and in order that I don't miss anything out, let's go back a day to the night before, the Friday evening, when we had first intended to take off. On that evening, a major unserviceability had prevented the departure.

CHAPTER 1

Ikeja, Lagos International Airport
Friday, 18 May 1984 – 17:15 hrs

It was around 5:15 pm at the general aviation area of Lagos International Airport. That part of the airport was called Ikeja after the village it was close to, just outside the airport perimeter.

As described earlier, Lagos is a very large, bustling international airport with aircraft arriving and departing with great frequency.

I glanced over towards the centre of the airport, beyond the first of the two runways. The setting sun was still just visible behind the huge international terminal buildings which flickered in the heat and dust haze. This gave me around half an hour of light.

The smell of Lagos was quite unique, even for Africa. It hit you when the doors opened after landing. It was one scent that you never really got used to. The smell was a combination of open drains, shit and urine, combined with the worst body odour you have ever smelt.

At this latitude there was very little twilight, so sunset to darkness arrived very quickly, within 15 to 20 minutes. I had timed our departure to utilise this short period of light to fly low and avoid the detection of my flight direction. I had not expected to use the low flight to avoid being shot down.

I was sitting in the captain's seat of the HS125 and glanced towards the co-pilot seat. Catriona was looking pale and anxious – well, wouldn't you be?

'Are you okay?' I asked.

'No,' she replied vehemently but was slightly grinning.

Catriona was a slim girl with long, dark hair and a pretty face with delicate features. There was just a hint of her Malaysian heritage. As I said before, Catriona was not a pilot; she had never flown an aeroplane. In fact, apart from a holiday flight, she had no experience of aviation whatsoever. This was her first flight with me as Captain.

However, Catriona came from a very brave female lineage. Her grandmother, Sybil Kathigasu, won the George Medal for bravery in the Second World War. Sybil, who was a doctor, helped the Resistance during the Japanese occupation of Malaya. She did this in the most extraordinary of ways.

Catriona's mother, Dawn, helped Sybil by carrying messages to various members of the Resistance. Sybil was eventually caught and tortured by the Japanese. At one stage, they hung Dawn (aged six) upside down and lit a fire underneath her in order to extract information from Sybil.

Although it is difficult nowadays, if you can, obtain a copy of Sybil's book *No Dram of Mercy*, it is the most astonishing account of events in Malaya during the Japanese occupation and of an *incredibly* brave woman – one of the very few people to be awarded the GM.

Dawn was clearly affected by her experiences. Whilst not wanting to go into detail here, of Dawn's four daughters, three left home at around the age of 16 – you can probably assume there were difficulties in their home life.

I chose to take Catriona because I knew she would trust my decision-making and she was a tough cookie. I could have taken a number of different pilot friends, but I felt that they would not necessarily be comfortable in the atmosphere in Nigeria (I had worked there and in West Africa generally for over five years, so I knew the ropes). They also might have panicked if things went wrong – this last thought was an example of intuition... Also, I knew that I could rely on Catriona's steadfastness, so the poor girl had to come along with me.

There was another strong point in Catriona's favour, my pilot friends would not be nearly as good in bed!

Sweating profusely in the 30-degree heat with almost 100% humidity, the timing of this readiness was not a coincidence. As previously mentioned, I had relied on intuition many times during my entire flying career (at this point, some 12 years); it had saved me on numerous occasions from hazardous situations and I felt strongly that the availability of light to fly low was an important option today.

I had been flying these aeroplanes for a long time and had flown a lot in Africa, especially in and around Lagos and Nigeria in general. This was why I had been chosen to take on the task of repossessing this particular aeroplane plus one other and bring them back to England.

I had been contracted by a company called Shirlstar Container Transport – but again, more of this later.

Frankly, in the early 1980s, the economy was in the shit. As usual, my aviation prospects had taken a plunge (as well as my overdraft) alongside the economy. So, this task seemed like an easy way out of my immediate financial problems.

Whilst it seemed a good idea at the time, it now looked like the height of naïveté.

Taking off in an executive jet without permission from a major international airfield (which was also the heart of the Nigerian Air Force), was a very, very dangerous thing to do. However, it was less dangerous than facing the two groups of Nigerians who were trying to find Catriona and me and kill us both.

I looked out of the front window and saw Ken and Angus standing in front of the aeroplane ready to help start the engines to depart. Over the past few days, the two of them had serviced the aeroplane getting it ready to fly.

Ken and Angus were very aware of the risk that faced Catriona and me, but they had insisted on helping. The preparation for flight was particularly important because the aeroplane had been virtually abandoned at Ikeja for about nine months.

This preparation included priming the aircraft hydraulic systems. These are used to raise and lower the main landing gear, wing flaps and air speed brakes. The engine's oil system continuously lubricates the engine's bearings but, most importantly, the rear turbine bearings at the back of the engine. If these do not get oil, the engine stops – this is an 'undesirable aircraft state'!

Ken and Angus were very experienced engineers; they worked for Bristow Helicopters in Nigeria.

Angus was short and stocky. He was a swarthy and slightly rotund man with a shock of thick, dark hair falling across his deeply lined forehead. Angus was blunt and definitely did not suffer fools gladly. He would exhibit a typical Glaswegian Scottish engineer's bad temper when presented with opinionated pilots who 'dina nor whet t' fuck they're tarking aboot'.

Ken, slim and fair-haired, was taller than Angus at around six foot. He was jovial with a calming influence and reminded me of a medical registrar in A & E who 'fixed' people without the slightest sense of being ruffled. Ken had moved to live in Aberdeen with his family to work for Bristows there but he was not a native Scot.

I had worked with Ken and Angus when I was employed by Bristows Helicopters, flying their HS125 a few years before. Ken and I had also worked together out in Borneo, based in a little town called Miri. Miri was close to Brunei in Malaysia. It was a huge Shell oil base, and I flew the Shell bosses to Kuala Lumpur and Singapore from Miri. It was great fun.

It was now nearing time to go.

As I switched on the battery master switch and electrics, G-LORI came to life. Then I went through the before start checks which I knew by heart, an almost automatic routine.

Once prepared, I put up two fingers to indicate to Ken and Angus that I was ready to start the number two (right-hand) engine – no, not the traditional offensive meaning but an *aviation* meaning! Ken was facing me in front of G-LORI, responded by putting up two fingers

25

and made a rotation movement with his other hand indicating it was ok to start the engine.

My hands moved across the upper panel and flicked the switch bringing the engine to life. The Rolls Royce Viper engine began to turn with a reliable heavy whine along with the *crack, crack, crack* of the engine igniters as they waited to light the jet fuel.

I placed my hand on the fuel lever at the bottom of the panel between the pilots' seats. I lifted the lever which opened the valve, allowing the fuel to be pumped into the engine. The cracking igniters lit the fuel. As the engine picked up speed, the instruments showed the temperature inside the engine increasing. I kept my hand on the fuel lever, watching the temperature, ready to shut off the fuel if there was a fault during the start. The engine settled nicely at a normal temperature.

Putting up a single finger to indicate to Ken that I was ready to start the number one engine, Ken responded by also putting up a single finger and rotating his other hand.

The starter selector for the number one engine was flicked, and again there was a deep whine and cracking of igniters as the engine started to turn. Again, I placed finger and thumb on the fuel shut-off lever and moved it to the 'run' position. The temperature of the engine began to increase, as the fuel burned inside the jet engine. The engine settled into its idle rpm, matching the other engine.

After a very short delay, the orange 'CAGS' (Central Attention Getting System) warning lights in the centre of the instrument panel in front of me began to flash. The CAGS monitored all the aircraft systems and brought the pilot's attention to any malfunction. The pilot would then look at the annunciator panel just below the CAGS. This panel had around 30 little lights that illuminated when there was a problem with an aircraft system (electrics, fuel, etc.), indicating a potentially serious problem with one of them.

I looked down at the main panel and saw that the 'Rear Bearing Overheat' warning light was illuminated on the left engine. This was a *definite* 'no-go' item; the overheating bearing meant that the oil flow to the bearing was not working. If left, the bearing would soon fail and the engine would be wrecked.

Clearly, the pressurising of the oil system Ken and Angus had carried out earlier on that engine hadn't worked.

'Bollocks!' I said out loud.I immediately shut down both engines, waited for them to slow to a stop and then turned off all the electrics.

There was now an eerie silence in the sweltering cockpit. Our adrenaline had been at maximum for the last half an hour in anticipation of the departure.

Catriona looked at me from the co-pilot's seat.

'What's going on?' she asked.

'There is a problem with the engine. We can't go with it like that,' I replied.

'You have got to be joking! Does that mean we can't go?'

'It's probably fixable, but not in time to go tonight,' I replied. 'I'll have a chat with Ken and Angus, and we'll make a plan.'

'Jesus!' Catriona exclaimed. 'Do you mean we've got to go through this again? I'm shaking.'

'Sorry, Coco, but yes. I don't think that we can get ready in time to go tonight. The sun has already set; it will be dark in fifteen minutes,' I replied.

I opened the main door and walked down the steps to explain to Ken and Angus what had happened. I had to go back inside to help Catriona out of her seat. Her knees were knocking.

When Ken and Angus heard what had happened, they said that the oil system on the left-hand engine would need to be reprimed and this would take at least an hour.

Now all four of us realised it was a 'full stop' situation for now.

I definitely did not want to take off in the dark, so it was decided to fix the aircraft the next day and go the next night – Saturday night.

It is difficult to explain how awful it was to have got that ready to go and then find we were forced to make the decision to stop, an adrenaline hangover of momentous proportions! I was also concerned as to how close the Nigerian pursuers were to finding us.

We closed up the aeroplane, locked it and went back to the Bristow Helicopters compound and had a massive party to offload all that the adrenaline; we all got well and truly pissed!

The next day it was back to Ikeja. We opened the cowlings on the left-hand engine. 'Priming' the oil system required connecting it up with a hosepipe to something similar to a big bicycle pump that was full of engine oil and then pumping like mad. We overdid it to make sure it was done properly.

There was lots of banter between the four of us, as is normal with the English (…and Scots!!) in tense situations. At the same time I was keeping a watchful eye around the section of the airport that we were in.

Ikeja was a busy area with lots of small aircraft and small jets coming in and out, dropping off and picking up passengers. There were also lots of Nigerians mingling around. It was supposed to be a secure zone, but I would never completely trust that here.

It reminded me of an experience a few years before this whilst in exactly the same spot as we were that day.......

I was standing beside my HS125 waiting for my passenger when a large Peugeot 504 estate rolled up and swung around so the back end was facing towards me. I was about to fly out to Kano in northern Nigeria. The vehicle had three men in it – two were very large, well over six foot tall, and one short and fat who bore lots of tribal scars on his face.

The short one was a gentleman called Chief Igbeninion. I had flown his aircraft for a few weeks around a year before that day.

The two big men strode with intent towards me, grabbing and lifting me up by the armpits and carried me towards the open boot of the 504. Worryingly, there were two cement bags in the back of the car.

These guys did not have this cement for doing a bit of DIY. The bags had holes in them ready for my feet. As well as 'necklacing', there was another common way of bumping people off here: setting their feet into concrete bags and throwing them in Lagos Harbour! I'll explain about necklacing later as I am a bit busy with the concrete shoe problem at the moment........

'SHIT!' I muttered.

You will notice that this term comes up again and again. In aviation it means 'a dangerous situation from which there is little option to avoid disaster'. It normally indicates a sudden and unexpected end to one's life!

So, clearly, their plan was to throw me into Lagos Harbour with trendy concrete shoes. I could feel another of my nine lives about to be ticked off.

Rather than going on about this now I'll expand more about this later in the book.....

We eventually finished the maintenance on G-LORI in the early afternoon and we then ran the engine for five minutes to ensure that the problem was solved. There were no CAGS lights this time – hooray!

We returned again to the Bristows compound for some lunch and a rest in the very hot middle of the day, ready for departure that night. I knew a lot of the Bristows pilots and engineers.. They were aware that I was there to collect an aircraft, but it was very much a case of no questions asked: it was best not to know.

We headed back to the airport at around 4:30 pm to be ready to take off at 5:45 pm There were many checks to carry out when preparing an aircraft and it was critical that the take-off took place with the right amount of daylight left.

It was always tense while travelling, being watchful that there were no 'followers' with 'ill intent'... My neck was always being stretched as my head rotated left and right. The traffic was always horrendous, so it was very difficult to spot a following vehicle.

We arrived at Ikeja and went through the same series of events to prepare G-LORI for take-off.

Before we carry on with this part of the story, I would like to give you some background. We can pick this up again a bit later on.

CHAPTER 2

My Early Years of Flying

I remember when I was 15 at Wymondham College in Norfolk, smoking a cigarette in the 'bogs' with my mate Andy Davidson.

He asked, 'Mike, what are you going to do when you leave school?'

'I don't know, Andy, but I don't really care as long as it's not boring!' I replied.

I can honestly say that, as I sit here typing, my life has never been in the slightest bit boring. Even at 64 years old, my life is still a fantastic adventure. Writing this story is a huge gamble – the chance of getting it printed and in the hands of someone like you reading it is very, very remote.

Finding a literary agent, much less a willing publisher, and actually getting something published is very difficult. If you are a 'nobody' like me who does not *have a name*, as it were, it is almost impossible – even if it is a great story.

If you are a 'Z-grade' celebrity – maybe on *Love Island* or something – it is easy; they will actually get a ghost-writer to write the bloody thing for you!

But hey ho, you have to have a go! If you are actually reading this, I have managed to overcome all those obstacles by publishing and marketing it myself.

I'm writing this story in my 'office' in the Imperial Grecotel in Corfu, Greece. It is hell! As I work a full-time job, time to write is very limited so I write during my two week annual holiday. All the staff have got used to me doing this and all want a copy of the book. They call me Corfu's answer to Oscar Wilde!

Quite a nice office!

I had just got married for the second time (you only do it twice!) and started a brand-new career as a flight simulator instructor the previous year – probably the most challenging training I have ever experienced. I am now a flight simulator examiner, too. I never imagined my life taking me in this direction.

Same thing happened after I got divorced from my first wife. I finished up teaching pilots to become flying instructors and was a presenter at special seminars for pilots in front of 20 of them over a couple of days. I've done around 60 of these seminars over 5 years. This was the sort of thing that would have given me cold shivers and I'd avoid at all costs but life threw it at me and, well, shit… why not? Now, I love it. I still get anxious, but I turn this into excitement.

I have been through some extremely tough times but have always maintained a very strong positive mental attitude. You never know where life will take you. No matter how bad things seem, believe me, there is always an 'UP'!

So, let's go back and fill in some of the background. Hopefully you will build a picture of how I finished up in this very unusual situation.

I did not do too well at school. A typical boy: only applying myself when stimulated in a subject by a great teacher. However, my first flight was at the age of nine.

My father Roy had been flying the Vickers Valiant bomber aircraft. The Valiant was part of the 'V'-bomber fleet; the Valiant, Victor and the Vulcan, The Valiant was based in RAF Marham in Norfolk during the height of the Cold War in the sixties.

To be selected as a captain of a Valiant at that time, was equivalent to being captain of a nuclear submarine now. It was part of the fleet of aircraft that carried the United Kingdom's nuclear deterrent and as captain you had to be relied upon to deliver this to the target destination without hesitation. Those pilots were especially selected as having 'exceptional skills'. Part of the selection process was to be interviewed by the air vice-marshal of the RAF.

Sadly, the Valiant had developed a problem with metal fatigue in the wing's main spar (the thing that holds the wing on). This meant that the wings would occasionally fall off. (Undesirable aircraft state?.... Just testing!) i.e. it breaks up into bits and falls out of the sky.

The result was the grounding of the Valiant fleet and Roy being posted on a 'ground tour' at air traffic control in Thorney Island, West Sussex. He absolutely hated this time – Roy was a natural pilot and lived to fly.

His solution was to teach the Air Training Corps cadets at weekends. This was carried out in a de Havilland Chipmunk, a single-engined training aircraft at Shoreham Airport in Sussex.

I was a diminutive little boy and the RAF required the use of parachutes, but these were full-sized parachutes with a reserve chute underneath; massively heavy and very bulky.

The ground crew strapped me into the parachute. I staggered out to the aircraft, waddling like a tortoise with an overlarge shell walking on two legs.

It required a couple of big lads to get me up onto the wing and into the seat, but they then realised I could not see out of the windows. They had to unload me, put another parachute onto the seat to pad it up and then load me in again.

Roy and I set off. My first flight and my first taste of aerobatics – loops and barrel rolls over Brighton and Shoreham beach – absolute heaven – and I wasn't sick!

By coincidence, the flying instructor courses and seminars I ran were out of Shoreham Airport in 2012. It was strange to go back and remember my flights with my dad there and doing aerobatics in the same place. There were Chipmunk aircraft in RAF colours there and it always reminded me of that flight with Roy when I saw them.

Later, at 15 years old, Roy regularly took me flying in a Piper Aztec aircraft. These were six-seater piston twin executive aircraft. Roy taught me to fly. So at that age, I could take off, fly it along and land it.

I did finish up working very hard at Wymondham College school in Norfolk, but my lack of attention between the ages of 11 and 13 at a boarding school in Sussex (where I did learn very effectively how to get into trouble but not much else) was a drag on my progress.

This meant that I failed most of my exams. For those of you who may have recognised my crap English grammar, I passed O-level English language on my fifth attempt – I think, in the end, they gave it to me for sheer tenacity. Just for your information, this book has been edited by two excellent Editors to correct my crap English grammar.

Then there was the impending 'leaving of school' and what to do next…

Roy asked me what I would like to do with my life in terms of a career. Like most boys, I responded with a blank face.

'Would you like to fly?' Roy asked.

'God, yes!' was my enthusiastic reply. 'But it is incredibly expensive to train.'

'I can lend you the money,' Roy replied.

And so a career in aviation began. I was 17 and it was 1972.

The first step was for me to go to the Norfolk and Norwich Aero Club at Swanton Morley in Norfolk, and there I completed my training to acquire a Private Pilots Licence (PPL). This was carried out in a Cessna 150 two-seater training aircraft.

I was sent 'solo' in 3 hours and 25 minutes – which was a record at the Norfolk and Norwich Aero Club. This sounds good, but it did not allow for the 200-odd hours I had spent with Roy in the Aztec. (Roy said it should have taken less!) I gained the PPL at 17 years old, before I passed my driving test.

I then built up enough flying hours to do the course to become an assistant flying instructor. The course took a few months of very hard work, and culminated with a day of flight and ground assessment by a senior examiner.

I began instructing before the age of 18 at the Norfolk and Norwich Aero Club's Norwich base (I had passed my driving test by then). This was mainly in the Cessna 150 and the four-seater, Cessna 172 aircraft.

In 1973, as an assistant flying instructor, you earnt £21 for a six-day week; not a lot of money, but it got you into commercial aviation. This was known in the industry as 'the hard way'. In other words, not paying £50,000 (nowadays £100,000) to go on a specific course for a year or so and come out at the end with a professional pilots licence.

This way, you built up 700 flying hours instructing, took a 'short course' for the commercial pilot licence and sat the same exams. The short course was eight weeks.

I worked with an experienced flying instructor called John Brooks. John was 23 years old, and I was 18. We became firm friends and had a gas – great fun – both flying and socially.

We are still in touch. John became a senior captain at Monarch Airlines (sadly not in business any longer). He has kindly been a 'test reader' for me, giving feedback on the book.

John was quite tall with longish, dark hair that dropped down over his forehead. He wore thick glasses with a slight tint to them and had a dark brown moustache that was always desperately in need of a trim, so it covered most of his mouth.

I used to take the mickey out of his moustache, but John insisted that the ladies 'loved' it… At that age, I did not have any concept of *why* the ladies might like it! However, I was not so sure myself! John also loved a Russian-style fur hat (complete with those ear flaps) in the winter with a long, thick, checked winter coat. John Brooks was never going to win any fashion competitions, but then again, neither was I.

With shoulder-length hair, a moustache that was trying (unsuccessfully) to compete with my dad's splendid handlebar moustache, I wore a jacket and trousers of the sort a Sandhurst Military Academy cadet would wear when 'off duty' – not exactly the height of fashion for an 18-year-old.

Me at 18 - I have a lot less hair now!!

On one occasion, John and I decided that our chances with the ladies were about to improve dramatically. We took the aero club's Nurdin & Peacock wholesale card (Bookers in today's world) and visited this massive warehouse on the Norwich Airport industrial site.

Having grabbed one of those huge trolleys, we – two rather odd characters – wandered around (you can probably picture the scene) until we found the rack with Durex on it. Putting a box of 144 on the trolley, we wheeled it to the payment point – I mean, a *gross of condoms*? *REALLY*?

Obviously, we chose the checkout with the very pretty girl on it. She looked at us two boys plus the gross of condoms on the trolley and showed absolutely no interest in us – I still can't understand why.

'Is that all?' she asked, unperturbed.

'Yes, thank you' I replied. 'Well, for the time being anyway, but we will probably be back after the weekend for another box,' I thought this was absolutely hilarious but the checkout girl just looked bemused and completely unimpressed with my humour.

Obviously, by any measure, the purchase of a gross of condoms by us was a serious case of undue optimism. Most passed their use-by date rather than being used by either of us!

So, the years instructing at the Norfolk and Norwich Aero Club allowed me to build up flying hours. I eventually became the chief flying instructor and an examiner for the Private Pilots Licence before the age of 21.

Around this time, I met and fell in love – my first love – with a stunningly beautiful girl, Lorna Folkard. She worked for Air Anglia in Norwich. Lorna was petite with very long, golden, curly hair and pretty, delicate features. The questionable photo above was at Lorna's twenty-first birthday. We are still close friends 40 years later. Lorna also helped with test reading and proof reading this book.

During this period there was an amusing incident. There was a school visit to Norwich Airport for sixth form students from a Norwich school. The weather was crap, so I was not busy and was asked to meet them in groups in the control tower by the senior air traffic control officer to answer questions relating to flying. I met a few groups and answered all their questions, then the teacher accompanying the visit came up the steps leading to the inclined glass room of the tower.

Well, well, if it wasn't Mr Purchase – the 'careers adviser' at Wymondham College while I was there. He had asked me what my plans were when I left school.

'I'm going to be a professional pilot,' I had replied.

He, of course, broke into fits of laughter.

'Howard, don't be ridiculous! You should aim for a career in estate agency, or insurance,' he had said.

Purchase entered the room and stood by the door listening to my answers to a wide range of questions.

Once the group left, I addressed him:

'Hello, Mr Purchase.' I did not say, '*Good to see you,*' as I regarded him as an arse.

'Hello, Howard. What you doing here? Helping the air traffic controller?' he asked.

Dave Cook, the ATC (air traffic controller) looked shocked. His eyes widened at this comment. He had known me for three years and respected my ability as a flying instructor.

'No, I am the chief flying instructor and PPL examiner at the Norfolk and Norwich Flying Club.' As I said it, I pointed towards the hangar with an array of training aircraft parked outside.

It was a truly WONDERFUL moment. Definitely an 'UP YOURS, MATE' without me having to say it. I just love karma. In my life it has always brought balance when people have been unfair to me.

The Norfolk and Norwich Aero Club decided to close their Norwich base and move to Swanton Morley. This was not convenient for me for a number of reasons.

I had met a guy called Tom Cree, and we set up an air charter company: Howard Scott Aviation. The operation was from Norwich and Aberdeen airports with six Piper Aztec aircraft, and we took advantage of the early years of the oil industry. It was a very successful small company which had contracts with major oil companies at the beginning of oil exploration in the North Sea. These contracts were with companies like Schlumberger International, Brown and Root, Decca Survey, Mobil Oil, and others.

My role was financial director and sales. Tom was in charge of the

CAA (Civil Aviation Authority) paperwork side and also involved in the sales side of the business.

Tom Cree grew up in Africa and had a completely unruffled approach to life and, more importantly, money. This was the reason I was financial director – I always said if you gave Tom £5 or £500, he would spend it in a day.

He had suffered with polio when young and had one weak leg. This meant he walked with an exaggerated, dragging limp with his right foot. He was a very handsome guy with an expansive moustache and craggy, sort of 'lived-in' features with literally life's scars from his adventures in Africa. Tom was always very popular with the ladies and used his disability to create a chat-up line with them.

Tom Cree and our chief pilot, Tom Gilligan and I had great adventures in Norwich and gave me lifelong advice with regards to the ladies. Both of them were 15 years older than me with considerable experience with girls. They were a bit like Derek Jordan, who I will talk about a bit later but was involved in teaching me to fly professionally. But the two Toms helped me with the much more challenging skill of handling the female race!

One bit of advice that I have never forgotten went as follows:

> 'Mike, this is VERY IMPORTANT. Always use a very expensive deodorant. Cheap ones smell like cat's piss after a few hours, and you will fail miserably when attempting to chat a girl up if you smell like shit!'

Apart from a short period of internecine warfare with my ex-wife (but this is another story), I have always followed this advice.

After it was decided by the Norfolk and Norwich flying club management that the Norwich base would have to close. When it was closed, I decided to set up my own flying school and operated that alongside Howard Scott Aviation, My flying school had lots of clients – mostly dodgy second-hand car dealers. This enabled me to carry on building flying hours. I also became formally 'twin-engined aircraft' qualified.

Not bad for a 20-year-old.

We had one unusual charter for Schlumberger. This was from Norwich to Stavanger Airport in Norway with a cargo of 500 kg of marine gelatine.

Marine gelatine is highly explosive stuff, but only when put under pressure. Basically, it is gelignite or dynamite for use in oil exploration – using an explosion to create a shock wave to measure the structure of the rock below the seabed to help find oil.

We were at the height of the IRA mainland campaign; the IRA would love to have got their hands on this stuff!

Schlumberger asked if I could go along on the trip as co-pilot because the cargo was of such significance. Special Branch at Norwich Airport was bugging Tom for details on the captain and aircraft registration, but Tom did his best to obfuscate the answer until we had actually taken off.

They were definitely not impressed when they learnt the captain's name. It was Captain Patrick 'Paddy' Callahan. This was also the name of a very famous IRA member! Paddy was the only pilot who was available at short notice. Also, it was a big paying charter as well as our first for Schlumberger and led to many more.

My only problem was that Paddy was a chain-smoker. In those days, it was considered okay to smoke in a small aeroplane; both of us smoked, although I smoked much less than Paddy. With all that dynamite behind me, I was a little uncomfortable but not too bothered.

However, when we arrived at Stavanger, ATC asked if we had the 'high-priority' cargo on board. When I answered yes, they informed us:

'Ah, roger, Uniform India (our registration), we have a special parking area for you.'

This parking area turned out to be in the middle of nowhere on the airfield, miles from any structure and near to where the fire service practised their firefighting tactics. Fire engines and police turned up to oversee the offloading of the cargo; they insisted I did this myself as none of them wanted to touch it. Once a flatbed van turned up, the driver said *I* would have to put the cargo on the van, as he retired to a safe distance. Paddy had headed over to the ATC tower, filing the flight plan for our trip back to Norwich.

So, with all the fire service, security, police and van driver as an audience, I started to off load the cargo. They were in cardboard boxes, the sort of size a new computer would come in, not too big and weighing around 15 kg.

So, with the van parked at the rear of the wing, near the door, I commenced 'lobbing' the boxes onto the back of the van. The boxes thumped down and slid towards the cab. As each box dropped onto the van, the whole audience kind of winced and sort of ducked.

I'd been assured by Schlumberger that the cargo was completely stable and only became unstable when put under pressure, therefore, it was safe. But the reaction of the audience put that into question.

I explained to Paddy when he got back.

'Looking at that, Paddy, I don't think we should have been smoking on the way over!' We were laughing.

Sadly, Howard Scott Aviation went bust due to two companies defaulting on substantial lease payments. We had been leasing a couple of Aztec aircraft. One was a company in Southend and the other was based in Edinburgh. The Southend company went bust on us and Edinburgh Flying Services tried to stitch us up.

Edinburgh Flying Services was run by a guy called Jonathan Turnbull... Turnbull put the aeroplane into his maintenance facility in Glenrothes airfield for a 50-hour (minor) check, and then stuck us for a bill of £5,000 instead of £1,000. Turnbull was after free flying for a few months! We argued about this during a phone call at around 9am but he was banking on the fact that I was in Norwich and the aircraft was in Scotland. Mmm... Turnbull banked wrong!

So, as it happens, the events in Lagos were not my first repossession...!!

41

Johnathan Turnbull thought my aeroplane was out of reach in Glenrothes Airport. This was a small airport with a grass runway which was the middle of nowhere, miles from Edinburgh. Yes, you guessed it, I went and got the bloody thing from right under his nose.

The moment he attempted the stitch up, I reacted very fast. I put the phone down on him in the morning in Norwich and asked my dad for a favour. Roy was flying scheduled flights for Air Anglia out of Norwich up to Scotland and as luck (Karma) would have it, he was going to Edinburgh, departing at 10am. So, I got a lift with him on his F27. (Can you imagine being my mum and dad? Mind you, I did entertain them – it was never a dull moment!).

I then got a taxi to Glenrothes from Edinburgh Airport. I was in that taxi less than five hours after putting down the phone. Turnbull would not have expected me to do anything that quickly.

I chatted to the receptionist, who knew who I was and said I'd go and check the aeroplane over. It was parked outside the hangar. The only problem was that the weather was really wild: pissing with rain and blowing a gale right across the grass and muddy runway. I jumped in, started up both engines and taxied straight away towards the runway. Various engineers came out of the hangar and ran around like headless chickens, but too late; I was off.

A major problem during take-off was the aeroplane weathercocking in the 50 mph winds and risking me 'going gardening' – remember that aviation term for going off the side of the runway and ending up stuck in the soft ground? Another undesirable aircraft state! The wind was pushing on the tail of the aircraft and pushing the nose into wind. The only way to control it was to throttle back the downwind engine to balance against the wind. Dodgy, but it worked. This was one of my first twin-engined aircraft flights.

When I arrived back at Norwich, Roy had just arrived back too. He looked at the aeroplane covered in mud and grinned.

'That's my boy!' He laughed.

Roy knew it was an exceptional bit of flying to get out of Glenrothes.

The other, more difficult problem was leasing an aeroplane to a company in Southend who went bust owing us £5,000 plus. This was an impossible position from which we could not recover and did the real damage. Cash flow was very difficult to manage, as we were doing a lot of flying. Also, oil companies paid after 90 days but fuel and salaries had to be paid straight away.

Tom went off to South Africa to start something new and left me to wind up the company.

The meeting of creditors and explaining to good guys that you know well that you owe money and that they would not get paid was a bad experience. We simply did not have the financial resources to weather that storm. Tom's decision to fuck off to SA meant he avoided that particularly challenging meeeting.

It was a great shame, because the company had the potential to become a huge success. It was probably the first example where I was *nearly* very wealthy – which has happened many times in my life!

So back to flying.

Once I reached the minimum of 700 hours, I could attend a short course (eight weeks) to take the exams for the commercial pilot licence.

Having obtained the hours to qualify for a short course, I went to the Sir John Cass School of Navigation in London for the eight weeks of very intensive learning, and then to Acton Town Hall to take the exams for the commercial pilot licence.

This involved taking 12 exams in four days. It was a massive challenge. If you failed more than two exams, you had to take the whole lot again. You could re-sit the failed exams but fail those two resits more than twice, and then the same would happen: you'd have to retake them all again. No pressure then!

The short course was more like an exercise in psychological torture. Every doubt about yourself came to the fore. The little voice that says 'You'll never do this, YOU'LL never succeed' was continuously whispering in your ear.

Thank God, I passed them. This was a huge confirmation of my father's confidence in me.

Passing all those exams was certainly a bit different from my schooldays!

Whilst instructing with John at the Norfolk and Norwich Flying Club, an executive jet used to come in and out of Norwich on its way to Rotterdam. This jet was owned by an American engineering company, Brown and Root, who were involved in the construction part of the North Sea oil business. John and I watched the HS125 slowly and majestically taxi to the parking area in front of us. Its Rolls-Royce Viper jet engines roared with the sound of the powerful thrust even at idle. It looked *sooo* cool!

I said to John, as I was hypnotised by this beautiful aeroplane in front of me,

'Ooh, John, that aeroplane is bloody cool! I want to fly one of those!'

'Knowing you, Mike, you'll be flying one in a week or two!' John Brooks replied.

As it happened, I became friends with a pilot called Derek Jordan who worked for Brown and Root.

Brown and Root built oil platforms and support barges, and had a large base in Rotterdam, hence the frequent visits by management. Derek flew a Cessna 421, piston twin aircraft for them based in Norwich. It regularly flew to Rotterdam carrying the management on board. The Cessna 421 was an executive, piston twin aircraft that carried up to seven passengers. It was normally flown with one pilot.

Derek was tall and handsome (he maintained) with thick and longish, fair hair that dropped slightly over one side of his forehead. He had clear, blue eyes and a rounded, slightly pronounced chin with a wicked smile – particularly if he caught you out.

Derek liked to be right – all the time – even if he was wrong! He loved it if you screwed up something or we argued and he won, which was what usually happened. Although he was usually right, he found great difficulty in admitting when he was wrong. But for all the bombasitic blustering, Derek was a good friend and a heart of gold.

He was ex-RAF and flew Lightening aircraft (another fantastic British aeroplane) until they were phased out. The Lightening could accelerate through the speed of sound in a vertical climb, astounding performance.

Sometimes though very occasionally, Derek got things spectacularly wrong. Such as one day when arguing with the security personnel at Rotterdam; he was refusing to let them search his passengers.

'It's a private bloody flight to Norwich! They're hardly going to hijack their own aeroplane, you idiots!'

Security at Rotterdam were not impressed and certainly did not feel that they were idiots. Derek was promptly arrested and stuck in a holding cell in the airport.

The heightened security was as a result of the new airport security that came into force in 1974, which followed the violent hijacking of airliners. After this, all aeroplanes and passengers – no matter who or where they were going – were subject to these rules. It's just that in Derek's mind it made no sense (and he was possibly quite right).

Fortunately, the passengers, who were very senior management, liked Derek and patiently waited until he was released. They had to wait on the aeroplane while Derek (slowly) recanted his position. You'd have thought they would have got pissed off and fired him but no, their attitude was tolerance. They were sort of amused.

'Why, that's just Derek!' (Imagine this being said with a strong Texan accent.)

I said to him later that he could not be King Canute trying to hold back the tide of security that was engulfing us in the wake of various hijackings.

The Cessna 421 was an executive, piston twin aircraft that carried up to seven passengers. It was normally flown with one pilot.

As it happened, Brown and Root had made a decision at the US head office that all their aircraft had to have two crew after an accident in the States due to the sickness of one of their pilots.

On the last day of my course, just before the exams, Derek rang me and asked if I had any plans after I'd taken the exams because there was a job for me, if I wanted one... This was a gift from God. Jobs in aviation are not easy to come by – especially for a very *junior* (lacking in experience) pilot like me.

This was just at the end of when I was taking my commercial pilot licence exams on the completion of my eight weeks at Sir John Cass College. During the course, I had been living with my grandmother just outside London near the Dartford Tunnel and commuting into the city centre.

'*Miiike*, there's a phone call for you,' she called in a shaky, aged voice.

It was Derek. 'Bloggs, have you finished your exams yet?'

I should explain that 'Bloggs' is a derogatory name for an incompetent and inexperienced co-pilot, a term originating in the RAF. I was, at this stage exactly that but the name never shifted with Derek, no matter how experienced I became. Whilst it was not exactly the most complimentary term, at this stage in my flying career I knew very little about the 'big wide world' of professional flying.

'Hi, Derek. Nearly. I've got the last ones tomorrow,' I replied. 'What's going on?'

'Brown and Root have decided I cannot fly G-BAGO on my own, so I need a co-pilot. What are you doing on Thursday?' he asked.

'Day after tomorrow?' I replied, not quite sure what was going on.

'Well, yes, Bloggs. Thursday generally follows Wednesday.' He took the piss, as usual. 'If you're not doing anything, do you want a job?'

'God, yes please!'

'Well, get your ass back to Norwich, because we're going to Stavanger in Norway at six on Thursday morning!'

46

And so I started my first job.

We flew to Stavanger on the Thursday morning and stayed the night in a very nice hotel. It was like a dream for me. He then explained the 'deal' when on a night stop.

'Now, Bloggs, the company pay the bill, so just charge anything to the room.'

We had a meal and then went to the bar. After a couple of lagers, Derek decided to go off to bed, leaving me in the bar – a big mistake, as it turned out.

I started chatting to two beautiful, tall, slender, blonde Scandinavian girls. Obviously, I thought they were overwhelmed by my handsome good looks and intelligence… (I know; same as the gross of condoms situation!). I was buying them drinks (brandies) and generally having a great time. It should be noted that alcohol in Norway was approximately four times the price compared to the UK.

When we were checking out the next day, Derek's eyes widened when he saw my bill.

'Not a cheap hotel, Bloggs!' he said with a hint of amusement in his eyes. 'What were you up to last night?' he asked.

'Well…' and I explained what had happened the night before.

'You daft bugger, Bloggs. Girls will have you over if they can,' he stated sagely. 'Did you get your leg over?'

'Not a chance, they went home – and I would have been too pissed anyway,' I replied.

'I rest my case,' he said. 'I should be able to get this bill approved, but don't take the piss in future, Bloggs,' he said with a stern look.

It was a very good-natured bollocking; I did not take the piss in the future. And I was a bit more realistic about *girls* in the future, too.

Derek was a very disciplined, exceptionally experienced pilot who taught his 'wet behind the ears' co-pilot how to fly as a professional pilot.

The stuff I learnt during these early days flying with Derek formed the basis of my ability to fly safely for the rest of my flying career. I am forever very grateful to him for his advice and patience in teaching me – even if it was not 'quiet advice'. It was generally delivered in a loud and uncompromising tone. Derek was a great teacher (if you could stand his manner!).

I was very lucky. Derek was a hard taskmaster and we were great friends. He continued to teach me over many, many years as our careers, as well as our friendship, kept us together.

Obviously, Brown and Root had the HS125 that I had coveted when I was in the Norfolk and Norwich Flying Club, watching it with John Brooks. I nagged the hell out of Derek to chat up the chief pilot. The aircraft was based at Heathrow, the head office of the aviation department.

Sure enough, within a few weeks, they had an empty sector on the HS125 back from Rotterdam. The Brown and Root boss had agreed (probably in a deep southern drawl).

So, I got to sit in the right-hand (co-pilot) seat of an HS125!

G-BAVB flew into Norwich Airport from Heathrow and carried passengers to Rotterdam.

It was a completely different world for me. This aircraft streaked across the southern part of the North Sea and we landed in just over 20 minutes – incredible. I had sat in G-BAGO to Rotterdam, which took 50 minutes and that seemed incredibly quick!

As there were no passengers on the way back, I got the chance to actually 'fly' it back to Norwich. This was the first time I had flown the aircraft that became my absolute favourite (until the Boeing 767) and one that I flew for many, many hours. My landing was good back at Norwich. I was like a dog with two tails when I got out of the aeroplane – John Brooks was very envious.

The Commercial Pilots Licence (CPL) allowed me to act as captain of aircraft up to approximately 18 passengers and to be first officer of any sized aircraft. I did have to complete a series of flight exams with a senior examiner from the CAA (Civil Aviation Authority) to obtain the actual licence.

On top of that, in order to actually fly commercially, you had to acquire another (very expensive) rating: the 'Instrument Rating'. This required even more training in a twin-engined aeroplane and another flight with a CAA examiner.

The instrument rating is another of those hurdles that a prospective pilot has to cross over. It is a flying exam which my wife (who is a professional licence holder) describes as 'having to drive down the centre lane of a busy motorway blindfolded, juggling six oranges and reciting the times tables whilst having a conversation on your mobile phone' – apart from that, it is easy.

After that, the next step was to sit even more exams to obtain an 'Airline Transport Pilots Licence' (The 'ATPL'). This allowed you to act as captain of any size of aircraft – it was another huge hurdle. But for now I, very proudly, had a beautiful blue 'CPL' and was now able to earn money as a commercial pilot.

I carried on flying with Derek for almost a year on the Cessna 421 until Brown and Root decided to sell it. I also undertook a lot of flights in the HS125.

This experience earnt me a job with McAlpine Aviation based in Luton, where I flew as a co-pilot on HS125s. This was a large company operating around 30 HS125s. However, I did so little actual flying that I began to worry I would forget how to do it. To get back into flying, I moved to Fairflight Charters, a small air charter company based in Biggin Hill.

With Fairflight, I flew single crew charter in Navajo Chieftain, de Havilland Heron, Shorts 330/360 aircraft around Europe and oil support in Scotland and Norway. Also, at a later stage, the Cessna Citation II jet. This carried up to eight passengers and was flown around the UK and Europe with a single pilot. This was a gratifying challenge to do professionally and safely (thank you, Derek!). It was all great fun, but the first time I went off on my own in a Navajo

Chieftain, with passengers in the back, to the south of France, was a real baptism of fire. There was no one else there to help you!

I worked for Fairflight Charters at Biggin Hill for a couple of years and had a wonderful time and during the time there,

I shared a flat with two pilot friends, Ian Faggatter and Gary Studd. It was in a block called Bramis House in Biggin Hill. We lived at number eight on the first floor. We often called it 'Brainless House' because of the amount of alcohol that was consumed there. Gary owned the flat but spent most of the year in Antarctica flying a Twin Otter aircraft supporting the British presence there. Between the three of us, we had a great time.

However, I do feel the need to tell you about the night 'a cat was strangled in Bramis House'. It is a mystery that remained unsolved, until now...

When I met some friends for drinks at a club, they had brought along an Anglo-Indian girl who had stunning good looks and a great personality. We hit it off, then at the end of the evening she asked, 'Is there somewhere we can go?' This was said with a mischievous grin.

Fortunately, at this age, I was not naive like I was five years previously and knew exactly what that grin meant.

'Well, we cannot go to my flat because Ian and Gary are there,' I mused. 'But, I do have a key for number two; it's the flat immediately below ours.'

This was owned by Fred Mulligan, the father of the guys who owned Fairflight and the chief engineer. I had stayed in the flat during the summer while Gary was home from Antarctica and had a family member staying. Fred had moved out of the flat and was getting ready to sell it.

'It is completely empty, though; there's no furniture at all,' I explained.

'Let's go!' was her emphatic reply. When we got into Fred's flat, her eyes widened with glee.

'Mike, I want to do it in every room!' she said in an almost reverent whisper, as she started taking off her clothes…!

Well, what is a chap supposed to do? I did not want to disappoint the young lady.

It would not be appropriate to go into detail here – it's before 9 pm – but the noise, *the noise* she made was incredible! I have never ever heard anything like it (I'm sure she didn't use the word 'disappointing' afterwards!). Her high-pitched howling and wailing was made much worse by the fact that the flat was empty; it amplified the noise, echoing around the rooms.

We had arrived there at approximately midnight, and I took her home at around 5 am. During our activities, from time to time, I heard movement upstairs (toilets flushing, etc.), so I knew there was some disturbed sleep in the flats above!

When I got to her home, she informed me that she could not see me again. 'My parents would not approve,' I was told! I felt so 'used' (not!).

Anyway, I got back to number eight, tiptoed in and slid into my room, just avoiding Gary staggering back from the kitchen. I quickly stripped and put on my dressing gown, then came back out and met him. Gary looked like crap.

'Christ, Mike, did you get any sleep? That noise – it was horrific, wasn't it?' Gary said, his eyes red with dark circles underneath.

'Noise? What noise?' I asked, busying myself putting the kettle on with my back to him – hiding my unsympathetic grin.

'It was like a cat being strangled – for four bloody hours!' he said. 'Sounded like it was coming from Fred's flat, but that's empty.'

Ian staggered out of his room, also looking like crap.

'What the fuck was that noise last night?' he said whilst grabbing a mug and helping himself to tea.

'Some kind of animal cruelty,' Gary replied.

'I'd like to meet that animal,' Ian said with a glint in rheumy eyes.

Mmm, I thought that might not be a good idea; 'the abused pussy' was a very close friend of his girlfriend! There was a lot of further moaning from other neighbours about the noise, so I have kept quiet, until now, about my responsibility for all those sleepless nights.

Sorry about that diversion, but moving on…

The problem with a career in aviation was that it suffered from the direct effect of the economic cycle.

Whenever asked, I used to call it the 'posh jet'/'night mail' cycle. When the economy was fine, I would find myself flying an executive jet and accommodated in five-star hotels. When the economy went south, I would find myself flying 'Night Mail' and sitting around the proverbial 'brazier' in East Midlands or Liverpool airports (the night mail hubs) at one in the morning, wishing I'd trained as a barrister – or a barista!

Derek moved to Bristow Helicopters in Redhill, Surrey, as they had bought an HS125, G-BFVI. I joined Derek there as a first officer.

This aircraft was used to fly to Lagos, Nigeria, out to Dubai and Tehran, also up to Aberdeen and the Shetland Islands as well as flights relating to Alan Bristow's (the owner) business requirements. This was the job where I gained an enormous amount of experience. Indeed, it was during this period that I was shot at for the first time.

CHAPTER 3

The first time I was shot at!

Would you like to know about the circumstances that surrounded the first time I was shot at? Of course you do!

Bristows had a large presence in Iran supporting the oil business in that country. Derek and I flew into Tehran with G-BFVI before the revolution, late 1977. What a beautiful country. Then the revolution occurred. We flew back into Tehran a few months after that happened in early 1978. The change we saw in just a few months was astounding. There was a total breakdown in society that I would not have believed possible. From orderly behaviour by the people, to a comprehensive ignoring of the rules that had once applied. There was even a disregard for the signals on road crossings. I watched with fascination as accidents took place in front of us on crossings.

We did not stay long on this trip – just one night and then scuttled back to Dubai where we were temporarily based.

Shortly after that, Bristows decided to pull all its helicopters, crews and their families out of Iran. This decision involved Derek and I flying into various parts of Iran to bring the families out while the pilots and engineers came out in the helicopters.

We did this legally. Well most of the time!

It involved negotiation with the Iranian authorities to obtain permission for us to fly in their airspace. When we got the permission, we would shoot off (probably not the best adjective) towards Iran from Dubai. When we called Iranian air traffic control, they would either say carry on (in ATC lingo) or 'turn back or we shoot you down!' regardless of the permission obtained. We used to laugh at this.

Derek would call it Iranian Russian roulette.

This wasn't the event I'm referring to though.

I did say 'legally, *most* of the time' just now…

We had some families near Bandar Abbas Airport, very near the Iranian coast, a short flight from Dubai just over the Strait of Hormuz – so, no problem then? The problem was that they had closed the airport, and there were very few ways of getting the families out.

So, we cooked up a plan to 'pop' over to Bandar, rendezvous with the helicopters who would bring the women and children, get them onto the plane and 'off we go'! Simple? Mmm, I'm sure you can see this simple plan may have had a few flaws.

Well, we 'lobbed' into Bandar, parked and shut G-BFVI down. Within a short time, three helicopters arrived. What we didn't bank on was the helicopter pilots gossiping like fishwives.

Derek was outside trying to round up the women and children, but it was like trying to herd a bunch of cats.

He said to me, 'Bloggs, as soon as we have them on and I close the doors, fire up the engines ASAP.'

So, I'm watching helplessly from the co-pilots seat, as Derek tries to get some order whilst also scanning the airport around us. Then I spotted the guy on a bicycle carrying a huge gun strung over his shoulder. It looked like an old 303. He was dressed in the classic revolutionary guard outfit.

'Derek!' I shouted. 'We've got company, and he has a big gun!'

'Shit!' I heard him say. 'If you guys are not on this aircraft in ten seconds, we will go without you!'

You could tell from the tone of his voice that he meant it.

I punched the starter button of the right-hand engine, the one the other side from the main entrance door, without being asked. I *was not* going to spend an unspecified time in an Iranian jail. No, thank you!

Funnily enough, they were all on in less than 10 seconds. I could hear the helicopters starting. The guy on the bike was still a fair way away. I started the left engine as Derek closed the main door with a thump.

'Let's go, Bloggs,' he exclaimed, jumping into the captain's seat and strapping himself in. 'Get your belts on – it's going to be rough!' he shouted down the back to the passengers.

We started taxiing to the runway, away from the guy on the bike – problem was that the take-off direction would send us back towards him. He continued cycling whilst also unslinging the gun off his shoulder, trying to position his gun to fire at us, as we lined up on the runway.

'Can you see what he's doing, Bloggs?'

'Yes, he's kind of getting his gun out – we'd better be quick!'

We rocketed down the runway and immediately Derek turned left.

'That's all very well, Derek, but that means he's shooting at my side of the aircraft,' I joked. I could see him with the gun up and firing whilst unsteadily continuing on his bike.

There was not a chance of him hitting us. If there were 10 barn doors in front of him, he would have missed! However, I am sure this still counts as being shot at for the first time!

Derek was an examiner on the HS125 and eventually decided that I was ready for command training.

As the captain of a jet like this, you had responsibility for all aspects of running the operation. You did not have a large 'operations department' to assist with diplomatic clearances and general planning of flights. The maintenance programme had to be planned and adhered to, with periodic checks made by licenced engineers at the appropriate times. So, command training was very arduous, taking into account the flying and all this other stuff. There was a lot to think about, particularly when the training was being carried out by Derek Jordan!

This training was carried out in West Africa, the Middle East, the Far East and around Europe over six taxing months. It culminated in a sector from Kano, Nigeria, to Cairo, Egypt, which I flew faultlessly.

During this period, we spent six months in Borneo, flying around Malaysia. We had to ferry the aircraft from the UK to Borneo. This involved refuelling stops in Istanbul and Dubai; Karachi and Calcutta; and then Bangkok and Singapore. We stopped for the night in Dubai and Bangkok. Barry Glover, an engineer, was also with Derek and me on the aeroplane.

On the night stop in Bangkok, obviously, we had to go to a Thai massage parlour. What an experience. Unfortunately, Barry's and Derek's massages were 'finished' early. But I was definitely going to make the most of it. I did not understand what the pretty Thai girl meant by a 'happy ending' at first, but I caught on when she gave me some help understanding what it meant.

It was very difficult however, to concentrate when Derek Jordan peered under the gap at the bottom of the cubicle door shouting:

'Bloggs? Are you coming? What's taking you so long? We want to get back to the hotel?'

So my command training culminated in that trip to Lagos and back, via Cairo over two nights.

All went well until arriving in Cairo on the way home, when the Egyptian air traffic control asked me to 'hold' at a navigation beacon during the arrival procedure as they were busy.

A holding procedure is a 'racetrack', oval-shaped flight pattern that takes place over a navigation beacon nominated by air traffic control. When you are asked to 'join' the pattern, depending on the direction you approach the beacon, there are three very set ways to join. This joining procedure is designed to get you going the right way around the holding procedure.

Derek decided that I had not carried this joining procedure correctly.

'Ha, Bloggs, you've failed your command check. You joined the hold the wrong way,' he stated with glee.

We were sitting in the pilot seats of the empty aeroplane with just the little auxiliary power unit running to give us lights. The APU is a small jet engine at the back of the aeroplane that provides electrics and air conditioning when the main engines are shut down.

'No, I didn't, Derek,' I replied with certainty. Mainly because I was certain. 'Derek, you draw on a piece of paper what I did and also what you think I should have done. But I want a promise. If you are wrong and I'm right, you have to sign my command completion form.'

'All right, Bloggs, it's a deal.'

As usual, Derek was sure that he was right and I was wrong and applied himself to drawing a representation of our join to the hold, what I had actually done and what he thought we should have done.

'And do you agree that the joining procedure in our *Jeppesen Airway Manual* (which contained all the airport and airway charts for navigating the world) that depicts the ICAO (International Civil Aviation Organisation) instructions are unambiguously correct?' I asked.

'Yes, Bloggs,' he replied petulantly.

'Good. Now show me, and compare what you have drawn to the instructions in the front of the Jeppesen.' I handed him the large, leather-bound Jeppesen manual opened at the appropriate page.

Derek took the book and studied the page. His attention switched back and forth between his hand-drawn picture and the printed 'Holding Joining Procedures' from the ICAO.

As he did so, a deep frown gradually appeared across his forehead. The deeper Derek's frown, the wider my smile became.

'Well?' I asked.

'Hmm, Bloggs, it seems you are right,' Derek reluctantly replied in a quiet voice.

So, in a theatrical gesture, I handed the Command Training Completed form (that had been in my bag for months) to Derek to complete and sign.

It was done in a reluctant but proud manner by Derek, recognition of the years we had flown together and my achievement under his coaching.

Having achieved a command at the age of twenty five (probably the youngest on an HS125), I was then offered a job in Nigeria, managing an HS125 for AGIP, the Italian oil company.

This appointment was permanently living in Nigeria. The job offer was based on my flying experience with Bristows which had been regularly down to Lagos. The pay was significant: the equivalent of £250,000 in today's money.

As I did not have any particular ties here in the UK, I took the job. It would be lots of flying, so it meant lots of 'command' – captain jet hours in the logbook – gold dust!

I worked out there for a year, but then the 1980 recession hit and the contract with AGIP ended, so it was home to bloody 'night mail' again!

There are lots and lots of stories I could tell in relation to that year. For example, the group of Nigerians chasing a six-foot black mamba snake towards me; twenty or so robbers opening the baggage hold of an airliner while it was taxiing out for take-off and stealing bags from it just ahead of me in Lagos; and also scaring the shit out of first officers by flying very low and very fast down river valleys (a bit like one of those shots of helicopters in films about the Vietnam War). I may go into some of the other stories later in the book – I don't want to put you off too much at this stage!

During this time, I met and bought a cottage with Catriona. The address was 2 Titsey Road, Limpsfield, Surrey. I always felt the need to say *number two* Titsey Road when quoting my address, I cannot possibly think why.

Also, at this time, a beautiful golden retriever entered my life. 'Toppy Dog' was a delightful, always smiling puppy dog. As far as I was concerned, he was a puppy all his life.

I kept the proverbial wolf from the door with night mail runs and short contracts on HS125s, usually organised by a friend called Owen O'Mahoney (pronounce O'Manie). Owen was an aviation wheeler-dealer in the executive jet world, priding himself on knowing everything that was going on. I had met him through Derek Jordan; they had met in the RAF.

Owen was a tall crane of a man; a dapper individual but with a slight stoop, which was accented when you spoke to him. He had the tendency of tilting his head, rather like an attentive bird. The stoop was probably there from childhood; a tall boy avoiding bullying by trying not to appear too tall.

He had slightly thinning, medium-length, sandy/ginger-coloured hair which fell over his forehead, slightly disguising an elongated face with a prominent, long nose. His skin was very fair with freckles that denoted his Celtic origins.

Owen would ring me up and say he had a *job* for me, usually in Nigeria, flying some Nigerian chief around West Africa and sometimes back to the UK. They normally lasted for one to two weeks, maybe a month, and paid £100 per day plus expenses. However, there *ALWAYS* seemed to be some catch or other with the contracts that Owen introduced me to.

I took these jobs because I needed to pay the mortgage on the cottage. Normally, they would pay some in advance, and I would pay this into the mortgage account. On return, the extra cash would pay for the other living expenses. However, and slowly over time, the overdraft increased.

One of the jobs was for a Chief Igbeninion. He was the guy in the Peugeot vehicle I spoke about earlier. Igbeninion had a very old HS125 and wanted a month of flying and paid for 21 days. So, £2,100 was duly paid to me (very handy) and off I went to Lagos with a young first officer, Jeremy Palmer. I thought of Jeremy as young, but at this time I was only 27!

Jeremy was the sort of first officer you would not leave alone in an aeroplane for fear of him touching something!

I had learnt that very quickly.

I left him alone on the aeroplane in Kano, while I went to the control tower to arrange a flight plan to Lagos. As there was no APU on this aircraft to make a cup of tea, I was in the habit of starting a main engine to get the electric power to boil the kettle. Probably the most expensive cup of tea in the world – yes, I know – but I was not paying for the fuel! Problem was that you used a lot of fuel from the right-hand wing fuel tank, so you have to 'transfer' fuel from the left wing to the right, with the electric fuel pumps. Jeremy did this but then forgot he was transferring.

As I walked back to the aeroplane, the fuel began to piss out of the right wing tip. I sprinted to the aircraft and jumped into the cabin. Looking to my right, Jeremy was sitting enjoying his tea.

'Jeremy, what the fuck are you doing?' I shouted.

'Drinking tea?' he replied, not quite understanding why I was shouting and completely unaware of the chaos he had created outside.

My hand grabbed the fuel transfer lever and quickly lifted it to the 'off' position.

'Yes, and flooding the apron in jet A1. Have a look out of the right window,' I said, barely containing my anger.

He looked outside, just in time to see the fire engines turning up to wash the fuel away from the apron.

'Jesus! Sorry, Mike,' he said as he peered at the mess he had created. 'I forgot.'

'In future, Jeremy, do not touch anything while I am not on the aircraft,' I stated flatly.

I believe Jeremy finished up as a captain on a major UK national carrier – which makes sense! I will not state the name for fear of being sued for libel.

Igbeninion was a truly nasty piece of work. At one stage, we finished up staying in his compound in Edo State. The compound was full of statues holding severed heads and other horrific things.

I had previously heard that Igbeninion was deeply into black magic.

People do not believe in such things. However, if you are in an isolated bungalow somewhere in Nigeria, miles from any town with no phone and surrounded by statues displaying various black magic rituals, and others holding severed heads, that belief might change. It was like a scene from a James Bond film – except this was real.

This was a one-night stay in the small bungalow. I organised myself to get some sleep as it was an early start the next morning.

I regard myself as being rather psychic (or as Heather says 'Whacky'!) or probably more accurately 'very in tune' than being a full-on medium. As I said earlier, my intuitive sense had saved me on a number of occasions. That night, my psychic antennae were twitching in warning. I was not scared, but I felt very uncomfortable. However, I did manage to get to sleep.

At around two in the morning, I awoke very suddenly. Opening my eyes, I was confronted by a large African face with many tribal cuts over his cheeks and forehead. His eyes were completely black and piercing.

It was such a fright to find this face literally inches from mine that I reacted instinctively. My hands thrust towards his throat in a defensive response. As I did so, the face broke into a grin and dissipated, the image distorting as it moved away from me, disappearing into and becoming part of the floral pattern of the curtains.

I was in a state of absolute shock; adrenaline rocketed around my system. Obviously, I did not sleep any further.

In the morning, when I met Igbeninion he was grinning.

He said: 'So, Captain, I think you met one of my house guards last night!'

I did not answer him, but any doubt I had about the vision that night disappeared.

I asked Igbeninion for the remaining 10 days of payment for Jeremy and me, but he was not coming up with the money. I felt that it was not going to be paid and had decided to return to the UK once the 21 days were up. I didn't like the guy anyway!

The twenty-first day came up and still no money.

I had lots of friends in companies like British Caledonian Airways (BCal) who operated DC-10 aircraft to Lagos. I parked and locked up the HS125 at Lagos and arranged for Jeremy and me to climb up the rear steps onto the BCal flight to London and home.

It was a relief to get out of the place – I should have been wearing a 'Happiness is 'V1' Lagos' T-shirts the local pilots wore – this was most apt today. I did need the money, but not that badly!

I heard that Igbeninion was furious, mostly because he had failed to cheat me and I was reluctant to go back to Lagos because of the threat that Igbeninion may have posed to me. I turned down a few jobs because of this.

* * *

About a year later, Owen rang to see if I wanted to take on a short trip to Lagos. This was after many, many long nights of night mail. Having turned down lots of HS125 work, I reckoned that enough time had passed and the threat Igbeninion presented was probably reduced. The dust should have settled.

There was also the ongoing overdraft situation; £40 a night flying mailbags around or £100 a day in a posh jet? Well, obviously the posh jet and £100 would win, wouldn't it?

This was for a Chief Francis Arthur Nzeribe. Now, Nzeribe was a different kettle of fish entirely. He had a regal aura around him, not the dark, brooding danger of Igbeninion.

Nzeribe was running for governor of Imo State and later went a long way in Nigerian politics. He was a tall man, educated in London and spoke with a very good English accent, but he amended this accent when speaking at the political rallies in which he was engaged.

The contract was for a three-week period. During that time I got to know Nzeribe well and respected 'Fanz', as he was known.

Fanz tended to be late for the flight times that he had arranged with me (he was running for president of Nigeria), but that did not bother me much. I was enjoying the relaxed atmosphere compared with night mail. Also, this time my first officer did not do stupid things like Jeremy Palmer spilling 50 gallons of fuel onto the apron at Kano. No, this chap was competent!

I was waiting for Fanz at the parked jet in the general aviation area of Ikeja, which, as usual, bustled with activity. This was exactly the spot that G-LORI was parked those few years later.

There were Twin Otter aircraft supporting oil company activity; other jet aircraft; Bristows Helicopters aircraft; and a bundle of Nigerian boys working to clean the aircraft, organise refuelling and supply bags, etc.

Everything was fine...

The little jet APU was singing, keeping the cabin cool and electrics powered up and ready. I was chatting to the young Ebu tribe boy (about 12 years old... and, obviously, with spear) who guarded the aircraft for me. It didn't really need guarding, but I gave him money for sleeping under the aircraft. This tribe was very poor.

So, I started describing this story earlier. The beige Peugeot 504 estate car rushed up to the parked jet and out jumped these two huge Nigerians, both over six feet tall and strode with intent towards me. They both had typical scar patterns, lines and spots of their tribe, both on their cheeks and forehead. Their black, curly hair, cut very short, revealed a pronounced, bony skull covered in a shiny scalp; funny how you notice small details when you are in danger. Their black eyes were fixed on me with expressionless attention.

Instinctively, I backed away from their approach, but they grabbed me. Immediately, my feet were off the ground. *Shit! What the fuck is going on now?* I thought to myself, but I bloody knew this was danger.

As the Nigerians picked me up, I was hit by the horrendous rank smell of body odour – "I know that smell" I thought to myself "it's the smell when you open the door after landing in Lagos". Strange what goes through your mind in these situations.

Then I saw my 'old friend' Chief Igbeninion slowly stepping out of the rear of the Peugeot. The answer became clear.

As the huge Nigerians carried me towards the Peugeot, Igbeninion opened the boot where lying inside were two cement bags.

Now, you do not need to be Einstein to work out the plan that was in store for me; we were not that far from Lagos Harbour!

The other funny thing about being in danger is that (normally) humans will still plan for survival, even if it looks like the odds are really stacked against them. I was doing exactly that.

'So, Captain Howard, I hear you in Lagos. You should not have come back if you want your life!' Igbeninion said with a heavy Nigerian lilt. 'You are a *thief*! You OWE me ten days' work!'

He spat the word 'thief' as if it filled him with disgust. Igbeninion clearly wanted a rant. I decided the only option was to go on the attack.

'What the fuck are you talking about?' I shouted back at him. 'I have not stolen anything from you.'

I knew EXACTLY what he was talking about, but at this stage it was a case of playing for time. Letting him rant would very likely buy me a few more minutes before being bundled into the boot of that bloody Peugeot.

'You *stole* ten days. You work for me a month and leave after twenty days. You *steal* from me!' Again, he spat the words 'stole' and 'steal'.

'You paid for twenty-one days, and I worked for twenty-one days,'

I stated flatly. 'I asked for the money many times, but you did not pay. I work only when paid in advance. You didn't pay. I went home.'

This reply (the truth) infuriated Igbeninion; he almost foamed at the mouth with rage and frustration.

This conversation took a few seconds, during which time I was heading inexorably on my way to the Peugeot.

The little Ebu boy was shouting in a high-pitched, adolescent voice, as he ran to confront the thugs carrying me to the car.

'You leave my captain! You leave him! You no kill him!' He bleated.

The boy then threw his spear at the massive man on my right, who just brushed it away like an annoying fly.

'I save you, Captain!' the diminutive boy shouted, as he rushed up to the huge Nigerians.

He then attempted to climb one of them like he was scaling a wall, fists waving. It was like watching a replay of David and Goliath. In a strange sort of way it was a rather bizarre and amusing sideshow to this serious situation.

They swatted the little chap off them with a spare hand. He fell to the ground but got up straight away returning to the offensive.

God, I was touched by the boy's commitment and saw that he could get seriously hurt, but I was unable to do anything about it – my feet were about six inches above the ground.

As the boy climbed again, he was swatted but much harder this time as Igbeninion was continuing his rant.

'Thieves die. You steal from me – you die.'

In all of this rather incongruous scene – Igbeninion ranting, the Ebu boy climbing, trying to save me and the approaching open boot with the two bags of cement – a slightly irrational thought went through my head: *I should have gone into law, medicine or be a barista? Why flying?*

As I reached the Peugeot, a large, black Mercedes limousine with blacked-out windows serenely rolled up to the aircraft.

Shit! I thought. *Fanz is on time – Christ, that's a first!* I directed a look to the heavens. *Maybe I'm saved?*

Fanz climbed out of the limo with an air of absolute calm control. He was a man with massive confidence. Taking in the scene, he walked with a magisterial manner over to Igbeninion.

'What are you doing with my captain?' He asked.

Fanz, a good foot taller than Igbeninion, then turned to the two men holding me and signalled for them, with a small movement of his hand, to put me down. The two men clearly recognised Fanz and lowered me to the ground.

'He steal from me, he pay,' said Igbeninion flatly.

Fanz turned to me. 'What happened?' he asked.

After I explained the background, Fanz took Igbeninion gently by the shoulder and led him away from the audience that was growing around the scene of my potential death. All the handling agent boys and other sundry workers from the general aviation area were assembling to witness the drama.

There would always be an audience for something like this.

As mentioned earlier, the other 'instant justice' was a 'necklacing'. Someone would be (fairly or unfairly) accused of theft by a vigilante mob and an audience would quickly form baying for blood. Some old tyres would be dropped over shoulders and arms so the 'criminal' could not do much to get away. They would then pour diesel fuel over the head and shoulders of said 'criminal' and set fire to the whole thing. The tyres would blaze with a sickening smell of burning rubber and roast pork. The crowd would then watch/listen to the result; truly awful.

I had inadvertently seen this a couple of times. The smell was bad, but it was the screaming that made this very difficult to forget.

I watched as Fanz and Igbeninion discussed my life expectancy; Igbeninion in an animated fashion, while Fanz stood imperiously in control. My life expectancy depended mainly on which of the two was more powerful.

After 10 minutes of barter, they walked back to the jet. Fanz said to me. 'Let's go to Kano, Mike!' He said.

As it turned out, Fanz was the stronger man, So, I lived.

Igbeninion went back to the Peugeot and got in with his henchmen; the disappointed crowd dispersed.

The Ebu boy was beside the wing of the HS125. I gave the little chap a paternal hug and said thank you, that he was very brave and a credit to his tribe. I gave him $10 US, a massive amount of money for him, and said I'd see him in a few days.

I climbed into the captain's seat, having pulled the main door shut, fastened my harness and for the first time in the last twenty minutes allowed my shoulders to drop.

My first officer was still sitting in the co-pilot's seat where he'd been during the whole episode.

I turned to him. 'Shit, that was close!'

'I didn't know what to do, Mike. I called the tower and asked for security, but nothing happened. They just said to stand by!' He replied, clearly shocked by the events.

'It would have been too late anyway. Thank fuck Fanz turned up when he did! Call for start for Kano, please. Let's get the fuck out of here!'

We duly got start clearance and went through the routine of starting and taxiing out. I made a point of taxiing very slowly to let the adrenaline dissipate.

We got take-off clearance and the HS125 slid down Runway 19L. We lifted off the ground, and I executed a smooth, left-hand turn through 180 degrees and headed north to Kano.

When we got to a cruise altitude of 35,000 feet, Fanz came up to the flight deck.

'Mike, a bit of advice, Igbeninion is a bad man, and he holds a grudge for a long time. You are safe while you are working for me, but be very careful if you come and work for someone else here in Nigeria. You may not get to go home!'

We both laughed at the final sentence; it was funny, but serious at the same time. When you work in Africa, particularly flying executive jets around the continent, the risks are not just the general risks of flying – weather, bumping into other aircraft, mechanical failure, etc. – it was the risks of just living on a continent where life is of so little value.

I worked for Fanz for a few more weeks and then went home, with £3,500 in my hand. It was cash I desperately needed to pay off that bloody overdraft.

CHAPTER 4

Leading Up to the Contract

So, after this little adventure, it was back to night mail. I had decided to avoid Nigerian executive jet contracts, as I suspected a dramatic downturn in the state of my health if I did so.

Also, the economic decline from 1980 had a long-term effect, particularly on the exec jet world, so opportunities were harder to come by. This was an example of that posh jet/night mail way a pilot's career following the economic cycle.

So, it was Biggin Hill, Stansted, Liverpool, Gatwick, Biggin... Or Southend, East Midlands, Brize Norton, Southend. Or Southampton, Liverpool, Southampton.

You guys still posted letters, and I needed the income!

It was such an impressive system: aircraft from all over the country would drop into one of these hubs with mail from their area and leave a couple of hours later returning with the first-class mail for their part of the country.

I had to sit with the other pilots, chewing the cud for a few hours, although it wasn't that bad once you got acclimatised to the continuous night work. But again, slowly, the overdraft went up and I needed cash to stop the rise. Catriona also ran into some serious problems with her family, which caused great distress and sent her towards chronic anorexia/bulimia.

CHAPTER 5

Catriona's Story

Catriona was one of four daughters of Dawn and Bruce Spalding.

Bruce was a barrister specialising in the field of patent and intellectual property rights; he was very successful and earned very good money.

As mentioned earlier, Dawn had a very dramatic and dangerous early life, and this probably affected her behaviour towards her daughters. This was so bad that three of her four daughters, Catriona, Gervaise and Simone, voted with their feet and left home at around sixteen years old to fend for themselves.

Catriona's younger sister Simone was living in a horrendous bedsit in London. When I saw the place, I insisted she came and lived in the cottage.

This was not necessarily the best idea. Simone was 16 and loved fashions like rah-rah skirts (remember them?). I had absolutely zero experience in managing a 16-year-old, but she was, on the whole, a good kid.

Bruce's father died and left his estate to various people including his grandchildren.

The family owned DC Thomson, the publishing company who owned *The Beano* and *The Dandy* as well as some very reputable Scottish newspapers.

So, the bequest was worth a great deal of money. Trouble was Dawn did not want Catriona, Gervaise or Simone to benefit. Dawn announced that three of the girls (not the one still living at home) were *not* Bruce's children, making them *not* eligible to claim under the estate.

Then Dawn and Bruce went off to the register of births, deaths and marriages and made a joint statement saying that Bruce was not the girls' father.

Apparently, if both parents do this, the birth certificate can be changed (without the knowledge of the child).

Dawn then announced that each of the girls had a different father! Nice!

This all finished up in the high court where a very small sum of money was finally awarded to the girls, but a fraction of the amount they were due.

To be fair, the main Thomson family did not approve at all of this action, but there was little they could do.

A lot of assistance was given to the girls by the *Mail on Sunday*. There were a couple of great reporters; unlike some reporters that I have come across who are of a truly 'low' character. One of whom wrote a highly defamatory article about me. But, my God, did I get my own back! This is a story in itself, but I do not want to divert too much from the central tale, but it helps to understand Catriona's character.

As I said earlier, and as a result of the terrible psychological punishment inflicted on all the girls, Catriona did succumb to chronic anorexia/bulimia and was violent and suicidal at times. In the others, it manifested itself in different ways.

I began studying psychology to help her (and survive myself), and had terrific help and advice from superb bereavement counsellors at that time.

But the girl had the genes of Sybil Kathigasu and was, therefore, made of strong stuff.

CHAPTER 6

A Call from Owen Spells Trouble

Life went on and the overdraft went up.

It was post the 1980 recession, the interest rates were 17%, reducing to 10% by 1982, and unemployment was up to 12% of the working population… The economy was bad and opportunities were very limited.

But, as usual, I did not sit on my arse doing nothing. At one stage, because the flying opportunities were so bad, I was selling door to door. These were hand-drawn pictures of people's houses for £100. It was quite successful, and I sold, on average, one in a 10-hour day and made £50 per commission. It helped a lot.

I'd met some artists living in a squat in Vauxhall while they studied art. I would take a photo of the house and hand it to these guys who would produce a drawing from the photo. I would then frame the finished picture and deliver it to the homeowner. If they liked it, they would buy it.

It turned out that I was a natural salesman.

Catriona decided that she would set up a driving school for her and Simone to run from an office in the cottage. I did the naming and the marketing for this: 'Bentleys Motoring School'. I emulated the logo style of a well-known bank – they probably paid millions for their styling, so it had to be good! We worked extremely hard to earn cash, but any income was difficult to come by.

The overdraft was £5,500, but I had a great bank manager – Charles Gaskill (remember those old-fashioned bank managers?). But even Charles's explanations to his bosses were starting to wear thin.

So, when a call from Owen came through with an *easy* repossession job for a British company, I knew this was 'manna from heaven'. My internal 'Owen O'Mahoney warning system' was clearly not working properly that day.

The fact that £25,000 plus expenses was the figure on the table may have influenced the operation of *that* particular warning system – needs must, as they say!

Owen said that he was busy with another contract, so he could not do this one. (The O'Mahoney alarm should have been screaming!)

'Mike, this is an easy job,' Owen had said in his typically quiet and reassuring tone. 'Ben Slade, who owns Shirlstar Container Transport, has leased two HS125s to a couple of Nigerians, but they have stopped paying. Ben has taken all the necessary legal action to recover the money through the UK courts and now has legal right to repossess.'

'Are these aircraft on the Nigerian register?' I asked, sort of searching for an 'Owen' catch.

'No. They are to UK limited companies leasing the aircraft and making the payments,' Owen replied.

'Who are the Nigerians involved with the two aircraft?'

Owen replied, 'One is Prince Olori.'

'Never heard of him, do you know him?' Frowning, I was trying to recall any mention of his name.

'No,' replied Owen. 'All I've heard is he's a decent guy.'

'What about the other aircraft?' I asked.

'Well…' He paused. (The 'Owen alarm' should have been red lights flashing and bells screaming.) 'That one is being used by

Victor Vanni.'

Owen exaggerated his soft, reassuring tone, trying to sound as if Victor Vanni was the kind of guy you would leave your kids with.

Trouble was I had met Victor Vanni, and Vanni was considerably more dangerous than Igbeninion.

He ran a private security firm in Lagos, which had tentacles – 'influence' in both the military and civilian government, mostly by acquiring information on people's activities that they would *not like* to become common knowledge.

'Victor Vanni? Jesus, Owen, the guy is really dangerous! Why on earth has your mate Ben been dealing with him?' I asked.

'Money?' Owen replied.

'Yeah, okay. That was an unmistakable reason, but Ben Slade should know the Nigerians will never pay if they can get away with it!' I said, stating the obvious.

This was true, but what I did not know, and wouldn't until sometime later, was that Slade was up to an awful lot of 'no good', mainly carrying out illegal currency transactions. Ben had a sophisticated money laundering operation in place.

He would use Nigerian naira from wealthy Nigerians to 'bunker' (refuel and restock his ships as they sailed to and from the UK to different parts of the world). This would then be repaid to the Nigerians at the black market rate in London. This would enable the Nigerians to avoid the stringent currency restrictions imposed by the Nigerian government.

Later, I would find out that one of these transactions had gone seriously wrong… which was the catalyst of this whole story.

I mulled this over while Owen tried to explain (persuade) how good and *simple* it would be.

In the end my confidence in Owen's knowledge of Nigeria, plus my experience gained from six years of flying in and out of there, living there for a year, and of course that bloody overdraft, swung it.

'Okay, Owen, I will see Ben Slade at his office and discuss it. Let me know when it's convenient for him to meet me.'

'Oh, he'll see you tomorrow. Ben is an impatient man and wants his aircraft back!' Owen replied.

'Okay, where's his office? I'm happy to have an initial discussion, but I will not commit myself until I've thought a bit more about the whole thing.'

'He's in Swallow Street, off Regent Street.' Owen told me.

After giving me the address, he said he would call Ben and set up the meeting. He did so and called me back.

'It's all set for tomorrow at 2 pm. I will be there but cannot help other than introduce you to Ben.'

So that was that. I thought the whole thing through and decided to go ahead and discuss the matter with Shirlstar.

My experience in West Africa was high, and I was confident in my ability to work around and sort out problems. What I did not take into account were the other factors which were unique, completely unpredictable, and associated with international crime committed by state operators – such as the two Mossad (Israeli intelligence) officers who had, a week or so ago, entered the carpentry/joinery workshops in Tottenham, London, and ordered the construction of two large, wooden crates to be made to a very specific design.

CHAPTER 7

Discussion with Nick the Lawyer

The next day, I went up to London by train to meet Slade and his team.

Prior to that, I spoke to my close friend and lawyer Nick Munns to discuss the conversation that I'd had with Owen.

Nick was an overweight, bustling, energetic individual with loads of energy and a penchant for high-calorie snacks and beer. He had a habit of leaning both elbows on his desk and almost talking to the desktop and then suddenly rocking back in his chair. I had known him a long time. Nick wore thick glasses in dark brown rims, with longish brown hair that was receding, giving him an intelligent high forehead; he also had a neatly cut ginger coloured beard.

Around this time, I helped Nick refurbish his new office in Redhill, Surrey when Nick had run out of money and I was out of work. This had taken about six weeks of hard work, but the two of us would do anything for one another. Nick had also helped Catriona with her travails during the awful difficulties caused by her parents.

'Whatever you do, Mike, *do not* take this on without a really watertight contract in case it all goes wrong.' Nick was emphatic.

I was really relaxed about it, and we had long discussions surrounding the negotiating and writing of a contract. In the end, I went along with Nick's advice. It turned out to be the best advice I'd ever had from any lawyer. Mind you, Nick was the best.

'I'll go tomorrow and let you know,' I said. 'Can you do a watertight contract?'

'Tight as a duck's ass,' joked Nick, with his usual informality.

I went up to London by myself the following day. My intuition was howling in my internal ears, so I was still in two minds over the whole thing. On one side, I needed the cash. On the other, I had been bitten by Owen's contacts. (The main being Igbeninion, but there were others: the Dantata family from Kano and those flights to Switzerland, with very small, incredibly heavy boxes.) My instincts told me to be wary. (YOU SHOULD ALWAYS LISTEN TO THOSE!)

I'd looked up Ben Slade in reference material, and to all intents and purposes he seemed an upstanding member of society (literally, he was a baronet) with distant connections to the royal family.

Ben is a descendant of King Charles II, King Henry I and King George IV. He inherited his title aged 15 when his father died of a heart attack.

Sir Benjamin was married for 12 years but divorced after he became frustrated with his wife's seventeen cats. Ever the extrovert, he said the divorce made British legal history as it's the only case where a cat is cited as the co-respondent.

He married again, this time to an actress, but this wife ran off with the estate handyman. The whole thing sounded like a bad plot from a comic *Downton*!

Unknown to me, Ben had a reputation as the black sheep of the family because of getting involved in this sort of bad publicity. He invested money in the name of his dog, Jasper. This dog figured in some legal action that Ben was involved in and was subject of some funny newspaper articles. Unfortunately, the investments would effectively evaporate when Jasper died because dogs usually do not make a last will and testament!! Ben tried unsuccessfully to 'clone' Jasper like Dolly the sheep so he could argue that Jasper was effectively still alive though his DNA! Ben seemed to like the infamy.

As Owen had said, the office was in Swallow Street, which was a little walk-through lane off Regent Street at the end near Piccadilly. The office was through a nondescript entrance off Swallow Street on the fourth floor.

Owen was there to meet me and introduce us.

Owen leaned down, tilting his head towards me in that birdlike fashion:

'They're upstairs, Mike.' Owen had met me in the lobby. 'I'll introduce you.'

'Have you done any actual flying for Shirlstar, Owen?'

'No, I've just acted as an adviser for the leasing of the aircraft. It was all fine for the first few years, but the two owners have run out of money,' Owen said in a passing comment, as if it was just one of those things. Bullshit!

'Okay,' I said. 'Let's get on with it.' I said.

We went up in one of those rickety old lifts, the ones with two sets of steel concertina doors, one outside and one inside. When both were slammed shut, the lift groaned its way to the fourth floor and the 'lair' of Benjamin Slade.

Owen led the way to the office. This was effectively the head office of Shirlstar Container Transport and Ben's very efficient (and probably long-suffering – or very thick-skinned) PA, Jenny. Jenny was an older lady, brunette with business like reading glasses perched on her petite nose. She wore an understated business dress, which helped to hide her slightly full figure. Jenny turned out to be a great help to me.

I was led into Ben's office. There were three men in there waiting for me. The office was a bit tatty, with slightly worn carpets, and a feeling of being a bit dusty. Nevertheless, it was overall sort of, plush. The walls were lined with oak panels and oil paintings dotted about of anonymous (to me) people standing with dogs or horses (or both); presumably, some of Ben's aristocratic family tree.

Owen stepped forward and introduced Ben to me first. Owen extended a hand between us.

'Ben, this is Mike Howard.'

'Mike, this is Ben Slade.'

Although Ben was a baronet, he preferred to be referred to as 'Ben' rather than 'Sir' Benjamin.

'Pleased to meet you, Ben,' I said, as we shook hands.

I took in Ben's appearance, trying to gauge his character. He was dressed in bright red, corduroy trousers, a checked shirt and a lightly checked sports jacket; the kind of 'uniform' that came from the prep school his parents had sent him to when he was seven and had never quite grown out of.

Ben was slightly rotund, but not fat, and had medium-length, fair hair – a bit like Michael Heseltine – with a hint of ginger. He reminded me of a combination of Billy Bunter, Billy Butlin and Rupert Bear all rolled into one; an almost comical figure.

'Good to meet you, too,' Ben replied, shaking my hand with a firm grip.

Ben's voice boomed with imperious, rounded vowels filled with an aristocratic confidence that was not used to being told no or disagreed with.

Owen introduced me to the other men in the room.

'Mike, this is Mark Tolner, Shirlstar's managing director.'

'Pleased to meet you, Mark,' I said, as we shook hands.

'My pleasure,' replied Mark.

Mark was tall, with a serious face and short, dark hair, dressed in a dark business suit with an understated tie and an air of competence and capability. He seemed to me to fit the position of MD.

Owen continued, 'And this is Stan, Ben's company lawyer.'

I shook Stan's hand. His full name was Stanley Beller, but somehow Stan's surname seemed to have been omitted by habit, so he just accepted 'Stan' as a name.

'Stan' I paused, shaking his hand, 'good to meet you, too,' I said.

Ben said, 'You've met Jenny, my personal assistant?'

'Yes I have,' I said, but completed the formality by shaking her hand, a little more gently than the others.

Jenny addressed Ben. 'Ben, I've just had word that the agents in Southampton are refusing to release those containers until the account for last month is cleared.'

'Bloody hell!' Ben's face changed colour to a ruddy hue. 'The bloody account has nothing to do with the release of the bloody containers. That is pure bloody ransom.'

His voice went up an octave, as he spluttered at the indignity of the insult. He turned to Stan and shouted:

'Stan! Sue the bastards. Sue them, Stan!' Spittle sprayed from his lips as he barked the words.

Apparently, this was a frequent order from Ben to Stan. Ben was a regular and, some would say, vexatious litigant. I would discover this for myself, first-hand later in these events.

We discussed the whole situation. Ben explained that he had leased these two 'jets' to Nigerians with whom he had been involved in his shipping and container business. They had been fine until a year ago (Vanni) and six months ago with Prince Olori. Shirlstar had gone through the usual methods of attempting to recover the outstanding money.

'But in the end, to protect our interests, we had to go "legal" on the bastards,' said Ben.

There were other explanations and background information, but I'll not bore you with that. Needless to say, I was still slightly unconvinced about taking it on.

'So,' Ben continued, 'are you going to take the job? For twenty thousand pounds, it should be an easy job!'

'Firstly, I am still thinking about it,' I replied. 'This is a fact-finding meeting. Secondly, my price is thirty thousand pounds for each aeroplane.'

I hated the word 'jet'. My father, Roy, had always insisted on using the word 'aeroplane', and I went along with that description.

'HOW MUCH?' Ben choked as if I was strangling his wallet. 'You must be joking.'

'With respect, Ben,' I replied, 'I've worked in Nigeria for six years, and it is a difficult place at the best of times.'

I paused for effect, holding Ben's gaze with deliberate, strong eye contact. I wanted him to be in no doubt that I was very firm in my position and to undermine any idea of him being able to bully me into doing his bidding. From the way the people around him behaved, Ben was used to getting his own way.

I continued, 'On top of this, and I shouldn't need to remind you, there was a military coup last December and the whole country is in complete upheaval.' Again, I paused. 'This makes doing anything more difficult – especially negotiating the release of a couple of executive jets with the government as it is at the moment. It is a very fluid situation with many risks.'

It all sounded very reasonable, but I had in fact called a good friend of mine in Nigeria who ran Tradewinds Airways, David Fagan. Dave was a dyed in the wool Nigerian 'hand' who had been in the country for many years. We were great friends and had some great times together.

Dave had said the country was a mess, so when I mentioned the two aeroplanes and the owners.

Dave warned, 'Olori's okay but, as you know, Vanni is a dangerous man, especially at the moment. He is well in with the new military government, so I would be very careful on that one.' Dave had spoken in a very serious tone.

Ben was getting a bit cross and blustered:

'Negotiate?' He added, 'If it's a repossession don't you just go in and grab the bloody things?'

I was amused at the naivety of the suggestion.

'With respect Ben, Lagos is a huge international airport. It is also the main base of the Nigerian Air Force. You just simply cannot go and *grab a jet* and take off without going through normal aviation procedures. So no, you cannot just turn up and grab them.' I continued, 'Anyway, I will not commit myself to anything now. I need to make a decision as to whether I want to take on what might be a risky and very difficult job, and you need to reconsider what it's worth to you for me to recover your assets. On top of that, there will be expenses at a rate of one hundred and fifty pounds a day.'

I finished setting out my position firmly. I was not going to be bulldozed by a baronet!

Also, my internal warning system was sounding louder and louder... Trouble was it was not as loud as my overdraft warning alarm. My internal intuition system was giving rise to serious concerns about the background to these aeroplanes, just a feeling that perhaps I was not getting the entire story.

I knew that I was pretty well the only guy in the executive jet world with enough African/Nigerian experience to do this job. That is why Shirlstar had gravitated to me through Owen's recommendation. I had in fact made up my mind, but I was not going to say so at this time – as a negotiating ploy, like Poker. Keep a straight face!

I decided to employ the leverage that was in my hands to find out as much as possible about these lease contracts.

'I will also need to have *all* the background files and information for these two aeroplanes. This will also have to include all the court evidence and the judge's decision on authority to repossess *if* I decide to go ahead. I will think about it over the weekend and come back to see you next week to discuss this further. *If* we go ahead, I will bring my lawyer, Nick Munns, to put together a contract for each aeroplane.'

I was quite blunt. It felt good to be in control. Not my usual rush in, devil-may-care way. Taking Nick's advice seriously, I was going to make sure that this was going to be very much on my terms.

Clearly, Ben felt that he needed to sound reasonable. I think in the back of his mind having a bunch of money tied up in those jets was something he wanted to get back. I was probably the best chance he had of getting it.

'Okay, I will get my PA to do that,' replied Ben.He then picked up the phone on his sumptuous oak desk.

'Jenny, please can you get all the stuff on these jets together for Captain Howard and have it ready for our next meeting?'

'Yes, Ben. I will attend to that as a matter of priority,' Jenny replied.

Fortunately, Jenny was *very* efficient, so for us this was the biggest godsend in the whole sorry tale.

We will return to the negotiations in due course, but at this time events not related to me, were creating a series of events that would give good reason for my 'warning systems' to be activated, so let's move on to those.

CHAPTER 8

The Nigerians and Israelis Move to London

Mossad were in Tottenham, plotting to kidnap a Nigerian in London, a Mr Umaru Dikko.

Umaru Dikko was the transport minister in Nigeria before the coup in December and had run off to London to avoid the revenge of the new military rulers.

Yes, you heard it, but this gets more bizarre as we go on.

Whilst I was negotiating with Shirlstar, Mossad and a Nigerian secret service team had come to London.

They arrived in early May 1984. This was the culmination of very high-level and clandestine meetings between the prime minister of Israel and the president of Nigeria.

Major Mohammed Yusuf and his Nigerian secret service team rented an apartment on Cromwell Road and posed as refugees from the new regime whilst the Mossad agents, Alexander Barak and Felix Abithol, posed as anti-apartheid activists and rented rooms in hotels catering to tourists from Africa.

Working separately but in close contact, the two teams searched among the Nigerian expat community in London, gradually narrowing their search to West London, to the area around Hyde Park where many wealthy Nigerian exiles lived.

Between them, they looked through the electoral registers available in the area's town halls and other freely available databases, but they could not find any trace of Dikko.

Mossad used their many and sophisicated sources of information to locate Dikko worldwide and had narrowed down the options. They were not sure, but it was very likely that he was in the UK, and probably in London. They were pretty sure that Dikko was there somewhere.

Around two weeks before my first meeting with Ben, Mossad agents Barak and Abithol walked into the workshops of a joinery/carpentry business tucked away off Tottenham Court Road.

These Mossad agents were some of the best that the Israeli secret service had to offer. Both moved with the quiet confidence of men who could cope with any aggressive situation that was presented to them.

This workshop was rather like Dr Who's Tardis. From an unassuming entrance on a Tottenham Court Road side street, it led into a very large workshop.

There were two large workbenches in the centre of the room. Surrounding them, hitched onto the walls were the various tools of the carpentry trade. Sheets of wood of different types rested in frames to keep them tidy.

At the far end, there were both finished and half-finished projects. The workshop had the distinctive smell of pinewood and wood glue. The mossad agents met the owner, Johnson Odahlu. Johnson was working at one of the workbenches on a large cabinet with a hand plane. He was bent over the piece, carefully sculpting the timber.

He was a tall, handsome African with classic, powerful features. He had very toned and solid muscles, exposed by his white T-shirt. His curly, brown hair was shaved fashionably close revealing a broad skull with an exaggeratedly rounded rear. His forehead was both high and broad, and he had dark brown eyes with slightly indistinct pupils. He gave the impression of a powerful and very strong fighter.

Apart from a few visits to Nigeria, Johnson, at 28 years old, had been in London for the majority of his life. His mother was a poor lady who sold beer at the side of the road in Lagos. Over the years, before Johnson was born, she saved her money. When she was eight months pregnant, like a lot of other Nigerian ladies, Johnson's mother bought a Nigerian Airways ticket and travelled to London.

This meant, as well as having her baby courtesy of the NHS, Johnson was born in the UK. This also meant he was automatically eligible for a British passport giving Johnson and his mother access to massive benefits from the UK.

Johnson's mother was banking on him providing for the rest of the family in the future. Indeed, this is what happened. He now worked with his other four brothers in London. Their mother was also now in London and the family were doing very well.

Both Barak and Abithol had seen active service in the Israeli army before joining Mossad. Which was why they moved with the absolute confidence of men who were extremely able to look after themselves; they had the aura of men who feared nothing, nothing at all. Both had killed many times in their careers.

Other than that fact, they were both typical Israeli men; not too tall, swarthy, dark complexions, and very short, dark hair cut in the way of the military. Their hair was so short that their scalps were clearly visible. Both had scars showing on their scalps from different episodes in their military lives.

Although young, both were experts in Krav Maga and had spent years teaching this in the Israel Defence Forces. Krav Maga is a self-defence martial art developed in Israel. It is a mixture of wrestling, boxing, ju-jitsu and karate. Krav Maga, whilst definitely not very pretty, is very effective. The aim is to end an attack, even if that attack involved a gun or knife, in less than a few seconds.

Both felt that this was a very odd job their boss, Mossad Director General Nahum Admoni, had sent them on. They were to work with a number of Nigerian security service agents, led by Major Mohammed Yusuf once of the Nigerian Army, they were to 'facilitate' the kidnapping of the former civilian transport minister, Umaru Dikko.

Apparently, Dikko had fled Nigeria at the time of the coup five months previously with a few (actually rumoured to be six) billion US dollars. The carpentry business had been researched and recommended as 'discreet', with indirect family links to the Nigerian military government. So, if necessary, Johnson could be leaned on to keep quiet.

This family were linked to a second-tier general in the new military government. So they had been flagged when Buhari, the head of this new government, found out that Dikko had made off with such an enormous sum of money. Buhari and his advisers had cooked up a plan to kidnap Dikko and ship him out in a box as 'diplomatic baggage'.

The plan was to bring him back to Lagos, give him a fair trial, after which he would be hung on Bar Beach, Lagos.

A bit of (boring but necessary) background: an intelligent and normally quiet, thoughtful man, Buhari was effervescent with rage when he discovered the extent of dishonesty perpetrated by the civilian government that he had overthrown using the power of the army.

In fact, on day two after the coup, Buhari made a list of ex-ministers of the civilian government who had cheated the country and made off with large amounts of cash.

Dikko had been an influential transport minister in the civilian administration of President Shehu Shagari (his brother in Law) and due to the missing $6 Billion US, Dikko became the main focus of Buhari's anger and easily made it to the top of this list.

As I said earlier, Buhari wanted Dikko found, brought back to Nigeria to face a 'fair' trial and then that public execution (after returning the money, of course).

I imagine Buhari would have probably liked the cash for himself.

The planning for getting Dikko back to Nigeria started very soon after the coup in a daring plot.

Buhari's advisers in the secret service suggested using their 'friends' in Mossad to help with what was going to be the most outrageous and (diplomatically) offensive act by the Nigerian government carried out on British soil, i.e. kidnapping Dikko and shipping him back to Nigeria drugged and in a box marked 'Diplomatic Baggage'.

To put all this into context, as a major diplomatic incident, these events were probably second only to the shooting of PC Yvonne Fletcher by the Libyans from their embassy in London on 17 April 1984, earlier that year.

Obviously, this would be a flagrant breach of the Vienna Convention on Diplomatic Relations of 1961. In fact, it would be famous in this regard, and the Nigerians knew full well that the diplomatic shit would hit the diplomatic fan when news surfaced of what they had done. This would have been a bit obvious when poor old Dikko was dangling from a rope after his very public hanging on Bar Beach, Lagos, after that *very fair* trial!

The link between the Israelis and the Nigerians was surprising. It exploited the subtle (clandestine) working relationship, the 'you scratch my back and I'll scratch yours' arrangement. However, the power was more in the Nigerians' hands.

Nigeria's relationship with Israel was very complex and largely unknown. It would even have surprised the general 'in the know' political/establishment class around the world. In actual fact, at the instigation of the Organization of African Unity (OAU), Nigeria had terminated diplomatic relations with Israel in 1973.

Although there were no official diplomatic relations between Nigeria and Israel, the two countries continued to conduct business deals with each other out of public sight.

Nigeria supplied more than 50% of Israel's crude oil in exchange for military hardware. From Israel's perspective, the continuation of the oil flow from a country with a high Muslim population did have a strategic advantage.

The continuation of that flow was cast into doubt on 1 January 1984, when news of the coup reached Israel, and Israel became aware that Nigeria's new military regime would be led by another Muslim. Israel unsuccessfully tried to make contact with the new military regime.

In his book on Mossad entitled *Gideon's Spies: The Secret History of the Mossad*, Gordon Thomas claims that Israeli Prime Minister Yitzhak Shamir was concerned that the new regime might interrupt Israel's oil supply from Nigeria. This would be disastrous for Israel.

Through their extensive intelligence gathering of 'assets', Israel saw an opening to gain favour with General Buhari. Nigeria began to arrest leading politicians from the former government for corruption. Dikko was still at large, but the regime was unaware of his whereabouts. Israel offered to track Dikko down using its formidable intelligence agency, Mossad.

Although oil was doubtless a factor, it seems illogical that Israel would independently offer up the services of its intelligence agency solely to maintain the supply of oil it was already receiving. More likely was the strong economic benefits to the relationship between Israel and Nigeria over the years. So, it was more probable that the new Nigerian regime solicited Mossad's intervention through its network of contacts among the Israeli security establishment to capture Dikko (and probably others too).

Several senior officers in the Nigerian army had long-standing associations with Israeli businessmen and security agents. For example, former head of state General Olusegun Obasanjo had established an agricultural farm with the assistance of Israeli experts, including a contractor named Elisha Cohen (although Obasanjo did not necessarily have any involvement in the Dikko affair).

Cohen, and his company Solel Boneh, had operated in Nigeria for decades carrying out construction work. An article in the Israeli newspaper *Haaretz* claimed that Cohen was instrumental in securing Israeli cooperation.

Mossad's director Nahum Admoni travelled to Lagos on a Canadian passport to meet President Buhari – Mossad agents were fond of travelling on forged diplomatic passports of friendly countries.

Admoni made Buhari an offer he could not refuse. He offered to find Dikko and repatriate him to Nigeria to face justice. It was at this meeting that the two countries hashed the plot to find Dikko and deliver him back to Nigeria to face that sensational show trial. It would be a *cause célèbre* for the new regime's war on corruption.

However, Buhari wanted more. He didn't just want physical custody of Dikko, but the location of the offshore accounts where Dikko had deposited the loot he had embezzled from Nigeria, an undertaking by Israel to cooperate with Nigeria's National Security Organisation (NSO), and for Israel to take no credit when Dikko was eventually captured. In actual fact, the last requirement was to the advantage of Israel – they would have anticipated the diplomatic stink that would follow these events.

For the long-term benefit of Israel, Admoni agreed and put his formidable resources within Mossad to work.

If the plan succeeded, it would be a pivotal moment for Nigeria's almost hereditary battle against corruption; and it would symbolise a once and for all break with 'the corrupt politicians of the past' (Yeah, right!).

Because of this arrangement, the kidnap of Dikko, who was likely to be in London, was not going to be an easy task. It was not something that the Nigerian secret service had ever done, but Mossad, of course, had been known to get up to all sorts of questionable 'black ops'.

In these circumstances, the Nigerian military government sent their secret service to offer whatever assistance they could to the Mossad agents and to take the flack if it all went wrong. However, that did not work out as planned!

So, all of this high-level skulduggery culminated in a plan that required the two Mossad agents to be standing in Johnson's carpentry workshop ordering two boxes that were very similar to the size of a double coffin.

'Mr Odahlu?' asked Barak.

'Yes.' Johnson placed the plane to one side and turned to face the two Mossad agents.

'I am Alexander Barak, and this is Felix Abithol. I believe you are expecting us.'

'Yes, I am.' replied Johnson.

Johnson was aware of the visit but had not been told too much detail by his uncle, who had rung him a couple of weeks previously.

Barak pulled some drawings out of a briefcase he was carrying.

'These are the plans for two boxes that are required to be ready for collection in two weeks' time,' said Barak.

The boxes were to be 1.2 metres in height, 1.2 metres in depth and 1.8 metres in width. The interiors had a central piece dividing both in half. Imagine two coffins joined together but with straight sides. One of the centre dividing sections did not go all the way through, leaving approximately one third of this container open. Both boxes had many small holes in the exterior; small so as not to be obvious, similar to crates that are used to transport animals, which is what, effectively, these were for.

'The boxes are similar but with significant differences,' stated Barak. 'You will be paid in cash – one third now, the rest on delivery. This *must* be discreet and *must* be on time,' he emphasised.

Johnson registered the cold, flinty look in the eyes of the man opposite him.

As I said before, Johnson was very strong and, like a lot of black men, had a powerful, very lean physique and was more than capable of looking after himself, but he registered that no-nonsense look and decided that he would definitely not be inclined to let these men down.

Indeed, the way the job paid, he would be glad to get it done and out of the way as soon as possible.

CHAPTER 9

Negotiations Continue with Shirlstar

The search by the Nigerians and the Israelis continued while my negotiations proceeded with Shirlstar.

It was a difficult negotiation because Ben wanted me 'to just go' and I was (as was said earlier) paying attention to Nick Munns' advice.

Nick (fortunately) was taking the whole thing in a slow and methodical manner. Indeed, Nick was present at all the meetings that followed. So it was Nick Munns, Ben, Stan and I who attended these meetings, thrashing out the basis for the contract to repossess the aeroplanes. As a compromise between Ben's £20,000 and my £30,000, a price was reached of £25,000 plus expenses of £150 per day.

Ben moaned like hell about the £150 per day.

'You could just go to the beach and enjoy yourself and bank a hundred and fifty a day,' he said, sounding as though I was squeezing him until the pips squeaked.

Ben had no conception at all about how that part of the world worked.

'I can assure you, Ben, Lagos is not a favourite holiday destination. Entertainment on the beach is usually watching a man or woman swinging at the end of a rope,' I explained with a bit of humour. 'I want to be in and then out as quick as possible,' I finished flatly.

After much discussion with Nick, who had a friend in corporate law, the contract was written so that it would be 'seen to be completed' when the aeroplane left Nigerian territorial airspace.

Although Ben squawked at this, objecting to potential abuse, he gave way.

I had successfully argued that because the aeroplanes had not been flown for some time, and also hadn't had any maintenance work carried out on them for some length of time. There was no way of knowing the actual physical state they would be in. It was very likely that the aeroplanes would have to undergo scheduled maintenance in whatever country they first landed; they may not be in a state to embark on a 2,000-mile journey back to the UK. Plus, any insurance would be invalidated by their maintenance state.

'Ben, it is possible that engineers would have to be flown out of the UK to do this,' I explained.

The timing of this and how long any maintenance would take was not my problem.

'Although I would almost certainly oversee the maintenance and fly them back to the UK, this is not part of the actual repossession contract,' I said. 'Also remember, as these aircraft have not flown for some time, there is no guarantee that they will be in a fit state to fly at all. I will not know until I get there' I added as a warning.

Ben was certainly not used to being dictated to; you could see the discomfort from his body language. He frequently shifted position, leaning forward frowning and then leaning back with hands clasped behind his head. But, in the end, he had to accept my terms if he wanted his bloody 'JETS' back!

So, the contract was constructed to reflect this. One payment of £12,500 immediately on departing Nigerian airspace, the other tranche of £12,500 would be paid on reaching UK airspace, or 21 days after departing Nigerian airspace.

Gradually, the contract was hardened up. This involved me, Nick Munns, 'Stan' and Ben Slade meeting several times, and the use of motorcycle couriers flashing about with draft contracts.

Obviously, I had agreed to go. Ben was absolutely focused on getting me on the way to Nigeria as soon as possible, but the negotiations had frustrated him because of the lack of real progress.

Almost every time I went to the offices in Swallow Street, bizarre and entertaining events were happening, with Ben's most used phrase echoing around the office: 'Sue him, Stan!'

At the final stage, when on a time limit to get up to Swallow Street, the motorcycle courier was late from Nick's contract law friend, and the whole transport timing thing dissolved into chaos.

This was the 'final' copy of the contract and it needed to be signed by Ben Slade with witnesses. For various reasons, it had to be done by a certain time.

Having been back and forward to Swallow Street, I had found a great route by car into London. This took us just west of Thornton Heath along Portland Road, making use of unknown but direct roads through housing estates. It was taking 45 minutes on a good day, and I had got to know the route well.

Trouble was, on this day (Sod's Law), there was a huge funeral procession travelling at 10 mph on Portland Road, leading into Beulah Hill.

'Shit! Bollocks!' Nick and I both said in unison.

'Where's the nearest crematorium, Mike?' asked Nick.

'I don't know, Nick. Can you smell burning?' (Yes, I have a bad sense of humour, but I couldn't resist it.)

'You know it will screw the whole thing today if we cannot get there on time,' observed Nick.

'Nick?'

'Yes, Mike,' he replied.

'Close your eyes!'

I had one of those souped-up Renault 5 cars; very quick. It was metallic blue with 'La Barouche' written on the sides. (Yes, I know, a bit over the top, but it had been Catriona's idea.) Although I was no Lewis Hamilton, I was capable of very fast (safe) driving.

What happened here was not one for the Institute of Advanced Motorists or, indeed, the British way of driving – demonstrating manners, tolerance and patience to other drivers – mind you, you do not see a lot of that at school run times with women in Chelsea tractors!

So, I started overtaking the funeral procession, driving in the middle of the road, very close to the many, many cars containing the bereaved family and friends of the dear departed.

'Christ, whoever it was must have been very popular,' I said out loud.

The car horns of the procession began as soon as the overtaking manoeuvres first started.

'Shit, Mike!' said Nick. 'I cannot believe you're doing this!'

'You're supposed to have your eyes closed,' I replied.

Nick was holding onto the sides of his seat as the speed increased to 60 mph to overtake before braking to 10 mph and pushing into the cortège. This was accompanied by even more loud and angry horns blowing. Not exactly a peaceful funeral, I'm afraid.

We eventually reached the hearse at the front of the procession and squeezed past. The look of the normally stony-faced funeral directors said it all.

'I believe they were swearing at us,' I said.

'I can lip-read,' Nick replied. 'They're not going to forget that funeral in a long time!'

'They'll get over it… Well, eventually! But at least we're on our way.'

We got to Swallow Street on time and the contract, watertight, as Nick had promised, was signed.

This was the moment that the whole thing was a 'go'.

Cash was handed over to me; enough for two weeks for two crew, around £2,500, and money for the airline tickets (first class) to Lagos.

The wonderful Jenny handed over a large Manila envelope to me.

'This is all the information in our files on the two aircraft,' she said.

I do not think Ben was party to or checked what was in that Manila envelope, but it saved our bacon in a lot of ways.

'Thank you, Jenny, much appreciated,' and I nodded to her in thanks for her help.

I would find out in Lagos, Abidjan and a few years later in the high court, just how much I would appreciate the work of the very efficient PA Jenny!

CHAPTER 10

Who Comes with Me as My First Officer?

There was a big problem. The problem was I had worked in Nigeria (and Africa in general) for many years, and it required a different mindset to operate aircraft in these parts of the world – mainly a lot of patience and also caring about 'where you are and what you do' in relation to self-preservation.

As I have said, I had flown around Africa for many years, gaining the necessary experience to cope with the esoteric difficulties associated with operating a sophisticated jet in these challenging parts of the world.

This was all about self-preservation. Nowadays in flying they refer to it as Threat and Error Management (TEM), but this is just a modern term for what I had always done – consciously or subconsciously making sure I ended the day safe and going on a job like this had a lot of unknown risks.

So, selection of a first officer was a problem in terms of the overall 'who was in charge', as this related to making decisions, both on the ground and in the air. The people around you and how they react to situations can affect your own decision-making immeasurably.

Friends who were pilots had not flown out in Africa and did not have experience on the HS125. Also, because the flying environment, both on the ground and in the air, was so different, that person could then add another management dimension – distraction – for me. The end result could mean that the other person may become a problem if things became difficult, which was entirely possible.

Unfortunately, all the guys I could think of to take with me would almost certainly freak out if things went wrong. Please don't misunderstand me, I did not intend to get into a dangerous situation, it was just that Africa had a habit of throwing unexpected stuff at you. And Nigeria was top of this 'unexpected stuff' tree. Then, add to that the nature of this particular job and a military coup on top of that.

This problem was considered and mulled over until, in the end, Catriona was the only person that I felt had the capacity to cope. This sounds strange, considering the weaknesses she had, but Catriona had an underlying strength and resilience.

It should be noted that all my 'friends' turned on me after this event – jealous that they did not have the chance to come with me. I was effectively 'sent to Coventry'. Aviation is always wise after the event.

I never quite understood this behaviour until many years later when a mutual (non-flying) friend explained that, as well as my infamy, they were jealous of me flying jets when they were flying piston-powered aeroplanes – how sad.

Catriona jumped at the chance when I suggested it. We had long discussions about the threats and difficulties of being in Africa. I described to her some of the distressing events that I had experienced: necklacing – as mentioned earlier, instant justice by the mob; bodies lying by the side of the road for days, plus if you reported them, you were arrested for murder, and then responsible for removing the body and the disposal of it. Stuff like this was so far removed from our normal lives that it almost sounded like a fantasy such was the cheapness of a human life.

But Catriona understood. And it was decided that she would come with me.

The minimum legal requirement for sitting in the co-pilot's seat in an HS125 was a Flight Radiotelephony Operators Licence – an

RT Licence.

Obviously, Catriona had no flying experience whatsoever. So somehow, I would have to get her a radiotelephony licence. As we were going to leave very soon, it was not possible to put her through a formal radiotelephony training course and exams...

'Mmm... What can I do to get you a licence?' I mused, thinking out loud. Then it came to me: Ivan Palmer!

Ivan had been a student at the Norfolk and Norwich Aero Club when John and I were instructing there. He was a very likeable character, about 30 years old then, tall and slightly overweight due to bad eating habits with long shifts at 'Comet Electrical Warehouse' (a forerunner to Currys PC World). He had an early receding hairline above a broad forehead, thick, dark eyebrows over brown eyes, and a large hooked nose. Ivan had pale skin because he hardly ever managed to get out when the sun was shining – he worked and worked to support his family. Ivan was married with a little baby, so all his (very) limited income went on them.

Although Ivan was penniless, he was absolutely determined to become a professional pilot. He was a 'charity case' for John and me. As manager of the Comet warehouse in Norwich, he did have the flexibility to 'disappear' for a few hours without much problem.

As the four aeroplanes at the Norwich base needed maintenance every 50 flying hours. This maintenance had to be carried out at the club's Swanton Morley base, about 20 minutes flying away, and we always had to bring an aeroplane back to replace the one that was off on maintenance.

Every time this happened, I would ring Ivan:

'Ivan! Get your arse over here. We have a ferry flight in an hour!'

This meant Ivan took advantage of 40 minutes' flying and, as he was with either John or me, a free flying lesson. In fact, he more or less did his PPL for free.

I know, I know. You're thinking, '*What the hell has this got to do with the RT Licence problem, Mike?'*

Well, the answer is that after many free flights and obtaining a PPL, Ivan then went on to obtain a Flight Instructor Rating.

Ivan eventually became the chief flying instructor at a flying club in Southend in Essex. And... *guess what?* Ivan was also a *Radiotelephony Licence examiner!* And he obviously owed me BIG TIME!

So, I called him, having not spoken for a few years.

'Hi, Ivan, it's Mike. How you doing? I need a huge favour...'

'Hi, Mike, long time no hear! Nothing is a problem. What's going on?' replied a curious Ivan.

'I've got this one-off job to collect a jet from Africa' I explained 'and I need another member of crew to sit in the right-hand seat...'

Ivan interrupted, 'I'll do it!' He was effervescent with excitement.

'Sorry, matey, but I've got someone lined up already and, for a number of reasons, it has to be her. Trouble is, she hasn't got a pilot's licence, and I need to get her a Flight Radiotelephony Operators Licence... and fairly quickly! That is the favour!'

'Oh, I see,' replied a very disappointed Ivan. 'When do you need this? Has she got any RT experience?'

'By the end of next week, we're departing at the weekend – and no, she hasn't a scrap. She doesn't even know the phonetic alphabet!'

'Shit,' replied Ivan. 'That *will* be a challenge.'

'I knew it would be, and I knew you would move mountains for me!' I replied. 'I will go to the CAA in Kingsway to get the licence issued when we have the paperwork.'

'Okay,' Ivan said, 'leave it to me. I'll sort it out.'

Aviation is a funny game, you get to meet people and become friends, and time and space does not change that relationship. I had not seen John Brooks for many, many years, but we are in touch now and the same with Ivan, there's no difference to the friendship we had in

Norwich all those years ago. In fact, there will be a proper reunion when this book is published. I am so looking forward to that.

John became a captain in Monarch Airlines (now retired) and flew with Ivan who became a first officer at Monarch with John. As I write this story, I'm about to get in touch with Ivan again. It will be great to chat to him once more and catch up.

Sometimes you meet friends in the most remote places on earth as you do 'trips' – extraordinary. I met a mate in Tamanrasset in the middle of the Sahara Desert at five in the morning. Tamanrasset is an oasis city in southern Algeria, high in the Ahaggar (Hoggar) Mountains.

The airport was my regular fuel stop northbound for the UK. I always loved the vista of Tam, where the mountains were of volcanic origin. Watching the sun rising while the guys were refuelling was one of those incredible views that's one of the gifts of being a well-travelled pilot.

'Shit! Hi, Mike. What the fuck are you doing here?'

'God! Hi, Mark.'

Mark had been my first officer years before and turned up with his own aeroplane.

'I'm trying to work out how to get to Palma, avoiding landing at Algiers – I've got no landing clearance here and Air Traffic Control have said I've got to go to Algiers to do the paperwork. That will take bloody ages!'

'Oh dear. What are you going to do?' Mark asked.

'I'm going to file a flight plan for Algiers with a diversion airport of Palma, and then divert to Palma above Algiers – that should do it – they're hardly going to shoot me down!'

We both laughed and chatted. I did do exactly that. Algiers air traffic control just happily cleared me to Palma and didn't query my actions. It was so much better than being stuck on the ground negotiating with a reluctant civil servant in a dusty, sweltering office for hours.

Sorry, I digress (again!).

We successfully obtained Catriona her RT Licence. It was a posh, silver-grey cardboard version, like my green airline transport pilot licence. I had no idea the CAA had specific stand-alone radio licences.

So, Catriona was qualified and, therefore, a licenced first officer (of sorts). I had a signed contract and cash in hand and tickets to Lagos. Pretty well every detail had been covered.

No more fucking about; it was time to go and do it. It was Thursday 10th May 1984.

CHAPTER 11

Travelling to Lagos

Nigerian Airways planes smelled 30% of Lagos, which meant a slight mixture of foul body odour and sewerage, along with the smell of women feeding their babies and changing nappies yuck! This took place without taking into account other travelling passengers – nice! It was always recommended that you were careful to check that your seat did not have the remains of a previous occupant's baby's nappy. Expeditious use of a blanket was the only way out of that problem.

I had rung David Fagan in advance and sort of explained the project; thankfully, he had kindly offered us accommodation for the stay.

On the flight out to Lagos was the first time I'd looked at the documents that Jenny, Ben's PA, had provided.

I had already seen the court documents relating to the right to repossess the aeroplanes, but I couldn't put my finger on that nagging, red light my intuition was causing to flash.

Catriona was sitting next to me. We had club seats, but that did not mean much on Nigerian Airways; it was still not particularly comfortable.

I pulled all the documents out of the large Manila envelope and started to go through them.

The most interesting was a series of Ben's desk notepapers. These were A3 size and came on a large pad. He clearly used these to make notes during telephone calls and were rather chaotic. When this whole mess ended up in court, they were a godsend to have and very enlightening in the end.

There were a number of these, and I looked at them in order. What I noticed first was the reference to the '*Yona B*' and a cost of bunkering in Nigerian naira, with 'Prince Olori' written next to it. Next to that was '£75,000', then 'Lloyds' and a group of figures that looked like a bank account number.

'Mmm… it looks to me like Shirlstar were carrying out illegal currency transactions,' I said to Catriona.

'What do you mean?' she replied, clearly curious.

'These are copies of Ben's jotters from his desk, and I'm finding references to ships and refuelling, and the replenishing of supplies all paid locally, and then references to amounts paid in London that equate to the black market exchange rate,' I replied. 'Works for them all.'

'Oh, does that happen a lot?' Catriona asked.

'Oh God, yes, it's an ongoing market. There are very tight restrictions on exchanging naira into "hard currencies", so the black market is used in all sorts of ways to filter money into places so that wealthy Nigerians can spend it. It's gone on for years.' I added, 'Ben Slade is milking this and getting cheap refuelling of his container ships.'

We were getting close to landing at Lagos, so I left analysing the paperwork until later. At least I had a bit of an idea about the background and what had been happening. I felt that one jet being repossessed was (sort of) understandable. However, two at the same time, from two different parties seemed very unusual. Although the notes of transactions on Ben's jotter may have contained something of an explanation.

The 747 touched down at Lagos and taxied towards the stand. Whilst still moving, everyone started getting up and pulling various bags from the overhead lockers.

'Keep your head down, Catriona! These guys don't respect the seat belt signs.'

It was chaos – and then funny. We stayed in our seats; the aisles were full of sweaty bodies eager to get off the aircraft.

When we got to the stand, the brakes were slammed on and over they all went, just like a line of dominoes. I was laughing because it was so predictable.

Eventually, the doors were opened, and then the disgusting smell, that I mentioned earlier, hit you.

'God! What a smell!' Catriona said, as she held her hand over her nose and mouth.

'I did warn you,' I replied, 'but you will get used to it.'

The throng were all pushing towards the door, eager to disembark. This nicely left space for us to stand and retrieve our cabin bags – with appropriate British calm. We would see them all in the baggage collection hall in a moment anyway, there was no rush.

I carefully put the Manila envelope containing the documents into my cabin bag and moved ahead of Catriona, as we headed off the aircraft.

We passed a picture similar to the Somme, which was famous for muddy trenches, although, this was not mud! The mess in the cabin was unbelievable. There were always lots of babies on UK to Lagos flights for the reasons explained earlier.

Knowing what we were about to walk into the terminal building, I said to Catriona to stay close behind me, the terminal building was always a complete nightmare.

As we passed up the ramp into the arrivals area, the picture was, as usual, incredible. It was a huge terminal building with baggage conveyors dotted along the hall. Inexplicably, there always seemed to be vast quantities of abandoned baggage strewn around, all wrapped with the traditional cling film.

Crowds of people milled around looking for their baggage. Once they had found it, they very reluctantly made their way to the passport control and customs.

The heat in the terminal was stifling – over 45°c. This temperature was exaggerated by the number of humans in the hall, all generating heat and adding to the already very hot air. The humidity was 100%. The air conditioning never worked – or if it did, it was completely ineffective.

The economy of Nigeria is built on a lot of 'dash' (or bribes). When Nigerians go to London, they come back with a fantastic array of goods (as well as the babies).

Coming off the baggage conveyors were microwaves, televisions, small cookers and other indiscernible goods. All these goods and normal bags too, were wrapped in cling film. The cling film was to prevent the baggage handlers from opening the bags and nicking their stuff.

The reason for the reluctance to approach customs was understandable. As people got to the front of the queue, their bags were opened with forensic attention, everything taken out and each item had a price, a 'dash tax'. Then, particularly the women passengers would argue, scream and shout at the customs men and women, who generally remained impassive.

Nothing would happen until they paid the dash tax.

We retrieved our bags and went through passport control. I had arranged for visas to be issued using a company in London that went to the embassy – again, it was a horrendous process and took a huge amount of time; it was just better to pay.

When we got to customs, our bags got the same treatment.

'You pay two hundred naira,' barked the customs man with a deep, throaty, African lilt.

'Okay,' I replied and handed it over.

He looked shocked that there was no dispute. Previously, I would have argued, but I just couldn't be arsed that day. I just wanted to get out of the place; it gave me the creeps. I knew people had inexplicably disappeared as they were going through this terminal. I had, for most of the time, managed to fly myself out of the country.

Looking around, there were staff that were not in uniform but clearly not the 'normal' security. They could be identified by their watchful and menacing stares; black, cold, expressionless eyes and impassive faces. They were military government agents and a law unto themselves.

It has to be remembered that the rules in Africa, particularly Nigeria, run in a wholly different way to anything that happens elsewhere. There are no legal niceties here. That is why I was reluctant to bring another pilot with me.

Eventually, we escaped the main terminal and made it out to the 'ground side' of the airport. Here, the cacophony was different with hundreds of cars and taxis fighting for space and crowds of black faces shouting for your attention.

'You want taxi?' was the mantra. 'I take you, I take you. No problem.'

Others would be doing the classic West African high-pitched *hiss*, created by their tongue and teeth, to get your attention.

I pushed through the crowded area outside the terminal building with Catriona close behind. Poor girl. I had warned her, but the first two hours (it had taken that long to get through) were clearly a shock.

'It still smells,' she said with humour. 'I thought you said you get used to it!'

'Just give it a few weeks,' I joked in reply.

CHAPTER 12

Getting Settled in Ikeja

Standing outside the terminal, I was sweating. The 100% humidity makes you sweat with the slightest exertion.

Scanning the sea of humanity, I was looking for our name on a card. Dave Fagan had said he would send a driver for us. The driver should recognise us easily. We stood out like a sore thumb here.

The view from outside the terminal was a sea of corrugated iron roofs flowing into the distance like a brown, rusty lake. The colour was formed from a combination of the rusty iron and that deep red Harmattan dust that covers everything here.

This was very similar to Soweto, only bigger; full of humanity fighting for a little space. This was the outskirts of Lagos and populated by the people who used to work on the land up country. Nigeria was, at one stage, the largest exporter of cocoa beans in the world and sits on one of the world's largest areas of that famous stuff called black gold. Oil was now the only focus of this nation. It became the largest *importer* of Cocoa beans after oil was discovered and of more value.

Nigeria abandoned its history as a major producer of agricultural goods of all sorts. If you shoved a lollipop stick in the ground there, it would start sprouting. Anything planted there shoots up like a rocket, growing to twice the size it would anywhere else. I had seen huge warehouses next to the Niger River whilst travelling up river in the past.

Some Nigerian friends who fished the river took me on a boat trip up the river. It was a fantastic opportunity. They showed me the warehouses and substantial docks for loading the cargo. It was like the docks in East London: huge. But all that infrastructure was abandoned and just left to rot.

A consequence of this was the movement of people to the big cities searching for alternative incomes. Fighting with millions of others, they came and occupied this sprawling mass of corrugated iron shacks to scratch a living.

These shanties gradually expanded outwards from the outskirts of Lagos. In the murky distance, through the dusty haze, the skyscrapers of the main city could be made out, rising out of the orange haze; the other side of the coin to the poverty directly in front of us.

The roads to and from the airport were full of holes. Tarmac was laid, but this had worn away with no maintenance; a bit like the UK, but the holes here were a few feet deep! The ground underneath the tarmac was just red earth – as with everywhere in this area of the world. Vehicles had to pick their way carefully around trying not to damage their wheels and tyres. These holes filled with water from the frequent and torrential rains, making the depth of them concealed. Occasionally, a wheel would drop into a hole with a huge splash, chucking red, muddy water high up in the air.

It didn't really matter what colour your car was here, they all finished up a mucky, dusty red colour.

A cheerful, smiling chap then came pushing through the masses:

'Captain, Captain! I am here for you from Mr Fagan. I take you, I take you.'

Wearing a pilot's shirt with four gold bars on it could get you through pretty well anywhere around an airport here, as long as you walked with a confident stride. We had travelled out dressed this way. It had also helped Dave's driver to identify us.

Great, I thought, *we can get out of here at last.* 'Thank you. What is your name?'

'Captain...' he bowed very slightly in greeting '...my name is Sammy.'

'Well, Sammy, we are very pleased to meet you. Where is your car?' I asked.

'Follow me, Captain, it is not far,' Sammy replied, gesturing with his hand. He then headed off past the crowds outside the terminal.

Following Sammy, Catriona and I picked our way through humanity, trailing our wheelie bags behind us.

It was quite a long way to the car. Parking was not like Heathrow; you had to try to find a suitable place. Fortunately, Sammy had intimate knowledge of the airport. Tradewinds Airways was based there and their aeroplanes frequently flew through with cargo. He had parked down a secret entrance to the freight apron. After a few hundred yards, it was a relief to put the bags in the boot and get into the back seat.

Catriona looked exhausted; we were both dripping with sweat.

'I'm not looking my prettiest,' she commented.

'Neither am I, darling. My hair! I just can't do a thing with it,' I joked, framing my head with my hands.

Catriona *did not* burst into laughter... As I said before, I'm not very funny.

'The next experience is the driving,' I said. 'That is an experience in itself.' I continued to explain to Catriona, 'I should warn you that the roads here were designed for right-hand driving, but the government decided to switch to left-hand driving a few years ago. The accident rate, which is very high anyway, spiked by hundreds of per cent that year. This was mainly, and you will not believe this, because they switched cars on one day and trucks a few days later – it was absolute carnage!'

Catriona looked bemused. I did when I heard about it. Imagine in the UK that you want to join the motorway, but instead of joining to drive in the normal direction, on the left lane, you had to join to go on the other lane. This would involve a sharp turn to travel down the 'off' slip road. Then, after travelling along the right-hand carriageway, when exiting the motorway, you would have to make a sharp right turn to exit off the 'on' slip road. Only in Africa! Driving in Nigeria was always chaotic, with enormous traffic gridlock, but these changes really did not help.

We set off. Sammy was actually a very good driver (Dave Fagan would always find good guys); he picked his way through the morass of traffic quite safely. Catriona sat silent, fixed on the view ahead, tensely holding my hand.

Each expanse of road was a logjam of cars. Nigerian drivers were not the most patient in the world, with revving engines and incessant blowing of horns – all, of course, to absolutely no avail. Eventually, you would make progress past whatever the hold-up was, but blowing horns did not speed things up.

As you sat in the jam, there were hawkers selling all sorts of crap, from local newspapers to fake Rolex watches. They usually did not say anything but just stood impassively by the car window holding up their wares.

The smell from the fumes was awful whilst in the traffic jams, and you were surrounded by corrugated iron shanty houses and shops with masses of people wandering around.

I had friends, aircraft engineers, who, in this situation – effectively trapped in traffic – had been attacked by robbers wielding 20-inch parang knives. There had been 15 to 20 of them who appeared out of the crowds beside the road. They were determined and violent, chopping into windscreens and the A-pillars between the screens and doors of the cars. The engineers were robbed of everything they had, as were others in the same jam. They rightly felt that they were lucky to survive. As engineers, their VW Beetle was then adapted to withstand a similar attack by welding thick steel into the A-pillars, steel mesh into the windows and deadlocks into the doors.

I saw the vehicle just after the attack, and it was shocking to see the damage.

Mind you, you think that was bad, a similar thing happened to a commercial aeroplane, a DC-9 with around 90 passengers on board, taxiing out to depart on Runway 19 Right (19R) at Lagos. This taxi route required a long trip down an isolated and deserted taxiway. The robbers (posssibly the same ones) came from the bush nearby, down onto the taxiway and opened the freight doors as the aircraft was moving.

The captain did not know it was robbers – he just saw a cargo door annunciator in the cockpit. The captain then sent his first officer (as you would) to close the door. They stopped the aircraft, and then the first officer opened the main door and went out to shut the cargo door. He was then grabbed by the robbers.

They dragged him around to the front of the aircraft and held him with a parang to his neck.

It was Christmas, so the robbers were after the passengers' baggage that would have contained lots of Christmas gifts. I was just taking off from Runway 19L on the other side of the airport, for Port Harcourt, at the time, listening.

The captain came up on the radio:

'Tower, this is an emergency. We are being robbed on the taxiway.' Obviously, he sounded very distressed. 'The robbers are holding my first officer at knifepoint. You must send army/security/fire service.'

Air traffic said it would be a long time, as they could not help quickly.

The captain then asked, 'What shall I do?'

Air traffic control replied, 'Rev up your engines and kill them! KILL THEM!'

The reply was one of the most bizarre and funniest things I heard in my time in Africa.

'I am an aircraft captain; I am not authorised to kill anyone!'

The incident finished with the passengers also being robbed of their wallets and watches. After that, if you used Runway 19R, ATC would ask if you needed the whole length, advising, for safety, to take off at an intersection near the terminal, avoiding that isolated taxiway.

Anyway, enough of the war stories (for the time being).

We were heading for the residential district of Ikeja. Ikeja had some decent houses and a lot of the expatriates working at the airport lived there. You could also access the general aviation area of Lagos airport.

Importantly, this was where the two aeroplanes were supposed to be located. It was also where David Fagan's office was.

David had arranged accommodation in Ikeja. I'd also had a comprehensive telephone conversation with him prior to my departure from the UK. I'd asked him to use all his contacts to find out as much as possible about the two aircraft.

Eventually, after the usual game of cat and mouse through the traffic, we arrived at David's quite large office on the edge of Ikeja. Brick-built and single storey, it was a wide bungalow-style. There was a veranda that ran the width of the building with a few chairs outside that were occupied by a couple of Dave's staff. It had the mandatory corrugated iron roof.

The office sat amongst a few other commercial buildings. These offices with brick-built walls sat in the red, dusty earth that was a

Dave Fagin and his team outside the Tradewinds office in Ikeja

little churned up by the coming and going of vehicles. It was quite a tidy area, even though the buildings had the dusty, red coating, and appeared well organised amongst the few trees dotted about.

Dave and I were great mates and spent a lot of time together when I lived out in Lagos. It was like seeing a long-lost brother again. We gave each other a man hug, and I introduced Catriona.

'Pleased to meet you, David. Mike has told me lots about you and your adventures.'

'Yes,' I said, 'Dave is fearless when someone else is near the danger.'

Dave and I laughed like schoolboys.

'What are you two laughing at?' Catriona demanded.

'It's always a challenge to make good time driving into the main city. However, there are often military escorts for ministers or some other dignitaries. There is always one of them going somewhere. The escort is usually large trucks with lots of flashing lights and sirens. This opens up the traffic jams.' Pausing, I pictured the scene. 'What Dave does is follow *very* close, tucking in behind the escort. The guys in the rear escort get very angry and try to whip the car with their Sjambok whips. Sometimes we would get stuck too near the escort; it always seemed to be me who was closest. Then Dave would shout abuse at the enraged police escort and the whips would be cracking inches from me,' I explained. 'But it was funny.'

Catriona warmed to Dave. He was a very likeable character. Clearly of a Jewish background, he was not tall, about five feet eight inches, good-looking with a mop of fair hair and a deeply tanned face. Dave's uniform was a pair of khaki trousers and a white shirt. He reckoned it was the most comfortable in this environment. Dave had been in Africa – mainly Nigeria – for many, many years and knew everyone. Also, more importantly, he knew everything that was going on.

'Dave, have you found out anything about these two aeroplanes?' I asked.

During our call, I had asked if he could glean any background information from his contacts.

'Prince Olori's aircraft G-LORI is over in the GA (general aviation) parking area, just over the back here. Victor Vanni's aircraft hasn't been here for a long time, and nobody knows where it is,' Dave replied. 'Do you want to have a look at G-LORI? It's been pushed back off the main parking area out of the way – she looks in a bit of a sorry state,' he went on.

'Yes, let's go and have a quick look, Dave,' I said. I wanted to see without drawing attention to the fact that someone was looking at it.

The three of us walked from the Tradewinds office towards the General Aviation area. As we entered this area, it was immediately familiar. This was where I flew the HS125's from when I lived in the engineers staff house and was employed by AGIP (the Italian oil company) and the Nigerian state bank – flying banknotes around the country. (*What? Trusting me with a planeload of cash?*)

There were some very funny stories attached to those flights. The aeroplanes had been based at the hangar of Aerocontractors – a Dutch company that looked after the maintenance, handling of passengers and, of course, the banknotes.

Aerocontractors' hangar was off to our right, with a mix of half a dozen Twin Otter and HS125 jets parked outside.

A similar-sized building to our left was Mobil Oil's hangar, also with a few Twin Otter aeroplanes sitting on its dispersal area.

The Twin Otter is a Canadian short field, take-off/landing aeroplane that carries 18 passengers, the same load as a Puma helicopter. These two aircraft were used in the logistics of taking personnel to and from the oil rigs. These were the bread and butter of transport from main airfields to small airfields and out to the rigs.

Looking past Aerocontractors were a couple of other hangars and past them, nestled into the corner of the Ikeja general aviation area, was the Bristow Helicopters' hangar. Again, they had Twin Otters there, but usually only for maintenance. Their fleet was based in Warri, 150 miles east of Lagos. Warri was easily within Puma range of the rigs.

On the opposite side to these hangars was a wide parking area for other aircraft, and in the centre was the taxiway towards Runway 19L over to the left. This is where the tarmac ended and the bush began.

'Bush' was a mixture of quite dense, tropical grasses which grew to a height of 15 feet. As I looked over to the far side, I saw G-LORI for the first time.

I loved these aeroplanes. They were designed by a British team originating from the renowned de Havilland aeroplane company, a very famous (only amongst pilots, of course) aircraft designer. The Heron and Dove I had flown whilst at Fairflight in Biggin Hill were from that company.

De Havilland said that the HS125 was 'a jet replacement for the Dove aircraft'. I had spent many, many hours sitting in an HS125 and I loved them.

To see G-LORI sitting rotting with its tail stuck in the bush was a tragedy.

'I've been keeping an eye on it since you called, but no one has taken any interest in it at all,' said Dave.

'Where is Prince Olori?' I asked. 'Any idea?'

'He's in his place up country, in Ilorin. As far as I can find out, he hasn't been down to Lagos for quite a while – not since the coup,' Dave replied.

'What about Vanni?' I asked.

'That evil bastard! He's in London at the moment. I rang his office anonymously to find out,' said Dave.

Vanni was my big worry, if he found out I was here to take his plane that could get very messy, and not in a nice way.

Both Dave and I knew he was a dangerous man. With his private security company, Vanni Security Services, he was reputed to have compromising information on just about every Nigerian politician. There were pretty much no strings he could not pull.

Also, Vanni had a small airline, Intercontinental Airlines, which operated freight and passenger flights around Nigeria and to Stansted. Unfortunately (or fortunately for the people living near Stansted), Intercontinental Airlines was banned from UK airspace due to the incompetence of its operating crew after a number of serious near accidents.

'I got one of my lads to have a look at the fuel state of G-LORI as you asked, Mike. It has full wings.'

'Oh, that's great. Thanks, Dave. Knowing that helps a lot,' I replied.

This was *instinctive* stuff that I was working on. My sole intention was to get permission to fly them out, but my self-preservation instinct was working overtime.

I still felt, even at this early stage, that the situation was dodgy. Ben's A3 pads were giving a bit of background, but there was a lot more poring through those and other documents to do.

'Let's walk down and see who's around at the Bristow hanger,' I said.

Having worked for them for years, I knew lots of guys there and had some really good friends, and I was keen to introduce Catriona to them.

We walked down past Aerocontractors' hangar. I looked to see if Mike Coleman or any other guys who I was friends with were there, but none were visible.

While I was based with Aerocontractors, I lived with the engineers in Ikeja. This was my accommodation when I was managing the HS125s.

I had started out in the pilot staff house, but quickly realised that there was no backup generator (very necessary as there were many power cuts), the beer was warm and the company was generally pretentious ('I'm a pilot, you know' – yuk!).

117

So, after a few days in the pilots' staff house, I arranged to move to the engineers' staff house. It was not easy. All engineers think – normally quite rightly – that pilots are pompous twats. I had to go through a formal interview by the guys. Fortunately, they quickly realised that I was not a 'normal pilot'.

The engineers' staff house had a working backup generator – as I said, this was absolutely essential as the main power failed several times a day. They also had a huge, American-type fridge (God knows where they found it) that was always stocked up with very cold Star beer. Also, the air con worked. This was pure luxury after a day in a hot aircraft cockpit.

There were twelve of us living there; we had a great time and lots of fun. For all these reasons, the engineer staff house was the place to be.

Soon after I arrived, the backup generator broke down. Disaster!

I called the company who had contracted me and chatted them up. They were making a lot of money from my efforts and agreed to pay for a new generator. It was a particularly good one.

Everyone was extremely grateful when it turned up a few days later on a Tradewinds aircraft (of course). It was a beautiful piece of engineering, and huge. Mike Coleman was so pleased. He used to polish, cuddle it, and often talked sweetly to it, calling it 'Jenny' obviously!

The engineers used to go out to clubs when off duty, and some were partial to 'night fighters'. These were prostitutes who were only seen at night, hence the name. Mike Coleman was a very sensible chap, but after a few Star beers he was prone to making bad decisions.

After one night out, he woke up and found a huge wig beside him. It was like a monstrous tarantula. Jumping up in fright, he then found this shaven-headed, very ugly girl next to him.

Girls were given a star rating by the engineers. Four or five stars depending on their looks – this was the number of Star beers that were needed to be consumed before they looked acceptable. Mike was sure this one was definitely a 'ten Star plus'!

'Fuck off! GET OUT!' Mike shouted, pushing her out of the bed.

'Give me my money! You owe me money!' The girl was very aggressive with a deep voice, almost sounding like a man.

Mike was sure he had done nothing to the girl for her to earn any money, purely due to the amount of beers he had consumed before he got her back to the staff house. However, he offered 200 naira to get rid of her.

She stood with her back to the door and shouted,

'Five hundred, you give me five hundred!'

'No! Two hundred and fuck off!' he repeated and grabbed her by the scruff of the neck, trying to force her out of the door.

It then got really out of hand. She fought back, punching and scratching at him, so he finally had no alternative but to punch her back…

This vixen fought like a man. As this fight took place, a random thought went through Mike's head: *If only my mother could see me now!*

It was one of the funniest stories I'd heard whilst out there. It still makes me laugh now.

The other funny/tragic story from the engineers' staff house was from another friend, Malcolm, who was in the Beetle when it was attacked by the robbers in traffic. Malcolm had been in Nigeria for many years and was prone to 'going bush' towards the end of his two months on (they all worked two months on and one month off – normally back in the UK).

Going bush for Malcolm usually involved wandering around the staff house in the middle of the night making the sounds that the locals made when you asked them to do something for you – it was a sort of moaning, yawning sound: *'Eeeeoooow!'*

He was also found to be stealing other people's underwear. 'Malcolm has gone bush' we would say. I never did quite understand the underwear thing, but if you had missing smalls, you would check out Malcolm's room.

Having survived twelve years in Lagos, he decided to chuck it in, get a sensible job and get a flat in Edinburgh. The plan was to do up the flat himself.

I saw Mike Coleman during one of my Lagos trips – probably with Nzeribe.

'Have you heard about Malcolm?' he asked.

'No, what's happened?' I replied.

'His flat in Edinburgh had high ceilings and tall windows. Malcolm was fixing a wall light. He was high up a ladder, and the ladder toppled,' Mike explained, 'catapulting him out of the window. It was a third-floor flat. Malcolm finished up being impaled on railings below. It killed him.'

'No!' I was stunned and truly shocked.

Then Mike and I started laughing at the same time. We both visualised Malcolm as the ladder was toppling towards the window with him making the famous '*Eeeeooooow*' sound.

As I recovered, I said, 'Fuck me! After all those years here, and he dies falling out of a window in Edinburgh! Doesn't make sense!'

We both knew he would laugh with us; it was the way he was. The engineers' staff house was full of fun and sarcastic humour – the irony of Malcolm's demise would have been met with huge laughter.

The Bristow hangar was in the corner, another large hangar, large enough to accommodate a couple of Pumas and Twin Otters stripped down for their annual maintenance. Sure enough, there were some friends there who I'd known for many years.

Firstly, I introduced Catriona to Barry Glover, who was the chief engineer in Lagos. Dave already knew him. I had worked with Barry in London and during that six-month detachment to Miri in Borneo where we had the HS125 operated for Shell by Bristows . Barry was the engineer looking after the aeroplane, and I got to know him very well.

Derek, Barry and I all shared the same hotel in Miri, the Gloria

Hotel, but it was not particularly glorious!

Generally, we ate in the 'sheds', a vegetable/fish market during the day, but at night it was converted to an eating area. Local chefs would turn up with Calor gas burners and woks and produce fabulous food, particularly fish and prawns fresh from the South China Sea.

However, sometimes we had to eat in the restaurant at the hotel. This was okay, but at 10 pm the staff would stop serving, turn off the *mood* lighting and turn on the strip lights in the ceiling.

As well as flooding the area with stark, white light, it was the cue for the well-trained cockroaches to come out for tea. Literally, hundreds of them would appear from behind the seats you were sitting on, from the walls and under the benches. They invaded every surface.

As you walked out of the restaurant, they cracked under your shoes, covering the soles in sticky, white cockroach guts. It was a bit like Harrison Ford as Indiana Jones in *Raiders of the Lost Ark*. 'I hate snakes!' I have a strong stomach, but I can assure you it was horrendous. 'I hate cockroaches.' Funny to think that in the event of a nuclear war, they would be one of the few creatures to survive.

There was not too much to do when we were not flying so Derek and Barry did try to teach me to play bridge, but that did not work. They both enjoyed playing but could only do so with three, so I was a very reluctant 'third hand' – it reminded me of playing excruciatingly boring card games at Christmas with my grandmother. They would both shout at me for playing the wrong card, I never sussed Bridge.

As with the Dutch security incident in Rotterdam, Derek got himself arrested in Singapore (I can't remember for what) – but then, why change the habit of a lifetime! Derek also did his absolute best to piss off all the locals in Miri. This was the most worrying.

'You're going to get yourself opened up on a dark night if you carry on pissing people off here like that, Derek,' I warned him after he had sworn at somebody for not doing very much.

'I don't care, Bloggs,' he responded. As usual, he was completely correct in every way.

'Trouble is, this is a very small town, and they will get their own back. I'm very worried about the fishermen coming after you,' I responded.

There was word that the local fishermen were going to 'have him'! They were going to get revenge for his behaviour. This was taken very seriously by Shell and Bristows . For his safety, Derek had to be quickly taken off the contract and sent back to the UK.

The fishermen had a special little tool they used to gut fish. It was a quaint, little 'knuckleduster', which had a very sharp, upward aligned blade welded to its centre. This was used with a quick upward movement of the fist to open up the fish.

In fights, this would be used with a quick, straight punch to the stomach of the opponent, and would then, with a similar sharp, upward movement of the fist, open the stomach wall, allowing the opponent's intestines to drop out.

Having done this, the opponent is too busy holding their guts in place to do anything to defend themselves. You would bleed out in around 20 minutes – job done. Not a nice end.

I was going to need engineering support before it would be possible to fly G-LORI out of Nigeria. Just seeing her parked, the back end pushed into the bush, told me that. Barry would have been the ideal person to help, however, he was a bit of a greedy sort. When he knew what I was there for, you could see the pound signs in his eyes. I was not keen on getting him involved for that, and various historical reasons.

My friends Ken Clark and Angus Patterson were also there, so I introduced them to Catriona. These two were best of friends but totally different types of characters.

Ken was a tall, slim, handsome chap with a rather calm and studious air about him. He had short, blond hair above a serious and fine-featured face with light blue eyes. Ken's family were in Aberdeen where he had first joined Bristows. He had taken the six weeks on, two weeks off cycle in Lagos to earn extra money.

Angus, on the other hand, was a typical Glaswegian, shorter than Ken with the physique of a brown bear. His shoulders were slightly rounded, like he was always ready to give you a big bear hug. Angus had a dark, swarthy and rough complexion, piercing dark eyes, and dark brows below a shock of dark hair dropping over his forehead. Angus's voice was typical of the comedy Glaswegian accent: 'YEW? Kin ya sue…? Will STEECH THAAAART!' said with a theatrical slicing movement of the hand. At one time, it was the fashion for Glasgow gangs to carry old-fashioned cut-throat razors.

Both were very experienced licenced engineers, and Ken was licenced on the HS125. They had not seen anyone near G-LORI for months either.

'Do you want some help getting it ready?' asked Ken.

'Aye, we'll geev ya a hund,' agreed Angus.

'Thanks very much, guys. I'm going to talk to the head of the Nigerian CAA and see what I need to do to get permission to fly it out. But depending on that, yes please, that would be a huge help,' I continued. 'I've got cash to pay for the engineering work.'

Ken and Angus looked at each other. As mates, they had a good understanding of what they were thinking – a bit like an old married couple.

'No, not needed, Mike. It would be good to work on something other than a "Twotter" or Puma! Anyhow, good to help – just as long as you buy all the beers while you're here!' said Ken.

'That's great, guys, it's a deal! Stars are on me!'

This conversation was the critical one, which I had to relay to their families, later in the story, to make them aware of the basis on which they had helped us.

The four of us chatted about the job I was on and arranged to get together at the Bristows compound for a drink later – obviously, I was buying. It was great to catch up and talk about old times and entertain Catriona with our 'war stories'.

As well as donating Sammy the driver for our use during the stay, Dave Fagan had put us in the spare room of his accommodation in Ikeja town. This was a bit like Ken and Angus; he would do anything to help. This was such a great thing, and I really appreciated all the help; such generosity of spirit.

However, in the long term for Ken and Angus, events would cause that generosity to explode in all our faces.

Dave's accommodation was a very large and comfortable bungalow-type building with a four-man staff to look after it, who lived in the grounds in a block-built house.

All the windows and doors were fitted with thick steel bars. Catriona asked what they were for.

'To keep robbers out,' I replied. 'This is a wealthy area where burglaries regularly take place. So we have bars on doors and windows, and patrols at night.'

I did not want to worry her, but more recently steelwork had been added to the inside of roofs. Robbers had entered a house by lifting the roof tiles and gaining access to the family home. This meant the family were effectively trapped inside with the robbers, by their own bars. As well as robbing them, they raped the wife and 15-year-old daughter in front of the husband/father. He had been strapped into a chair with duct tape and forced to watch. The wife and daughter died during this gang rape. Even by African standards, it was a most horrific event.

As I have said, life is cheap in Africa, so you had to be careful. There was little human sympathy in some circumstances. In another example, there was a kidnapping, but they got the wrong person. The family (Italian) had very limited funds. In the end, the gang decided to end the negotiation. They didn't kill the victim (an oil company employee's wife). They gouged her eyes out with hot spoons and left her staggering blinded and lost on the main road 10 miles north of Lagos until someone stopped and took the deeply traumatised woman to a hospital.

* * *

Back to that day, Sammy had taken us to the Bristows compound. This was a large, brick-walled area with 20-odd houses surrounding a large swimming pool. There was a nice air-conditioned bar and games room for the staff.

This was where we planted ourselves for an early evening chat and Star beers with Ken and Angus. Being an expat involves a lot of alcohol consumption!

Catriona enjoyed the evening. She said it was the first time she had felt safe since we'd got there. The Bristows compound was an island of security in the maelstrom of humanity that she had been subjected to since walking off the Nigerian Airways plane.

We were not there for too long, as it had been an exhausting day. We all agreed to meet up in the following few days after we had seen the head of the Nigerian CAA.

First, we visited the British High Commission and saw one of the senior staff there. Chris Haslam was the 'Second Secretary, Commercial' and he kindly gave us a letter of introduction for Hyacinth. We then went straight over to visit Hyacinth Odigwe for the first time. Dave assured me that Sammy knew where the Nigerian Civil Aviation Authority was.

After Catriona and I had visited Mr Odigwe, I had planned to take Dave for a good meal as a thank you for his help. A meal was a small thank you for the vast effort and help he had given us.

CHAPTER 13

Meanwhile… Back in Ben's Office

One of the stupidest things Ben Slade did was to make contact with Victor Vanni and invite him to his office for a meeting.

Catriona and I were in Nigeria for approximately 10 days before our unscheduled departure. The meeting between Vanni and Ben was around halfway through this period. I got to hear of it from two sources: Owen and, as it happened, Hyacinth Odigwe.

As I said earlier, I had asked Dave Fagan to, if possible, locate Vanni. Vanni was scary, so I wanted to know exactly where he was while I was in Nigeria. Although I had asked the whereabouts of his aeroplane (my second contract), this was down on my list of priorities for that reason. Dave had found out that Vanni was in London.

Vanni effectively had a private army, but I definitely did not have the resources to counter that. I was not an ex-member of the SAS with a load of ex-SAS mates to help out!

Ben made sure his 'aviation expert', Owen O'Mahoney, was there for expert guidance in this meeting.

As in many circumstances, Ben Slade was rather naive. Sitting in his ivory tower in Swallow Street, pulling the levers of his 'power' was one thing, but not understanding the consequences of his actions was quite another. Especially when it involved men like Vanni in Africa.

Vanni turned up and was invited into Ben's plush office with its air of 'the establishment'.

Baronet Ben, as black sheep of the family, was sent off to Australia (probably with a one-way ticket) at the age of 21. He is descendant of royalty, as mentioned earlier, but that did not make him a 'good guy'. He was both greedy and naive – as you will shortly find out. (I would also add 'a bit thick', but he would probably get Stan to sue me if I said that!)

Ben inherited his title aged 15 when his father, Sir Michael Nial Slade, a brewery director, died of a heart attack. Ben set up Shirlstar after returning to the UK in 1971 and actually made a success of the company.

Among the wood-panelled walls and old paintings were bookshelves with old novels and impressive small sculptures. It gave the impression of one of those archetypal old boys' clubs.

Owen was in one studded leather armchair. He stood up and offered Vanni his hand. Ben pointed Vanni to the other armchair and offered him a drink.

'Whisky?' offered Ben, pointing to the crystal decanter containing 12-year-old malt.

'I'm a Muslim,' came the growl of a reply in a deep African lilt.

'Oh.' Ben, confused, carried on, 'Well, tea, then?'

'No. What do you want?' Vanni barked in a deep, bass voice. There was almost a spit at the end of the sentence.

Vanni was not a man who had any fear. He was very powerful and very confident about his power. There was an air of intimidation around him, which garnered him respect wherever he was.

Vanni had taken the 'jet' from Ben and had basically shafted him. The HS125 was at a small airfield near Abuja in Nigeria. He'd used it a lot but had only paid peppercorn rent amounts to Ben after getting the aeroplane into Nigeria. Vanni owed Ben £120,000.

Ben sat in another armchair opposite trying to control the meeting. However, Ben, like others, was intimidated by Vanni in a way that he had never experienced. All Ben wanted to do was close the account. He did not want to lose all the money but was prepared to take a loss to not have any more contact with this man.

But Ben also wanted to make sure he got as much money as possible out of what had turned out to be a disastrous couple of deals. Leasing the jets had seemed like a good idea at the time. However, as no one at Shirlstar had any background knowledge or experience in leasing aircraft, they had not anticipated the problems that could occur – especially when dealing with Nigerians, for whom it was a national sport was how to get away without paying.

Of course, they had Owen O'Mahoney, but Owen had not been able to help them avoid the consequences of doing business with the Nigerians.

Ben had decided to offer Vanni a deal.

'Mr Vanni, as you know, you owe Shirlstar one hundred and twenty thousand pounds for lease of our aircraft.'

Vanni just scowled. 'I pay you when I am ready,' he said, snarling, as though he just didn't care. 'You said you have offer for me.'

Ben held up his hand and smiled, hoping this would calm the man opposite.

'Well, yes, as well as your debt, I have another jet that is causing me problems, and I want to get it back to the UK.' Ben replied.

Owen, who was there to give Ben support, suddenly took great notice. He had not been aware of the direction of Ben's mind. This was potentially not good.

Ben continued, 'Prince Olori, you know him?'

Vanni nodded; he knew everyone.

'He has my jet G-LORI. He owes me a lot of money, and I want the jet back. If you get the jet back for me, I will let you off the money you owe so far, and you can keep your jet.'

'I can get your jet for you, but I want that offer in writing,' stated Vanni flatly.

'Yes, yes, I will do that,' Ben said in a smarmy way. 'But if you want this to work, you had better be quick. I already have a pilot out in Nigeria trying his hand at getting the jet for me.'

Vanni was now paying attention. That would mean he'd effectively own £300,000 worth of aircraft for free. Bargain! Vanni liked that idea – a lot. He had got very angry when Shirlstar took out a court action against him. He wanted to keep his jet and would have also worked out that, if Ben had sent a pilot out to fetch Olori's jet, it was very likely he would have used the pilot to attempt to get his, too.

Shit, thought Owen, *Ben is doing a 'two-pronged strategy' on the Olori aircraft – with fucking Vanni involved in it. Ben is completely nuts!* Owen really could not believe what he had just heard.

For all his faults, Owen was a decent guy and had a lot of experience in West Africa. He knew Vanni's reputation as well as I did. He also knew this 'deal' would potentially put Catriona and me in serious danger.

Vanni accepted the offer and left Ben's office; he had to make some phone calls to Lagos. There was no time to lose. Vanni needed to get a plan into action if he was to get his hands on Olori's jet. This would clearly involve stopping me by whatever means necessary. I have alluded to how things work in Africa, so you can use your imagination!

It was likely that if Vanni got his hands on Olori's jet, Ben may not have got it back anyway. Vanni just might keep the bloody thing.

Owen asked Ben if he knew what this arrangement with Vanni could mean for my and Catriona's safety.

'What do you mean, Owen? They're only Africans!'

The naivety of the man was breathtaking. However, he had never been to Nigeria and didn't understand that Africa was completely different to Regent Street. As far as Ben was concerned, like a lot of his ancestors before him, it was just a place to milk for cash and fuck the consequences.

A dangerous series of events had been set into motion, so Owen decided that he had to warn me. Trouble was, in those days, there were no mobile phones. He did not know where I was (this was partly a decision on my part – a sort of low-level self-preservation). Owen set about trying to get in contact with me.

Vanni's plan, of course, was springing into action.

CHAPTER 14

Meeting Hyacinth Odigwe –
Head of Nigerian Civil Aviation Authority

I wasn't sure what to expect at the Nigerian Civil Aviation Authority (NCAA). It had never been in my sphere of experience or for anyone I knew. So we set off fairly early in the morning.

Sammy was outside Dave's house before eight. Unless you got the opportunity to 'ride the wake' of one of the ministers, it would take over an hour to complete the 10-mile journey. And, as far as I knew, Dave Fagan was the only one who partook in this highly irregular form of navigation. Sammy – definitely not.

It was a typical drive into central Lagos. A lot of jams and strange 180-degree turns to get on and off the highways and (distracting Catriona by getting her to look in another direction) a couple of bodies dumped and swelling in the heat on the Ikeja Highway.

After an hour and a half, we arrived at the building of the NCAA. The entrance was a typical multi-storey building, very large with high, glass windows and huge supporting concrete columns. The main difference here was the dirt and dust. It had not been cleaned for years, and I am pretty sure that originally it had (like the lifts) air conditioning that actually worked. This meant that the normal 32°C outside temperature was amplified by the tall, glass windows to a breath-taking and oppressive 42°C.

After we walked in, I asked a guy sprawled in a chair behind a desk where Mr Hyacinth Odigwe's office was.

He opened his eyes. 'Eight floor,' he muttered.

'Where are the lifts?' I asked.

'Over there,' came the surly reply, pointing to the far corner of the building. 'Lifts no worko!' he added, as if we should have known that!

'Oh God. An eight-storey climb in this heat,' I said to Catriona.

'Never mind,' she replied. 'It can be part of our fitness routine!' She always had a positive slant on things!

We started the climb. It was a wide staircase with plenty of human traffic up and down. The windows, reinforced with steel to support the glass, continued to follow the stairs. By the time we were halfway up, our shirts were sticking to our backs. *Must bring a towel next time*, I thought.

Along with the flight out, during the 'running around' I chose to use uniform shirts and trousers – I had four gold bars and Catriona two. This wasn't a matter of 'look at me, I'm a pilot!' As I said earlier, it genuinely helped you gain access to places. I am sure customs were more lenient with us, so here, as with the airport especially, I was pretty sure it would help.

We finally arrived at the eighth floor and went through a set of double doors into the main corridor. As in the entrance lobby, there was an atmosphere of dilapidation and lack of cleaning all around. There was dust and dirt everywhere.

The main reception area outside Odigwe's office had a couple of armchairs, a sofa and a desk. The two armchairs were occupied by a couple of young (20-ish) Nigerian boys sleeping soundly. The desk was occupied by a quite frightening-looking, very large Nigerian lady. She looked very much in charge.

I never did quite work out who the two boys were or what they did, but they were always there. They just seemed to be chilling... However, the lady was definitely the one with the power.

I had not made an appointment because this would have been futile. It was a case of 'turn up and be very patient'. This was the way it was.

'Please may I see Mr Odigwe?' I smiled pleasantly at the woman, hoping it may help.

'You have an appointment?' she barked.

'No, but I hoped he would have a moment at some stage during the day. It is a very important matter.' I said, smiling at her.

'You wait,' she replied, pointing to the sofa.

And so began the first of many patience-testing and boring waits – and for no apparent reason. We waited for about four hours the first day, but others were worse.

After a few of these mammoth sit-ins, suddenly out of the blue, with seemingly no phone calls to the secretary's desk or any other prompt, she said: 'He see you now!' and pointed to the door that had been shut all the time we had been sitting there. She made no attempt to move from her desk and show us in.

We got up from the rather smelly sofa and moved towards the door. I opened it and walked in ahead of Catriona, wanting this powerful man to see me first.

Surprisingly, it was an opulent office. Also, it was very clean and had an air conditioner thumping away in the corner providing a comfortable temperature. It was certainly a relief from the area outside.

Hyacinth Odigwe sat behind a dark mahogany desk in a comfortable looking, but old-style, office chair. I smiled at him warmly and offered my hand. He stood to shake my outstretched hand. My friendliness was deliberate. He was crucial to our getting permission to fly out of Lagos, and I wanted to make the best impression possible. A good handshake and a look into the eyes in this situation was a good start. He shook Catriona's hand, too.

Nigeria is a very large country that extends from the Niger Delta to Lagos and up to the edges of the Sahara. The countrymen from the

Niger Delta tended to be shorter with stubby features, whereas the northern Nigerians had a lot more of the nomadic Arabic in them.

I had worked for a lot of wealthy people from the northern areas of Nigeria and generally got on well with all of them. The people from the Kano and Maiduguri areas on the whole were very tall with a sort of aristocratic air. The Arab genes tended to give them fine features with high cheekbones and longer, straighter noses, and they generally had a high level of intellect. They also tended to have a pragmatic approach to life. The northern areas of Nigeria were mostly of the Muslim faith while the southern areas were mainly Christian.

Hyacinth Odigwe was from northern Nigeria. He was typical of the picture I've described. As well as that, Hyacinth had an open and very friendly smile.

After shaking hands, he gestured towards the two chairs opposite his desk.

'What can I do for you, Captain Howard?' He continued smiling; he knew exactly who I was.

'I am here to collect an HS125 jet for a British company, Shirlstar Container Transport. They leased the jet to Prince Olori, but he has not paid for it. The lease is to a British limited company that is effectively owned by Prince Olori. Shirlstar have taken action in the UK courts and have secured the legal right to repossess the aeroplane,' I explained.

I passed the court documents to Hyacinth as I spoke, pointing out the lease, the company details and the court order showing the right to repossess.

Hyacinth studied the documents one by one.

I remained silent while he did this. It was a deliberate omission of mine not to mention Victor Vanni's jet at this stage.

Finally, after a few minutes, Hyacinth spoke:

'This all looks in order, but you may be aware that the military government imposed a ban on executive jets taking off last winter when they took over?' He paused, smiling again. 'This was to prevent the removal of valuables from the county after the military took over the government...' He paused again. 'They know that these jets are a common way of smuggling,' he added in a soft, deep, smoky voice. 'Any jet taking off needs the permission of General Buhari's office.' He continued, 'I will submit your request. Unfortunately, I cannot say how long this will take. It could be a few days or a few weeks... or not at all. It is out of my hands.' He finished with his elbows on the desk and his palms facing upward in a gesture of uncertainty.

'If you were to guess, do you think it possible that we would obtain permission?' I asked, because if he definitely said no, there would be little point in staying.

Hyacinth thought about his reply:

'During the last few months, aircraft have been given permission to depart, so I would say that this situation will probably be looked on favourably.' He smiled again and continued, stating, 'It is a British aircraft on the British register owned by a British company. For all those reasons, it is very likely that the government will want to get rid of it. The jet should not be here. The new military government wants to remove the evidence of those who took advantage of the black-market currency in the past. So, yes, I think you will get permission soon.'

Hyacinth said that he would take the documents to the president's office and explain the situation. We agreed that I would come back every other day to see if there was any progress on the permission and to get an insight into the process.

We said goodbye to Hyacinth, thanking him for his time.

Walking out through his office doors, the two lads had not appeared to move and the secretary continued to scowl. We traipsed down the eight floors. The descent was much easier than the ascent!

Sammy arrived a little later. He had been doing errands in the city while waiting for us. As usual, he was in a happy mood.

'Where you want to go, Captain?' he asked, smiling.

'Back to your office please, Sammy.'

This would give me the opportunity to chat to Dave, and also let Ken and Angus know what had happened today. I was more confident that we would, eventually, get permission to take G-LORI out of Nigeria – although, it would take time.

The journey back was similar to driving into the city; the only difference was that I failed to distract Catriona at the critical time. Unfortunately, she got a close view of one the bodies. It was much worse because we were stuck in traffic very close to it, meaning we got an unpleasant whiff as well.

She went pale and was retching. Fortunately, she did not chuck up which was a miracle.

CHAPTER 15

Preparing G-LORI

As we arrived back at the Tradewinds office, Catriona was still, understandably, traumatised by the close proximity of the bodies. She had never been that close to a dead body before – or smelt the odour. I had to explain the way the system worked with bodies lying by the road.

'But how do they get there in the first place?' she asked.

Dave was listening to my explanation as we reached his office and continued the conversation.

'They either die of natural causes in the home, or they're bumped off by rival gangs. In either case, no one wants the hassle of dealing with the police. The poor people have no money for dash or, indeed, burials, so the bodies are dragged there or, most often, dumped out of cars as they go along.'

'What happens to them in the end?' Catriona was mystified.

Dave joined in the explanation:

'The Christian community, you see them around in bright white gowns, go at night and collect the bodies and bury them. Quietly. The police leave them to it.'

I left Catriona having a cup of coffee and went down to the Bristows hangar to see Ken and Angus to let them know what Odigwe had said.

They were on a break and offered me a coffee there. I described the events of the day and what a nice guy Odigwe was.

'It seems that I will probably be getting permission to take it – the odds seem to be seventy-thirty or sixty-forty. The fact that it's British registered and subject to a British legal recovery action may swing it,' I explained.

'So, shall we have a look at G-LORI and see how she is?' said Ken. 'She has been pretty well abandoned for quite a while, and it would be a good idea to see what needs to be done to get her into an airworthy condition,' he continued. 'Best if we drag her out of the bush and see if the tyres are okay and work up from there.'

I could see that he was getting enthusiastic about the project.

Angus piped in, 'Aye, we can borrow a tow truck from Aerocontractors – Glover has been moaning about us using Bristows gear for doing anything.' Angus was clearly unimpressed with Barry Glover's attitude. 'He's still shit-faced about not being involved.'

'We've told him that anything we do is in our time and nothing to do with Bristows. He cannot argue with that,' said Ken.

It was such a gift for Ken and Angus to help us, and great company too. Barry was such a miserable git!

'I really, really appreciate your help, guys, but are you sure that you want to get involved considering Glover is so pissed off? It may not be worth the aggro to help me.' I was worried about Ken and Angus being caught up in company politics. I knew what it was like having worked for Bristows for a few years.

'No,' said Ken, 'Angus and I have talked about it. Both of us have been around Bristows for many years, and much longer than Glover. We're both happy it will not be a bad thing for us.'

Angus joined in. 'Let *us* worry about Glover,' he snarled.

I arranged to meet Ken and Angus at the Bristows compound later on that evening for a chat and drink after popping into Aerocontractors to see about using some of their towing kit and specialist HS125 tools. Although I did not know any of the guys there at that time, the engineers at Aerocontractors were also very helpful, giving us access to any tools we needed.

G-LORI was parked almost opposite the Aerocontractors hangar; I had a closer, longer look at her. She was dusty, but the tyres were not significantly deflated. It would have been a challenge to get tyres refitted. I was also concerned about the aeroplane's general condition.

Aircraft frequently get broken into and damaged, but, from what I could see, G-LORI had not been affected by a third party. This was a relief.

We were going to pull her out onto the tarmac parking area the following afternoon, after we got back from our scheduled visit to Hyacinth. Timing was obviously flexible due to the 'office management style' of the NCAA; we were at the mercy of that huge, no-nonsense Nigerian woman!

It was like that too. Sammy drove us up there, and then we scaled the eight floors in the dusty, oppressive heat of the stairwell.

The two mystery lads were still sprawled in the armchairs; the secretary's face was still like a smacked arse – even when I employed my best winning smile. Then, as before, we sat.

Again, after around four hours, without any warning – seemingly by some kind of sixth sense – we got in to see Hyacinth.

He said that the documents were presented to the office of President Buhari, and Hyacinth had explained the situation to them. Hyacinth said the documents had been well received, and he felt that permission would be granted fairly quickly.

Although it was a relatively short meeting, we found ourselves chatting generally. I had begun to like Hyacinth; he came across as a very decent man, very helpful and friendly.

We left this short meeting feeling encouraged having agreed that we would come back and see Hyacinth in a couple of days.

When we got back to Ikeja later that afternoon, Ken and Angus had already dragged G-LORI out of the bush and onto the tarmac. She looked so much better parked on the apron near the taxiway with some chocks underneath her wheels.

I told Ken and Angus what Odigwe had said at the meeting, and then we decided to get cracking on checking out G-LORI.

There was also the question of whether or not Prince Olori would turn up at Ikeja and spoil the party. I had mentally prepared myself for that eventuality.

Whilst waiting to see Hyacinth, I had continued to go through the documents in the package given to me by Ben's PA, Jenny. There were some very strange notes on some of them that, at this stage, did not make sense.

One sheet had 'Prince Olori – 890,000 naira. Graham Bott, agent gone'. Along with '*Yona B*' and 'bunkering' with scrawled references to payments on other sheets, confirmed my conclusion that Ben was involved in illegal currency deals.

This was not a surprise. Whilst working up in northern Nigeria a few years before, it had been for one of the Dantata family from Kano. The senior family member was a billionaire in US dollars. It was through this family that Derek and I had met Owen. They had always been involved in 'strange' transactions.

I had flown for one of the younger sons for a while, Nasaru Dantata. Black market currency deals were an obvious part of financing his lifestyle. Ocasionaly flying to Zurich with small but extremely heavy boxes!!

There were always a lot of eager helpers around the Ikeja GA apron, so we got a couple of them to bring water and cloths to give G-LORI a clean. Slowly, as the grime and dust covering G-LORI's paintwork was washed off, she began to look a bit better.

Ken, Angus and I crawled about underneath checking the tyres and inflating them to the correct pressure with a pair of huge gas cylinders on a trolley containing nitrogen (you do not use air in a big aircraft tyre, only nitrogen).

Catriona watched, fascinated by our work. I wanted to open the door to get into the aircraft, but it was locked.

'Oh dear,' she said. 'How are you going to get the right key?' she asked.

'Now, let me see.' I was smiling as I said this, fishing a bunch of keys from my pocket. Singling one out, I proffered it to her. 'This,' I said, 'opens *all* HS125s.'

'You are joking!' Catriona was mystified. 'You mean that key works with *all* these aircraft?'

'Yep,' I confirmed 'It's not like aircraft get stolen'

As if to prove the point, I pushed the key into the lock on the main door pull-down release handle, twisted the key in the lock, removed it and pulled the door handle down. As I did this, the whole oval door moved up slightly and then majestically, on the gas strut actuators, opened outwards and downwards. The steps up into the cabin were part of the door.

Ken and Angus had come around to see into the aircraft.

I walked up and into the cabin. It was exceptionally hot inside and smelt very musty. There were eight armchair passenger seats in the cabin and a walnut rear bulkhead with a door that led into a small lavatory area.

Generally, the cabin was in a reasonable condition, but I was more concerned with the flight deck and what was (or wasn't) working.

Jumping into the captain's seat, it felt like pulling on an old, comfortable and familiar suit. Having flown many, many hours in this type of aeroplane, I could close my eyes and place my hand on any switch or lever that I wanted to.

I reached up and switched on the battery master switch. There was a faint *clunk* of a relay in the back, but no electrical power came on. This wasn't really a surprise.

'I think we may have to charge the batteries up,' I said to Ken and Angus with a comical tone.

'We'll drag them out and put them in the battery shop for a deep cycle and recharge. That should do them nicely,' said Angus.

I looked back and called to Catriona who was sitting in one of the armchairs in the rear of the cabin.

'Oy! You!' I jokingly screeched. 'Your seat is up here in the front! You'd better get up here and try it for size!'

Catriona came up, and there was a shuffling of bodies as Ken and Angus moved to give her access through the narrow entrance of the jet to the co-pilot seat.

This was the point where all the discussions that we'd had before coming to Nigeria came to a crunch point.

Catriona had the Radiotelephony Operators Licence, which meant she was licenced to sit in the co-pilot seat. Of course, sitting in the cottage in Surrey saying, 'Yes, I'll go,' is a lot different to actually sitting in a crew seat on a powerful jet which she was now doing.

It surprised me that the CAA had issued Catriona an actual 'stand-alone' RT Licence. It was a proper licence like my airline transport pilot licence. These licences were like the old-fashioned passports with a solid card cover. The ATPL was green, whereas Catriona's RT Licence was silver-grey. It was the first time I had come across a dedicated RT Licence. It looked very posh.

Catriona was now taking in her surroundings.

The pilots' seats were very comfortable. They were specially shaped for spending long hours in and had a thick sheepskin cover. There was also a 'crotch', waist and a pair of shoulder harnesses to firmly hold you in the seat, no matter what the aeroplane did.

In front of her was a 'ram's horn' control wheel shaped in a 'W', with various buttons on the top near where the pilot's thumbs would be. Obviously, Catriona had no idea what they did.

In front was the windscreen made of very thick glass, which was not very big, but it did allow a decent view once the pilot was sitting in the right place. The windows continued around to just behind her shoulder.

One window was openable. It was called the DV or 'direct vision' window. This window was intended to be used if the main windows failed for any reason. It was also used to chat to engineers outside and to ventilate the cockpit. It had a lever system to lock it in place.

There was an impressive array of switches above for all the aircraft systems: electrics, hydraulics, engine starting, de-icing systems, temperature, and pressure control of the cabin. All the flight instruments were below the windscreen coaming, and to her left was a centre console with levers and a bank of radios with rotary selectors. It was a baffling new world.

'What do you think, Catriona?' I asked.

'I'm impressed,' she replied. 'So, this is what your office looks like!'

Ken, Angus and I removed the batteries. They were located up in the rear equipment bay, sometimes called the 'hellhole'. It was a very awkward job to get these out, but we did manage it. Many of the bolts were seized and required careful freeing.

We then started checking various other bits and pieces: the oil levels in the engines, hydraulic levels and pressures, we drained some of the fuel out of the tanks to check/remove any water (there was quite a lot due to the high humidity), and then we went around the flight controls making sure they were free and had grease on the cable runs. We found no particular problems.

Ken then explained about the engine oil system.

'We will need to prime and pressurise the engine oil systems before doing an engine run to make sure the engine oil is getting through to the rear bearings of the engines, otherwise the bearings will overheat,' Ken explained. 'It's been standing around for such a long time, the oil will have all gone back to the reservoir. It kind of airlocks,' he continued.

I was not aware of this even though I had managed the maintenance on these aircraft in various places around the world.

'Shit! Didn't know that,' I replied. 'Glad you two are around; that would have fucked up the flight!'

We tidied up the aircraft, closed and locked it, dropping the three batteries – two big and one small – off at the Aerocontractors' battery shop, and then arranged to meet later at the Bristows compound for a drink and further discussions on what to do next.

Once Sammy drove us back to Dave's house, we ate some food – generally, I primarily recommended food with eggs while in Nigeria. Boiled, omelette, fried, scrambled. The theory was that these were safe if you wanted to be confident about your stomach.

So we tucked into an omelette, showered and changed, and then headed off to the Bristows compound and put some of Ben's money behind the bar.

Ken and Angus and a couple of other engineers were there; we had a great evening with, of course, more war stories! I also chatted with Ken and Angus about various practical considerations when preparing the aircraft, but also the potential problem of Olori turning up.

As far as I knew, from Dave Fagan and others, Olori was a decent chap. I also told them about the contract to repossess Vanni's aircraft and that I would not be touching it for reasons which everybody seemed to agree with.

I also expressed my concern about feeling that something was wrong. Certainly we were all on guard while working on G-LORI, and nothing out of the ordinary had happened, but I did, nevertheless, have that '*bad feeling*'.

We went back to Dave Fagan's in the early evening. Dave was about (he did do a lot of socialising), so I asked him if he'd heard of Graham Bott, the mystery name on Ben Slade's sheet.

'I've heard his name. He's normally involved as an agent bunkering ships for various customers, but I don't come into contact with that part of the business as I do mostly air freight,' said Dave.

'Clearly, Ben is one of them,' I said. 'Can you find out anything about him for me? I'm feeling unsure about this; I don't think I've been told the whole story by Slade.'

After I showed Dave the notepad, we both agreed it looked dodgy. Dave said he would make enquiries the next day with the bunkering companies at the main dock.

We went off to bed shortly afterwards; it would be an early rise. Over a few days a routine was established: work was carried out on G-LORI and visits were made to Odigwe in Lagos city for any news.

As I said earlier, we got to know Odigwe very well during this time. He struck me as a really decent and honest guy who was not at all involved in the events that transpired. Like me, he was an innocent victim of a conspiracy. He was used as a tool by the military government, same as the rest of us.

CHAPTER 16

Mr. Graham Bott

Graham Bott was the catalyst of one of the problems that caused my instincts to work overtime. I never met him, but he was someone that I would become very familiar with. Yet this would not be until much later, after I returned to the UK to face the fallout of these events.

Bott had been an agent working with the bunkering companies in the Lagos Harbour area. He ran his own company which arranged the supply of fuel, and other necessities, for not just oil tankers but also container ships transiting through Lagos. There were a lot of ships, so a lot of business.

On the side though, Bott was involved in a substantial amount of illegal currency transactions. These transactions were made relatively easy by the number of high-value bunkering contracts that occurred on a daily basis.

One of his customers was Ben Slade. Slade had set up a currency swap arrangement with Prince Olori (and others). Basically, Ben would get a ship bunkered with Prince Olori's naira, and then Ben would 'drop' an appropriate amount of UK sterling into an account of Olori's choice in London.

The 890,000 naira noted on Ben's desk notepad was one of these transactions.

Prince Olori handed the naira to Graham Bott. The black market exchange rate for 890,000 naira would have put approximately £400,000 into Olori's bank account in London.

Unfortunately, Graham Bott had a problem with managing his own cash flow. He was one of those who spent too much of the cash in hand and not the 'profit'. Because of this, Bott had been getting behind with payments for other contracts.

When he turned up at the bunkering company at the docks, the manager took Olori's 890,000 and said:

'Mr Bott, thank you for settling your outstanding account with cash. Now, what was it you wanted us to do for you?' The manager smiled. 'Obviously, we will require the cash before we can do anything for you.'

Bott had now got himself into an extremely precarious position. He did not have any cash to replace that 890,000 naira. Now there was one thing for sure, if he hung around, he was likely to finish up at the side of the Ikeja Highway on a Sunday morning. Bott had to do something quickly.

Bott, therefore, collected everything from his life in Lagos that was not bolted down and jumped onto the first available flight to Miami, Florida, leaving the fan running with the shit heading towards it.

As Prince Olori headed to London on one of his regular trips, he checked his London bank account and found it short of the expected £400,000!

He rang Ben. 'Where's my money?'

There was a hint of anger in the normally affable Prince Olori's voice. He didn't particularly like the arrogant Slade, but it was an easy way to get money to London.

Ben replied, 'Now hold on. You don't get the money until I get my ships sorted. I have not had my fuel and stuff. No bunkering, no cash,' Ben finished with that irritatingly head masterly tone.

'I gave your agent, Bott, the eight hundred and ninety thousand naira,' Olori stated flatly, sensing a serious problem.

The verbal tennis match went back and forward, but it did not go much further than that.

Ben would not accept responsibility for Prince Olori's money going missing in the hands of his agent. Therefore, Prince Olori was short of £400,000; a lot of money.

This impasse eventually finished with Olori stating that if he was not going to be given his £400,000, he'd make no more payments on the lease and would keep the aircraft as payment of the money. The aircraft was valued at £400,000.

Fair enough, I'd say.

Trouble was there was no evidence, in UK law, to show any background to the non-payment of the lease; therefore, Ben was able to take action in the UK courts to obtain the right to repossess G-LORI.

Clearly I did not know anything about this problem other than the note which did not make sense at the time.

Dave Fagan did tell me that he'd found out Bott was no longer in the country and had left suddenly, but he could not find out any more as to why.

Had I known anything about this, I would have headed home and visited Ben to give him a talking to.

Rather like Igbeninion, there was a bush telegraph in Nigeria, so it was highly likely Prince Olori would soon be aware that I was there to take his jet. And he wouldn't want that.

Also, Vanni and his band of 'private security agents' were somewhere in the background, working their way inexorably towards me.

CHAPTER 17

Odigwe's Warning

The last visit to Odigwe's office was a few days before we took off. He was not his usual jovial self.

'Captain Mike, I am very worried for both of you. I have heard very reliable information about your situation that you must take very, very seriously.'

'What is that?' I asked worried by the sound of his voice and the way he was talking.

'There are two different groups of people who know why you're here and are planning to harm you… These people are very dangerous, and you should take all steps to protect yourselves,' Hyacinth said emphatically.

I was very shocked at this; the implications were running around my mind.

'Do you know who these people are?' I asked.

'Personally no, but the source is coming from a very high place and is completely reliable,' Hyacinth replied. 'The main thing to understand is that we, the government, cannot protect you – it is not possible.'

Although my instincts had been warning me, it was a complete shock to hear this from Hyacinth. It was an unexpected development, and I wasn't sure what to say.

'Do you know if these people know where we are staying?' I asked.

'No, I do not know, but you should assume that they do.' Hyacinth paused. 'You need to plan to leave Nigeria as soon as possible, and it may not be a good idea to leave on a scheduled flight. People disappear in the terminal.'

Odigwe stated something that I already knew, but it was a surprise admission, nevertheless.

'The worrying thing is that from what I hear, these people are determined to ensure that you are permanently stopped from being able to succeed in your plan.'

When Hyacinth said this, I was completely taken aback. It was this part of the conversation that completely shocked me. The clues in the Shirlstar Manila envelope may have been far more important than I had thought. Even for Africa, this was a completely unique situation.

'Let's assume that you arrive at the airport one day and just flew her out of Nigeria. This has been done before' he paused 'in my experience, the government would make a fuss and write a few letters to the Civil Aviation Authority in London and possibly a few more to the British government but that would be the end of it.' He looked very serious when he said this.

It appeared that this advice was being given after a lot of consideration.

'These people are very serious about stopping you from taking G-LORI from Nigeria and they will use all necessary force to do so. They are aware of your progress and if you receive the permission, they will probably attack you as you approach the aircraft. I also believe that the closer you get to obtaining permission the more danger you are in'

As Hyacinth finished talking, he was still not smiling.

I thought the last bit was bad, but this was even worse. I was staggered by all this. It is astonishing to hear that someone actually wants to kill you.

'Take off without permission? Apart from the practical problem of taking off from a busy international airport, the legal issues are enormous.' I was leaning forward and speaking very earnestly. 'The *shit* would hit the fan, Hyacinth,' I stated.

Odigwe put his hands forward in that placatory gesture he had used before:

'Mike, you have been around Nigeria for a long time, as I have said, there would be some noise for a few days, but it would calm down. Then all would be okay; I am sure of that,' Odigwe said solemnly. 'But you would be safe. In the end, that is the most important thing.'

I had developed great respect for Hyacinth Odigwe. I judged him to be an honest and decent person in whom I had confidence. I also had to agree with him. When flying an aeroplane, I had control over events. The only other real alternative was an overland trip to Benin state. This was the next state along the coast to the West and a lovely country. It was not far – about 30 miles west of Lagos – but there was only one road. My worry was that this road would be easily covered by our potential (invisible and unknown) assailants.

My feeling was that Vanni had somehow got wind of our presence in the country and wanted to stop me from taking his asset. Obviously, I had no idea about Ben's 'backup plan' or the disappearance of the 890,000 naira in the Bott debacle.

'This is a shocking development,' I said. 'I will have to consider the options very carefully… but thank you for being so candid, Hyacinth.'

There was not much more to say, so Catriona and I stood up. I shook Hyacinth's hand firmly and repeated our thanks, wishing him well. It would be the last time we saw him.

The next day we did go to see Chris Haslam in the Commission after this meeting with Hyacinth and relay this shocking warning to him. Chris considered the situation and decided to give this letter of introduction to the airport manager at Lagos who was a good friend of his, asking 'is there any way to help these people leave more quickly?'

CHAPTER 18

The Shit Hits the Fan

We were both quiet on the way back to Dave's office. I was thinking about the implications of the information that Odigwe had passed on to us and the way he had framed his advice.

Apart from our direct safety, I had no way of knowing if the threat could affect Dave Fagan, Ken Clark or Angus Patterson, and what I could do to mitigate that threat.

The priority was to ask Dave if there was any other accommodation we could use. It was Wednesday, 16 May, and I did not think G-LORI would be ready to fly until the weekend – Friday at the earliest – based on the progress of the preflight checks.

I was very worried that Odigwe had confirmed my instincts. I wanted to get moving as soon as possible, but I needed to protect us all as much as practicable.

When we arrived at Dave's office, I explained to him what Odigwe had said. He looked as shocked as I did. He also knew that this sort of warning should not be ignored here in Nigeria – it should be taken very seriously indeed.

As well as this, Owen had called Dave, looking to make contact with me.

'Owen O'Mahoney left a message for you,' said Dave, 'and I quote "Vanni has been in Ben's office. Ben has offered a lot of money.

Be careful". I'm not sure, but it's very likely that Odigwe is talking about Vanni.'

Dave did have other accommodation options (well, he would, wouldn't he), so it was decided to use a different one each night. We went through the logistics of this.

It was also decided it was best not to use Sammy, as it may put him at risk. Dave gave us the use of an old, battered Peugeot 504 and some advice on routes to and from the accommodation to check if anyone was following us.

It was all a bit 007.

Catriona and I then went to see Ken and Angus at the Bristows compound to explain the situation with them. It was a moment to be very realistic about the risks that existed.

We sat in the Bristows bar around a table with some Star beers, and I explained what had been said by Odigwe.

'I am inclined to take the aircraft. It is the best way in my control to get out of Nigeria,' I started. 'Trouble is I'm worried that if I do that, it may be bad for you guys.' Continuing, I said, 'We do not know who has seen us working on G-LORI and if there are any serious repercussions.'

'Mike, we've all been working out here for a long time and know the ropes,' said Ken. 'As Odigwe said, they're very unlikely to kick up too much of a fuss. All we've done is help to do a couple of jobs on the aircraft,' he concluded.

'Yes, I agree,' said Angus in his growling tone. 'We're not directly involved. Anyhow, you guys are clearly in serious danger, so we cannot ignore that. Anything that happens to us is insignificant compared to that.' He finished with a deeper than normal frown on his swarthy forehead.

We continued to discuss the situation, all speculating on the news given by Odigwe and the best way for Catriona and me to safely leave Nigeria.

In the end, between us, it was decided that I would take G-LORI.

My own feeling, at the time, was that by flying the aeroplane out, even if that was without permission, at least I would be in control of our destiny. Going by road to Benin state or, indeed, by scheduled service from the international airport, there was no way of knowing who was watching us at any stage of either option.

I decided to depart on the Friday night at around 5:30 pm This gave me around 45 minutes of light, as the first part would have to be flown visually at lower altitude because I would not have filed a flight plan with air traffic control.

It had always been my intention to take the aeroplane to Abidjan. This was the 'friendliest' country in that part of the world with a reliable and sophisticated legal system. This meant that I would need clearance to climb to a high altitude (41,000 feet) in order to get the range to fly there – higher altitude means lower fuel consumption per mile. We had full wing tanks so only had a limited amount of fuel available. Too low for too long would mean we would run out of fuel.

We continued chatting and had a few more Star beers. As it was a few days before the Friday departure, we made a plan, so G-LORI was ready for flight.

Ken and Angus were discussing the various things that needed to be carried out: tyre checking and inflation, and priming the hydraulics and engine rear bearing oil system.

'I do not want to refuel G-LORI, as it may draw attention to what I'm (potentially) going to do with it,' I said. 'We could do an engine run for a short time, but this would need to be short, as I need to conserve fuel.'

'We'll have to do one engine run to check the engine oil system is all okay after we prime it,' Ken reminded me.

'Okay, no problem. We'll just keep it as short as possible,' I replied.

As I've banged on about here, there was a significant amount of 'instinctive self-preservation' involved all the way through this story and, as it turned out, this was very important.

If I had not been so conservative about the ground running of engines, I would not be sitting here typing; I would have finished up in the Gulf of Guinea having run out of fuel, a fond memory of my poor, long-suffering parents!

So, as described in the earlier part of the story, Ken, Angus and I got on with the preparations and gave a final engine run to check all the systems were working normally. This was engineer territory, so Ken and Angus were in complete control. I did what I could to help, but I did feel like a spare prick at a wedding!

We ran the engines for about 10 minutes to check for no overheating of the rear bearings – this was a check that the oil was making its way to those bearings. No oil equals very hot bearings, and eventually seizure of the bearings and engine failure.

Now we were all happy that G-LORI was ready for flight, all that was left to do was go back to the bar at Bristows for a couple of Star beers. This kind of catches us up from the beginning of the book…

CHAPTER 19

The Gulf of Guinea, at around 20 Feet and 400 Miles an Hour

So, where were we?

Oh yes, the Nigerian Air Force were trying to shoot us down with an Alpha Jet, and we were scaring the shit out of a crew member on one of the tankers sitting out in the Gulf of Guinea.

As the flash of the African's face disappeared, the next tanker appeared ahead. I climbed slightly and jinked right. I had to climb, because at that very low height, if you banked the aircraft steeply (as I was about to bank to around 80 degrees) the wing tip would impact with the water. This would have been the end of us, in a rolling ball of disintegrating aluminium in the Atlantic.

I continued using the cover of the numerous tankers in order to avoid the Alpha Jet getting either a weapons radar lock-on and firing a missile or lining up and taking a shot with cannons. I reckoned it would have been more or less impossible to do this with me dodging in between a whole load of oil tankers. Well, it would have ended in a spectacular firework display, not to mention the ecological disaster.

As I said earlier, my only countermeasure was to fly as low as possible, as fast as possible and throw up as much spray as possible.

In most cases with a fighter, you had to pitch the nose down slightly to take a shot. As they were probably also feet above the ocean and in between the tankers, I reckoned the fighter pilot would be swimming home if he got any of this wrong.

Anyway, I felt that I was probably far more focused on surviving than he was on shooting me down. Despite all the military training, it also took a very strong mental attitude to shoot down an 'innocent' civilian plane, killing the occupants.

It was ironic that some of these ships I was passing almost underneath were under the control of Benjamin Slade and involved in the illegal currency deals that I had very recently become aware of.

Half turning to Catriona, who more or less still had her head between her knees, I said: 'Can you have a look out of the side window to see if there's an aircraft?'

'What sort of aircraft am I looking for?' she replied, her voice husky from stress.

'I think it's a Nigerian Air Force Alpha Jet fighter jet,' I calmly explained.

As I spoke, I lifted G-LORI's nose slightly, preparing for another sharp, banking turn, lining up on the bow of the next tanker. This time the turn was to the left, giving Catriona a reasonable view out of the right-hand side of the aircraft – which wasn't the dark green Atlantic Ocean!

'A fucking what?' Catriona was not prone to use expletives, but in this situation it was hardly surprising.

'They had a fighter on standby holding to the north of the airfield when we took off, and now it's in pursuit trying to shoot us down. I have no idea why they're trying to do that, but they are... That's why I'm flying so low – it's the only way I can counter their attempt!'

Catriona lifted her head and looked through the front cockpit window to be confronted by a scene that was just indescribable: the sea just feet below and ships whipping past at a phenomenal speed. She swung around as far as she could to see behind out of the side window, obviously the HS125 was not designed for air combat and did not have a rear view, but she looked nevertheless.

'I can't see anything,' Catriona said very nervously.

I was concentrating while we spoke, still very calm. Uncannily calm. Again, I climbed a couple of feet and banked steeply to about 70-80 degrees as we roared past the next tanker to the left.

Catriona drew a sharp intake of breath at the extreme attitude that G-LORI was adopting to pass close to the next tanker. She resisted the desire to put her head between her knees at this next exceptional aircraft height. Her hand involuntarily grabbed the side of her seat as the aircraft banked dramatically.

I had her in my peripheral vision but obviously could not look directly at her. I thought: *anyone else would either be throwing up or screaming by now. I've definitely made the right decision in bringing her.*

Looking forward, I was continuously judging the best track through the tankers. My plan was to choose a line through them that would take us towards the south-east into the Gulf of Guinea.

My hope was to give the impression that I was heading generally in that direction and the following aircraft would not realise my actual intention was to head south-west then west-north-west in the direction of Abidjan on the Ivory Coast.

As I said earlier, the Ivory Coast was the best place in West Africa to reach. The president was known to be very fair and the treatment we could expect to receive would be the best on the African continent outside South Africa. This would give us the greatest chance of resolving any fallout from a situation that I was at a loss to fully understand.

I had started a stopwatch as we'd crossed the Nigerian coast; we had been over the sea for around 20 minutes now. Eventually, the tankers became fewer and farther between. We were now becoming exposed having lost the tanker 'cover'.

I did not know how long the Alpha Jet had been airborne before we took off, but it was possible that he would become short of fuel soon. Also, I really needed to climb before very long or we would finish up swimming to Abidjan. Flying this low and fast, we were throwing fuel out of the back in buckets and we would not have enough to get all the way there.

As this was the most worrying part, I pushed G-LORI even lower. Even in my experience, this was the lowest I had ever flown. We were very, very low – literally just a few feet above the swells.

The feeling of speed was most incredible. The dark greeeny blue of the Atlantic was contrasted by the yellowish-white foam at the crests of the rolling waves. I could see every single drop of water flicking off the tops of the surf as it was picked off by the wind. I actually had to adjust my height to allow for the Atlantic swells.

I don't think even most military pilots will have experienced that kind of speed at that height. It was the focus of survival that was driving me. Control of G-LORI was still with just my fingertips resting lightly on the ram's horn control column between my knees. I was consciously aware of my calmness and still surprised by this, considering the circumstances.

At this now lower height, the massive spray would have been even greater due to the mass of seawater being churned up by the jet quake and the effect of the airflow over the wings and tail. I hoped but did not know whether it had affected the pursuing aircraft or not.

I carried on jinking with up to 80 degrees of bank left and right every 15 to 20 seconds, hoping this would make it incredibly difficult for the Alpha Jet pilot to take a shot. The training pilots on these jets were very good, I was pretty sure it would be a training pilot at the controls.

Up ahead, about 30 miles, I could see a line squall – a line of huge, black cumulus cloud bubbling up from the sea with dark streaks underneath, the dark streaks being heavy rain falling from the clouds. At this distance, the rain looked like a dirty lace curtain hanging below the clouds down to the sea.

It looked innocent enough, but there would be zero visibility and very, very bad turbulence in there. Normally, pilots avoided such weather like the plague, but for me it represented sanctuary.

'Can you see anything, Catriona? We have some cloud up ahead with rain, so I'm going to fly into that and hopefully disappear from his view *if* he's still there. It will get very bumpy when we hit the rain.'

Catriona was still looking nervously out of the co-pilot's side window, scanning as far behind as possible.

'No, I cannot see anything at all, but shit, all I can see is water going past at an unbelievable speed!'

I said what I had thought a few moments earlier: 'Glad you don't get airsick!'

'I'm sort of beyond that,' she replied tartly.

Jinking left for a final turn heading almost east-south-east, we hit the rain. The moment we hit it, I pulled up into a rapid, steep climbing turn, towards the west. At the same time, moving the thrust levers fully forward, applying absolute full power. Now we were trading all of that low-level speed into height, climbing at almost 6,000 to 7,000 feet per minute for a few minutes until the speed gradually washed off to a normal climbing speed.

We were in solid cloud and rain the whole time, and I was counting on that rain and cloud to blank any radar contact that the Alpha Jet may have had. It was incredibly turbulent. Thunderstorms in Europe are bad enough, but tropical storms are incredible. The wings and fuselage were flexing with the rapid changes from positive to negative 'G'. To give you some idea, imagine the worst turbulence you have ever experienced on a plane and multiply it by 100!

I had selected the engine igniters 'on'. These are huge spark plugs to start the engines, but they are also used in rain and icing conditions to prevent the engines from stopping. The amount of rain was phenomenal and going into the engines. We were being bounced around in the up and down drafts of what was a very active thunderstorm, but at least we were safe.

As we passed 20,000 feet, I turned further right onto a heading of north-north-west; towards Abidjan. Yay!! We had not been shot down.

I was pretty sure, by this stage, that the Alpha Jet had lost contact with us. He must have been running low on fuel by now, especially if he'd been holding in the air for a significant time waiting for his 'target' to take off. They would not have known exactly what time I was going to go.

So, this was a moment for the pressure to come off a little and for me to collect my thoughts – back to the routine of flying a jet aeroplane.

The HS125 was designed as a two-crew aeroplane, but as Catriona obviously was not a pilot – I was flying it effectively as single crew, i.e. operating G-LORI on my own. Having said that, I could reach all the controls from the captain's seat except the pilot oxygen controls and the standby cabin pressurisation system over on the co-pilots side. However, if either of these were needed on this particular flight, it *really* would not be our day!

The next problem was that when I tried to engage the autopilot to give me a free pair of hands, it wouldn't engage, so there was no alternative but to 'hand fly' the aeroplane. Fortunately, as I'd flown old jets quite often with no functioning autopilot, I was used to hand flying at high altitude.

'Bollocks!' I said out loud.

'What's the matter?' asked Catriona.

'Bloody autopilot isn't working,' I replied.

'What does that mean?' she asked.

'Effectively, I have to work a lot harder hand flying at high altitude and navigating at the same time. It's not a huge problem, as I've flown lots of stuff without one working,' I replied.

All pilots use something called a 'Jeppesen' navigation chart to navigate the 'airways'. Airways are like motorways in the sky, following lines between navigation beacons. I'd had one of these on my lap since take-off.

During the low-level flight I was keeping a mental picture of roughly the direction in which we were going. Now I was climbing to a normal altitude (well, actually quite a lot higher than a normal altitude), I needed to engage myself with the problem of navigation.

I had to find somewhere to land. My intended destination was still Abidjan. However, approximately 120 miles at such a low altitude, and jet engines being designed to be fuel-efficient at a high altitude of say 30,000 plus feet, flying very fast at 20 to 30 feet increased the fuel consumption massively. So, G-LORI's range at this stage was very, very limited. Did I have enough to get to Abidjan?

I began tuning in navigation beacons to get some help with navigation. These were the beacons on the Jeppesen charts we were talking about a moment ago. Aircraft use these for navigating along the airways. Sorry to keep banging on about aviation, esoteric stuff. You'll be able to obtain your own pilot's licence by the end of this book – the exams are at the very back!

I selected various frequencies; nothing happened. It became apparent that the navigation equipment on G-LORI was not working.

This was something I hadn't anticipated. It was a serious 'doh' moment! After all, the aircraft had been parked more or less in the bush at Ikeja for a long time in very high humidity This clearly would not have done the electronics any good at all.

'Shit!' I said again out loud, realising I was now presented with an additional major challenge.

It was a very serious problem because we were out in the middle of the Gulf of Guinea, now at 41,000 feet, with limited fuel. We needed to land within the next two hours otherwise we would effectively be in a jet 'glider'. 'Gliding to the scene of the crash' was the phrase that came to mind.

I did have a 'dead reckoning', or a 'guesstimated' position. I had roughly kept track during the flight from Lagos, but it was *very* rough.

Now I would need to navigate – hopefully to Abidjan – without the assistance of navigation aids. In other words, continuing to do it by dead reckoning – estimating the wind, track, drift and heading required to make it to Abidjan. Even worse, because I was hand flying, maintaining the heading was more difficult – it wasn't necessarily as accurate as an autopilot because I had other things to do while hand flying the aircraft.

Fortunately, the winds at this latitude were very predictable. I'd flown lots of times over the Sahara from a little airport called Zarzaitine in Algeria to Kano, Nigeria, with no navigation aids whilst hand flying. Zarzaitine was the nearest airport to Kano on the north side of the Sahara. I had been regularly flying a very old HS125 (number five off the production line) for Nasaru Dantata, youngest of the very wealthy Dantata family, who lived in Kano. The range of this old thing was very limited, so I used Zarzaitine, an isolated Sahara Desert strip to refuel.

It was a strange place, just an airport surrounded by dunes. You had to take off before 8 am, otherwise the temperature became too high and you would be stuck there until it cooled. (High temperature equals thin air meaning less lift which equals? *More principles of flight lessons!* Zarzaitine airport primarily serves Algerian oil field support and associated air traffic. The airport was completely isolated so the guys at the airport hardly saw another human, let alone a woman. I used to pay my landing fees with a box of men-only magazines – they loved it when I turned up!

It was a 1,000-mile flight from Zarzaitine to Kano and I had to fly at very high altitude to make the distance. The autopilot on that old girl was very basic and at high altitude it was a bit rough, making too large control inputs; therefore, she had to be hand flown across the Sahara with no navigation aids. I always found Kano, usually landing with only 20 minutes of fuel left.

I was now using that same dead-reckoning technique. I started working out the mental calculations of our situation.

Abidjan was around about 700 nautical miles from our present position. About 1 hour 45 minutes' flying time. There would be about 15 minutes of fuel left on landing – if I could find the bloody airfield.

The winds at altitude were pretty light. I was slowly climbing to 43,000 feet, which was above the maximum altitude of the HS125, but the fuel flow up there was as low as possible. With only Catriona and me on board, the aeroplane was very light, so weight-wise the aeroplane was capable of flying at that altitude.

The 41,000 feet limitation was due to cabin altitude. So, I simply cranked the cabin up to 6,500 feet instead of 6,000 feet. Job done.

As well as the low fuel flow, the normally westerly winds are much lighter at that altitude, so less headwinds. The estimated track to Abidjan would also be the 'heading' because there was little or no drift (you will be asked questions on this subject at the back of the book!).

I set the heading cursor on the direction compass and began scanning the flight instruments to hold G-LORI's heading and altitude. The aeroplane was now flying in a straight line at a constant altitude. I had to prioritise scanning the instruments. At the same time, I carried out the other tasks involved with flying the aeroplane.

The next problem was that we were now flying along an airway without permission.

Before taking off on a flight, the captain would file a flight plan with air traffic control. This provided details of the aeroplane registration, point of departure, destination, route, speed, departure time and time en route. The information would be processed and used to coordinate with other traffic along the same route. This would enable air traffic control to stop aircraft bumping into one another. Yes, you are catching on… an undesirable aircraft state!

The problem for me was that I was flying along the airway without any coordination, so there *was* a risk of bumping into another aeroplane.

Although I had climbed to 43,000 feet, I was actually flying at 43,500 feet. This meant that the only person I would bump into was another smart-arse coming in the opposite direction.

However, I did have to try to get this flight into some sort of normality, so I began the process of contacting air traffic control to file an airborne flight plan.

Between Nigeria and the Ivory Coast there is a small country called Benin state, after which lies Ghana.

The capital of Ghana is Accra, which is the air traffic control centre controlling the airspace in which we were flying. I had tuned into Accra Radio, the name of the air traffic control centre at Accra, and was listening to the transmissions.

I took a deep breath and pressed the 'Transmit' button:

'Accra, Accra, this is Golf Lima Oscar Romeo India, do you read me, over?'

The answer came back quite quickly:

'Golf Lima Oscar Romeo India, this is Accra Radio, go ahead.'

'Accra, Golf Romeo India is an HS125 aircraft departed Lagos bound for Abidjan. Request file an airborne flight plan, over.'

'Golf Romeo India, stand by.'

I waited to see what was going to happen because I had no idea at this stage.

'Golf Romeo India, go ahead with your flight plan.'

I then passed all the information required to file the airborne flight plan to the air traffic controller.

'That was easier than I thought it was going to be,' I said to Catriona.

Communications between different countries in this part of the world wasn't brilliant, but I did think the shit would have hit the fan. However, it seemed that this bit was going to be easy.

The reporting points along the airway in Ghana's airspace were about 400 miles apart, this equated to about an hour of flying time.

The whole thing about the interceptor waiting for us to take off baffled me. It did not make sense to go to so much trouble when, effectively, the Nigerian government had told me to take off through the head of the NCAA.

Due to this uncertainty, and for the sake of ongoing self-preservation, I thought it possible that the military government of Nigeria would persuade the military government of Ghana to send aircraft to intercept us. I was not sure, but the whole situation was so strange; I would not put anything out of the range of possibilities.

As a strategy to avoid being found by some fighter or other, I gave a very misleading actual time that I had passed the first point of entry into the Ghanaian airspace and an equally misleading estimated time of the reporting point on the exit of their airspace. I then amended these times in an equally misleading way.

The effect of this was to give an area of about 2,000 square miles for them to look for G-LORI – a tiny needle and a huge haystack.

Having been at level flight for about 20 minutes, it was a chance to collect my thoughts properly.

Adding the fact that the radar controller at Lagos seemed to be awaiting our take-off, the gunnery crews were not, as normal, asleep, and the Nigerian Air Force had an interceptor aircraft holding, waiting for us, meant that there was a lot more to what had happened than met the eye.

This meant that the military government of Nigeria were well aware of my intention to take off, so there must have been other underlying agendas at play.

I thought back to the last conversation I'd had with Hyacinth Odigwe just a few days before. He had told Catriona and me that our lives were in danger and that we needed to leave Nigeria as soon as possible. He also said that our safety could not be ensured and encouraged me to take off without permission, effectively into the waiting trap of an air force jet. Needless to say, why this had happened will be revealed in due course.

'Golf Lima Oscar Romeo India, this is Accra Radio. The federal government of Nigeria instructs you, for your safety and security,

to land at Accra international airport. You must proceed to Accra immediately.'

I was completely taken aback – that word 'shit' sprang to mind again.

It was amazing for this to happen in this part of the world, especially because of the poor communication between states. Less than an hour after take-off, the Nigerian military government had contacted the Ghanaian military government, pressurising the Ghanaians to make me divert to and land at an airfield that was also under military control.

Again, this was more evidence that there was a lot more to all this than met the eye. There was absolutely no way that we were going to Accra!

In some ways, when that call came, I was not really surprised (considering the various surprises of this day).

The fact that I'd put in misleading estimated times at reporting points, which was really just spontaneous, probably meant that we now had a huge advantage. In other words, if they *had* sent up intercepting aircraft from Ghana, they wouldn't have the first clue where to find us.

As an additional precaution, I turned off all the cabin lights and external navigation lights, and then turned down the cockpit lights very low.

Sounding perturbed, Catriona asked:

'What's going on now?'

She was wearing a headset and listening to the radio. We were speaking through the intercom system, but she did not know the significance of the transmissions.

'That call was from the air traffic control centre in Ghana telling us we have to go there and land,' I replied.

'Are you going to do that?'

'Absolutely not,' I said bluntly. 'This is an unbelievable situation. It absolutely stinks that the Nigerians had military aircraft up and ready on a Saturday night at six o'clock waiting to intercept us, and the

Nigerians have been in contact with the Ghanaians within an hour.'

'You're not kidding,' Catriona replied. 'You smell it, I'm sitting in it!'

Catriona was repeating one of my very old and very bad jokes, but it did have the effect of making us laugh – releasing a massive amount of built-up tension.

'What are you going to do?' Catriona asked. She looked at me with a look of absolute trust in her eyes.

'We are still going to Abidjan,' I replied. 'Still the safest place to go, especially with what is going on. We are short of fuel, but according to my calculations we will land with twenty minutes' fuel. Not a lot, but enough!' I paused, and then thought out loud: 'There is definitely much, much more to this than meets the eye; some bigger issue than just us taking off without permission.'

Catriona nodded. She was at the meeting with Hyacinth Odigwe, so had heard exactly what he'd said.

'Golf Lima Oscar Romeo India, confirm you are proceeding to Accra?' Ghanaian ATC were now going to start pressurising us to divert.

Pressing the transmit button and making a static-like noise with the odd 'Golf' thrown in, I made it sound as if I was out of the Accra ATC transmission range.

Catriona was giggling at this rather banal but effective way of avoiding questions, like an errant husband answering his mobile phone from his wife on the way to the pub, not wanting his plans to go boozing with his mates spoilt.

As all this was going on, the nautical miles were streaking past; we were getting closer to the boundary between Ghana's airspace and the Ivory Coast's airspace – and hopefully (relative) safety.

I had been carrying out the normal process of flying the aeroplane, including the dead-reckoning navigation and monitoring the fuel consumption. I continued to tune in various navigation aids to work, but this was unsuccessful.

I estimated that we had just crossed the Ghanaian air traffic control boundary. This meant that there was approximately 250 miles to run to Abidjan (I hoped). This equated to about 40 minutes' flying time. Having calculated that we had just over an hour's fuel, one way or another, the aircraft was going to be on the ground somewhere in just over an hour's time.

Over to to right, there was a very hazy impression of a coastline. According to my calculations, the coastline should have appeared around now (ish). There was vaguely something that could be lights, but electricity was not comprehensively available in this area of the world. I stared, trying to make sense of what I could see. The impression was a slight curve of a light grey flowing into the distance, punctuated with odd faint dots.

It was time to be serious about our options; time (*fuel*) was definitely running out.

'Catriona, I've calculated that we've got forty minutes to reach Abidjan, but I don't know if we're going to find Abidjan. There are no navigation instruments working, and I'm doing everything by dead reckoning – or guessing,' I explained. 'In other words, I'm just calculating heading and speed, then converting that to distance and, therefore, a position/time. But there is no guarantee that I am correct.' I paused before continuing, 'I think Abidjan is directly ahead of us, but I don't know for sure. We must be prepared for landing somewhere other than an airfield, so I'm just warning you.'

I was speaking slowly to make sure she understood what I was saying. Being told we might have to crash-land when you're not an experienced pilot takes a bit of mental processing. Having said that, it was a new experience for me to consider too.

'When it comes to it, probably the best place to put G-LORI down is on the beach. If that happens, you must tighten your seat belt and shoulder harness very tight, and do not undo it until the aeroplane comes to a complete stop – it may bounce a few times before stopping completely.' I paused, thinking about the best way to explain how to get out. 'Then, we can get out through the main door or emergency exit. If I'm injured, just pull the big red handle upward on the main door. With the emergency exit, pull the handle down and let the door drop onto the cabin floor. We can also use these windows if the main door is not available.' I showed her the small DV windows beside each pilot's seat again and the handle to open it. 'They are small, but you can get through them if you need to.'

'Okay, Mikey, I do understand. How long before we know?'

'About twenty minutes or so,' I replied. 'I think I can vaguely make out the coastline in the distance on the right.'

As I spoke, I pointed to the vague, hazy, lighter area in an arc ahead with what could have been a line of lights in the distance. Encouragingly, the picture was becoming slightly more defined.

'We've been right out over the Atlantic Ocean, but we're closing with the coastline on this heading.'

I tuned in the Abidjan 'VOR' – more out of habit/hope than anything else. It was a normal thing to do, at this point, to continue with normal navigation. I then busied myself with the remaining normal operations of the aeroplane.

I selected the communications frequency for Abidjan air traffic control and made the call, based on the estimate of our position:

'Abidjan Control, Abidjan Control, Golf Lima Oscar Romeo India.'

'Golf Lima Oscar Romeo India, this is Abidjan Control, go ahead.'

This was good. At least the fact that I could speak to Abidjan air traffic control without any problem indicated we were relatively near!

I passed the relevant 'handshaking' information to Abidjan Control and requested clearance into their airspace and to proceed to Abidjan airport for the landing.

Abidjan confirmed that they had no traffic and that G-LORI was cleared for an approach without any delay. I indicated to Abidjan air traffic control that we had very limited fuel.

Those 40 minutes began to tick away; I knew it was time to start a descent, no matter what.

'Abidjan Control, Golf Romeo India requesting descent.'

'Golf Romeo India, you are cleared descent initially to flight level one hundred (10,000 feet in aviation-speak). Expect further clearance shortly.' I responded to the descent clearance that had been transmitted to me:

'Golf Romeo India, cleared descent to flight level one hundred, leaving flight level four four zero now.' (Yes, you got it, 44,000 feet! I'd crept her up as high as possible!)

So, I set up the altitude select to 10,000 feet on the autopilot selector. This instrument would illuminate a warning light as that altitude was approached to (hopefully) stop the pilot descending below a cleared altitude. If the autopilot had been working, it would have automatically levelled off at that altitude. Because of everything else going on, the benefits of the alerting system would ensure that I would not miss the cleared altitude or bump into someone else coming the other way.

Easing forward on the control column and gently reducing the power to idle by moving the thrust levers fully back to the idle position, G-LORI's nose began to pitch down. The altimeter responded by beginning to unwind down from 44,000 feet.

The start of our descent was also an indication that time was running out – fuel-wise. It takes just over 20 minutes to lose 40,000 feet; the fuel was about 40 minutes to running out.

The altimeter continued unwinding: 35,000 feet, 32,000 feet, 30,000 feet, 28,000 feet.

Sure enough, that vague shape was becoming more defined. I was looking out of the front window to the right, studying the view, trying to ascertain whether or not I could see the shape of the coastline properly, wanting to compare that shape to the navigation chart. This would help my confidence about our position.

Everything so far was based on a guess, seeing the shape of the coastline and comparing it to my chart would mean that I was somewhere near where I expected to be. Thankfully, there was an indication. The pale lights I had seen earlier slowly formed a shape, a sort of a line. Though I could not be sure that this was not 'anticipation bias'. Anticipation Bias is where the brain falsely fills in the details of a picture that it was expecting to see. It is something pilots had to be very aware of, as it could cause errors in judging position.

At 26,000 feet then 24,000 feet, I turned my attention back to the flight instruments to monitor them and carry out descent checks. This diverted my focus away from the view outside. Once I had done that, I turned my attention back to the outside. This meant that my brain could not infill the picture for me. I was desperate for that to be Abidjan!

Now I was convinced that in the view ahead there were lights along a specific line, forming a half-moon shape. I now referred back to my chart to hopefully identify it.

The shape of the lights definitely showed it was a coastline. YIPPEE! At least I could stick the aircraft on the beach and we might have a pretty good chance of walking away from it!

'Catriona, that is the coast somewhere near Abidjan airport, but I cannot yet see the city or the airport. I may still have to land her on the beach. When it comes to it, as I said, make sure your belt is really secure and hold tight if that happens. The five-point seat belt will hold you in position very well.'

'Okay, Mike. When will you know?'

'I hope to see the airfield soon. I can hear them well, but no navigation aids makes it difficult. I think within five minutes – I'm scanning ahead for the estuary of the river. Abidjan sits on what is basically a huge, natural harbour.'

As I was speaking, the CAGS started flashing. I scanned the instrument panel to find the source of the warning. At the top of the engine instruments was a red light marked 'Rear Bearing Overheat' – it was the one that had played up on the Friday night and had obviously decided to give up.

'Shit!' I said out loud.

'What is it?' Catriona asked cautiously.

The word 'shit' was the precursor to any number of problems. Catriona was catching on! Well, the day had not gone brilliantly so far...

'The rear bearing on the left engine has failed. I'm going to have to shut it down before it seizes up. It's got no oil flow through it.' I hesitated. 'We will be landing, wherever we finish up, on one engine.'

I went through the procedure to shut the engine down; there was no discernible change as both engines were at idle power during the descent. But this would change. When the flaps and gear were lowered in preparation for landing, the power would need to be increased – more if you're trying to fly on one engine. This was a fairly 'normal' emergency situation. Pilots practise this a lot.

'Mayday, Mayday, Mayday, Abidjan, Golf Romeo India – we've had an engine failure and are going to carry out a single engine landing.'

Abidjan confirmed understanding of the new situation:

'Mayday Golf Romeo India, this is Abidjan Control, cleared descent as required and priority landing for Runway Two One (21), call when on final approach with Abidjan Tower on one one eight decimal one.'

I felt it best to keep them in the loop – not that they could do much, except for getting the fire engines out in case I cocked it up!

Don't forget that I did not know exactly where Abidjan was. However, I did now see a larger town appearing out of the night haze ahead. I had been continuously checking in my head the dead-reckoning navigation, so that place ahead should be, according to my calculations, Abidjan.

I had arranged the descent to be quite high, to give the maximum options. If it was Abidjan then wonderful, but the only other option was landing on a beach if it wasn't Abidjan. So, the backup plan would then go into effect: a night crash landing to an African beach. The height would give me time to set up a crash landing.

22,000 feet. 20,000 feet. 18,000 feet......

As we passed 16,000 feet, an indication appeared on the DME (distance measuring equipment). This was a system that used a transmission from the aeroplane and a reply from a ground station which was converted to give you distance. It was a very handy bit of kit, as it also gave you a ground speed because of the rate of change of distance. (More help for your pilot's licence!)

As it happened momentarily, the 'inoperative' red bar on the DME shifted up out of view and the instrument showed three miles. This was the first navigation instrument to work on the whole flight and, as G-LORI was at 15,000 feet, the mathematicians amongst you will be able to work out that three miles (at 5,250 feet/mile) is indeed 15,000 feet – YAY!

Phew, I thought, *that is a relief!* The ground-based DME transmitter was on the airfield. We were overhead Abidjan airport! At that moment, the city was becoming clearer, so I could make out the shape of the airfield through the haze below me for the first time.

'That' I paused for full effect. 'is Abidjan, Catriona,' I told her. 'We *will* be landing on the airfield!'

'Thank God!' she uttered.

I had been flying the aeroplane, but poor Catriona just had to sit there, unable to do anything to help. The stress for her had been enormous. She looked at me and smiled.

It was strange, with all that had happened, I still felt ice cold, completely calm. I cannot explain this. I am not superhuman or a top military pilot. I had been like this for the whole flight, as well as the two weeks before. It was like my brain had entered a 'pure focus' mode.

Catriona said later that seeing this Ice-Cold Focus Mike was such a contrast to the guy who took Toppy the retriever out for long walks and did the supermarket shopping.

Of course, I was to pay for it later with severe PTSD.

I knew the runway at Abidjan was aligned more or less south, 210 degrees to be precise (hence, the shortened 'pilot's name' for the runway was '21' – pronounced 'Two One' as explained earlier)

Looking down, I could see the welcoming shape of the airport with the runway now visible. I'd been there several times before, so I was very familiar with the airfield.

From overhead, I took up a heading of 330 degrees with the intention of making a teardrop-shaped approach, staying close to the airfield. I began the procedure for landing and completed the approach checks.

As I was high, I needed to lose the excess altitude I was carrying. For your exams at the end of the book, there are three essential rules of flying:

• Air below you.

• Fuel in the tanks – not in the fuel bowser.

• Runway in front of you – not behind you.

There is one more, but this does not relate to safety: *always look cool*.

I selected the first stage of wing flaps, 15 degrees, ready for landing.

The flaps on the wing had the effect of creating the same amount of lift from the wing at a lower airspeed and, therefore, enabled the aeroplane to be slowed down to land at a speed that did not use too much runway – they are retracted at normal flying speeds to reduce drag and consequently use less fuel.

The moment I did that, the aircraft hydraulic system failed and the wing flaps did not budge.

'Shit!' I said out loud (that word again).

'What is it now?' Catriona again asked cautiously – the day

continued to disappoint!

'Now the hydraulics have failed and the flaps are stuck in the up position!' I started laughing.

'I'm sure it's not that funny,' Catriona said.

'Well, it's just that not much else can go wrong,' I said. 'apart from not being able to lower the landing gear normally but don't worry. I can lower it with the emergency system.'

I selected the landing gear lever to the 'down' position and then proceeded going through the manual lowering of the landing gear checklist. The landing gear *clunk* was heard as the gear dropped and locked into position. Three green lights showed reassuringly over the landing gear selector, confirming that the landing gear was now locked down.

The wing flaps indicated that they were in the up position but with the hydraulics failed the wing flaps could not be lowered any further. To allow for this, the landing speed would now have to be 150 knots (180 mph) instead of 110 knots, with the consequential substantial addition to the landing run. The wing flaps would normally be at 45 degrees for landing.

The checklist advised that with the landing gear lowered with the emergency system, there was no anti-skid system (aircraft ABS) when the main hydraulic system had failed. In this situation, wheel brakes would have to be applied carefully and also at a much higher landing speed. Bursting a tyre was a distinct possibility.

I would need to get the aircraft onto the runway very early and land firmly to start braking with the emergency braking system.

I completed the landing checks and began the turn to line up with the runway. I then selected the tower frequency.

'Abidjan Tower, Mayday Golf Romeo India turning final, request landing clearance.'

'Mayday Golf Romeo India, you are cleared to land, emergency vehicles are in position.'

'Cleared to land, thank you, Mayday Golf Romeo India,' I replied.

'That's the runway, Catriona,' I told her. 'We are almost there.'

Catriona had been praying for a safe arrival:

'Thank God!' she said. I could hear that her breathing was fast.

As I stabilised G-LORI on the approach at a speed of 170 knots, I intended to slow for touchdown at 150 knots in the last mile or so. It was a delicate job, with one engine failed, so there had to be a lot more power on the right engine to compensate. A boot-full of right rudder was needed to keep the aircraft in balance.

When that power was reduced, as we crossed the threshold of the runway, the aeroplane would 'swing' as the power came off, requiring compensation with the flight controls. This was made more difficult with the wing flaps up because the approach speed was so much higher than normal.

Up ahead, to the side of the runway, there was a sea of blue, flashing lights from the emergency fire and ambulance vehicles standing by in case it all went wrong…

I deliberately dipped G-LORI below the normal approach path, aiming for the very beginning of the runway (remember the rule?)

The runway threshold soon flashed underneath G-LORI, so I retarded the thrust lever on the 'live' engine to idle; hands and feet moving on the controls, maintaining the centre line of the runway and the approach path as I did so.

The HS125 hovered five feet above the runway, floating on the cushion of air under its wings – the ground effect I was talking about earlier. We were still travelling at over 160 miles an hour, but the runway was not of unlimited length – 8,600 feet. That runway was being eaten up at a worrying rate.

Finally, the cushion began to evaporate under the wing as the speed washed off. To get it on the runway as soon as possible, I eased the control wheel forward, resulting in the aeroplane dropping unceremoniously onto the runway with a very firm bump.

That old phrase 'Did we land or were we shot down, Captain!' went through my mind. I started to gently apply the brakes. They responded with a reassuring reduction of speed.

For the first time in this series of events, I began to feel in complete control of my life expectancy.

'That wasn't a very good landing,' Catriona teased in a somewhat unsympathetic tone.

I was proud of making good landings.

'In the circumstances, that was the best landing ever!' I replied, breathing a sigh of relief. 'Safely on the ground, not a beach, *and* at the right airport!'

We both laughed together – a physical release of an incredible amount of tension.

I continued gently applying the wheel brakes and brought the speed of the aeroplane down to a fast walking pace before starting the APU. Then I began going through the normal after landing checks in an automatic and well-practised routine.

At the same time, with a map of the airport taxiways on my lap, I taxied the aeroplane to the stand that had been allocated to us – this was in the freight area away from the main terminal parking area.

As we stopped, I applied the parking brake and looked out of the window in front of the aircraft. We were completely surrounded by a huge number of men in military fatigues, all sporting large rifles; they were extremely well-armed.

'God! What are we going to do now?' Catriona asked.

'Don't worry, Coco, this is Africa. It's more show than anything else,' I replied.

This was more to reassure Catriona, but the real answer was that I had not expected this reception either.

It was another example of exceptional communication in a part of the world not renowned for it. The Ghanaian ATC reaction and now this army reception in Abidjan were both a real surprise.

'Clearly, the Nigerians have been very busy on the phone – and all on a Saturday night,' I said sarcastically. 'None of this is normal for Africa, there is *definitely* more to this than meets the eye.' I was externalising the questions that were buzzing around my head.

This was the first time that Catriona had flown with me, but what a baptism of fire! She had been exposed to real danger, and the flight itself had been so extreme, yet she had maintained such composure during all these events. I was so impressed; this further reinforced the thinking behind my decision to bring her with me.

I continued to carry out the after-shutdown checks and secured the aeroplane. This took about five minutes. During this time, the reception committee remained, waiting for us at a respectable distance.

When ready, I told Catriona to stay behind me. Opening the main door, I stood on the top step and gave the army men a huge wave.

'Hello!' I shouted, along with the biggest smile I could muster.

All of the assembled group responded by raising their hands, huge grins showing bright, white teeth, and returned the wave with great enthusiasm.

Catriona was behind me, looking over my shoulder amazed, wondering what I was going to do.

'I cannot believe you have just done that!' she whispered with an air of incredulity.

'It's called "disarming a potentially hazardous situation"!' I replied. 'I had no idea it would work, but it seemed like a good idea.'

'More like gross stupidity, but you're right, it worked,' Catriona replied.

'Catriona, what do you call an African with a gun?' I asked.

'I don't know,' she replied, expecting a hugely philosophical answer.

'Sir,' I stated.

We both laughed – quietly.

I closed up G-LORI, locked the door and then went around the back of the aeroplane to undo the rear access door underneath the tail. Popping up inside 'the hellhole', I disconnected the 'Number 3 Battery'.

This little battery powered the start sequence of the engines – the electronics that enabled the start sequence to begin. It was a small thing, not something that would have stopped anyone with a reasonable amount of aircraft knowledge from discovering. At least I felt that I'd done something to secure the aeroplane, not knowing what was going to transpire from where we were now.

As I finished, the leader of the army escort walked over holding out his hand in greeting. As I shook his hand:

'Welcome to the Ivory Coast!' he said.

Typically polite, the Ivorians were lovely people in a lovely country. This was one of the main reasons for heading here.

I warmly shook his hand in return, smiled a big smile and replied politely:

'It is my pleasure to be here again, sir.'

The first impression in this situation was critical in setting the scene for how we were treated. Politeness is free and can only help in any situation. I also adopted a very relaxed body language to highlight that impression. I deliberately maintained eye contact with him during this interaction.

The sergeant asked us to walk in the direction he was pointing, towards the building that housed the control tower. The large group in fatigues, sporting their rifles, followed a little distance behind.

I said quietly to Catriona, 'Follow me!'

I peeled very slightly away from the direction the sergeant was walking, towards the customs entrance of the main terminal; the normal way you would enter the airport building.

Catriona followed looking a bit bemused. For a short time, we gradually diverged from the escort.

Slowly, the penny dropped with the escort and there were a number of high-pitched, hissing-type whistles. It was a typical African 'attention-getter'.

'Mike, they're whistling at us,' Catriona said in an urgent tone.

'Catriona, *Never Answer To A Whistle*!' I replied.

When I first arrived in Nigeria to live, Mike Coleman was with me on the apron at Ikeja when one of the ground-handling staff started hissing at us to get our attention. I turned to acknowledge the calling of the guy behind us.

Mike grabbed my arm and said, 'Mike, never ever answer to a whistle – wait until they use proper language.'

Sure enough, the chap then called:

'Excuse me, sir, can you help me?'

We both turned around and went to help him. I've never forgotten that little interaction.

The sergeant turned around:

'Please, Captain, this way.' He politely pointed in the direction of the offices at the bottom of the control tower.

'What were you doing?' Catriona asked, mystified that I could do something like that with all these armed men around us.

'Just seeing how serious they are,' I replied in a jovial tone. 'Just testing!'

'There are fifty of them, and they have *guns*,' Catriona stated.

'I know, but we mustn't take it too seriously,' I replied calmly. 'This is Africa. Different rules apply to anyone else with a gun... Mind you, wherever you are in the world, you always call a man with a gun "sir"!'

As I said earlier, in my opinion, I have a superb sense of humour –

although, this is not shared with all my friends and family!

My daughter, Victoria, once asked me: 'Dad, do you know why you're not a really successful stand-up comedian?'

'No, Victoria, I don't know why I'm not a really successful stand-up comedian.'

'Well, Dad, it's because you are not funny!'

Yes, I do have an esoteric (crap) sense of humour, but it had the effect here of de-stressing a very stressful situation.

In the back of my mind, I was still trying to work out how and why that Alpha Jet was waiting for us to take off on a Saturday evening. And this reception committee here in Abidjan were waiting for us. It simply did not make sense.

CHAPTER 20

Abidjan, Ivory Coast – Under Arrest

I had a feeling what was going to happen next.

The fact that the Ivorian army and security service had been waiting for us meant that the Nigerians had contacted the Ivorian government at a very high level.

This was not a surprise, as the Ghanaian air traffic control had been asking us to land there (definitely not a good idea).

So, the most likely thing to happen now was us being questioned by someone very senior in the police. Fortunately, I did have my briefcase with all the documents ready to justify our actions.

'Catriona, we are going to be questioned by someone senior. But don't worry, we have all our documents and the contract, so it will be okay,' I said, trying to forewarn her.

'This way please.'

The sergeant raised his hand and indicated to the door on the side of the building. We were led into the building that housed air traffic control.

We followed him into a corridor that had strip lights and pale green walls with industrial lino flooring. There were a number of doors either side of the corridor.

The sergeant led us into one of the rooms on the left.

'Please be seated,' said the sergeant.

He indicated to the chairs lined up in front of a desk in the centre of what was probably an airport manager's office.

Catriona and I moved to the seats and sat down.

It was quite large and, again, painted in an industrial light green but with the accoutrements of a management office, with grey filing cabinets and shelves displaying a few family pictures. The floor was covered in a light grey, hard-wearing carpet.

'Please wait here,' said the sergeant, still very politely. 'Someone will be coming soon to speak to you.'

One of the guys with guns was positioned in the room, but this was clearly a formality. There was a very calm atmosphere around our 'arrest'.

Catriona and I then had to make ourselves as comfortable as possible on a pair of basic, wooden office chairs. I must admit that I was quite happy: we were alive and in the Ivory Coast.

'I'm guessing that we are going to meet a senior member of the police or security service,' I said to Catriona, 'probably coming from the city, so they'll likely be here in half an hour or so.'

'What do you think is going to happen?' Catriona asked.

'Notwithstanding the unexpected intervention of the Nigerian Air Force, we do have all the legal documents and authorisation to collect G-LORI. It will be up to the Ivorians to decide, but we are in a completely separate country here, so it should be okay.'

Admittedly, this was a huge bit of 'glass half-full', but it was the only way to look at it in the circumstances.

We continued chatting about the last few days and the flight, trying to make sense of it all.

Eventually, we heard muffled activity, so I guessed we had company.

Patrice Koro walked into the room:

'Good evening, Captain Howard,' he said, offering his hand. 'I am Patrice Koro, senior officer in the security department of our government.'

As I shook Patrice's hand, smiling and looking into his eyes as I did so. This was the same technique to deffuse the situation that I had used with the sergeant. Patrice's eyes were classic deep black, with a twinkle of humour. I guessed that this humour was somewhat buried at that moment!

'Pleased to meet you.' I shook his hand firmly. 'This is my first officer, Catriona Spalding.'

'Pleased to meet you,' said Catriona as she also shook his hand.

As I said before, considering the bizarre events over the last few weeks, I continued to be so impressed with Catriona's ability to adapt to these events. After all, we were now effectively under arrest in a far distant, very foreign country.

Patrice, tall with ebony skin and handsome African features, was dressed in smart evening clothes. His attire seemed to indicate that his Saturday evening had been interrupted by our arrival.

He was frowning, clearly a little bemused by the summary of a story that he had been briefed on before being sent off to the airport to interview us.

'Well,' Patrice began, 'I think you need to explain exactly what has been the background to your arrival in the Ivory Coast.' His voice was deep and resonant. His English was extremely good with a flowery French accent.

We began to explain all the events, from seeing Ben Slade in London to the warning from Hyacinth Odigwe, and the decision to leave in the aeroplane. I also spoke about the pursuit of the Nigerian Air Force and my surprise that it had happened.

I opened my briefcase and began to pull out the documents and began going through them with Patrice; starting with those that related to the aeroplane lease and court order showing permission to repossess.

Patrice listened intently to my explanations with a frown furrowed deeply across his dark brow. He then studied the documents that I had handed to him, explaining the significance of each document so they made some kind of sense. Patrice continued to frown as he read them.

'Would it be possible to speak to the British Consulate, please?' I asked as he read.

Patrice looked up. I could see that he was making a judgement of us and the story. The Nigerians would have been in high-level contact and putting pressure on the Ivorians. Of that I was quite sure.

'Of course,' replied Patrice. 'I will call them shortly.'

I did feel that if he had not believed our story, that request would not have been so easily agreed to.

The study of documents and discussion went on for some time until Patrice seemed to decide he had seen enough and wanted to bring proceedings to an end. It was now nearly midnight.

He excused himself politely and left the room.

'What do you think is happening?' Catriona asked, frowning.

'I think he's going to speak to someone up the seniority chain,' I replied.

After 10 or 15 minutes, Patrice returned and sat down. He sighed and looked at me.

'Captain Howard, you have really upset the Nigerian government, and they are making very threatening noises about you to our government.' He paused and continued in that deep tone and French accent. 'The Nigerians want our government to hand you over to them...'

Catriona and I were intently listening to him. After all, to all intents and purposes, our lives depended on what had been decided.

'However...'

Both Catriona and I slowly let out the breath we were both holding.

'…the president of the Ivory Coast has taken this matter into his hands personally and has asked me to keep you under arrest… house arrest. We have arranged for you to stay at the Hilton Hotel in Abidjan,' said Patrice.

Our breath was now properly released. It had obviously been a very tense period after landing, not knowing what our fate would be following our arrival.

My knowledge of the way the Ivory Coast worked was turning out to be correct with that announcement.

Patrice also said that he had spoken to the British High Commission's duty officer and explained the situation. The duty officer had confirmed that one of their representatives could come down to the hotel to meet us in the morning.

It is an interesting comparison between the French and British colonial countries. I have travelled extensively and observed the differences as to how these countries work. Whether it is Nouakchott or Nouadhibou in Mauritania, or Bamako in Mali, compared to Accra in Ghana, or Lagos in Nigeria, what were previously French colonies seem to be much better organised. I eventually met an 'old' colonial hand and asked why.

He explained that when the British handed independence back to the colony, they pulled out lock, stock… including all the civil servants who were running the show.

On the other hand, the French handed political control over but left their civil servants in subordinate roles to maintain the management of the infrastructure. Hence, on the whole, the ex-French colonies remained pretty well organised.

Patrice left the room again and signalled that we should remain where we were. He returned about 15 minutes later and indicated that we should follow him.

'I have arranged transport for you. I will follow in my vehicle to the hotel and get you checked in,' he explained.

As Catriona and I picked up our little travel bags, I held tightly onto my briefcase containing all the evidence of our situation. We left following Patrice out of the air traffic control building into the car park outside.

It was again a point where we exhaled slowly and let our shoulders drop a bit more. There were a large number of police and army vehicles in the car park; clearly, these had brought our reception committee. But we were outside – and, for the time being, free!

Immediately outside the building were a couple of very large, posh Mercedes. Patrice again indicated to the first vehicle:

'I will follow in my vehicle and see you at the hotel.'

'Thank you for your help, Patrice. Yes, we will see you there,' I replied.

So, we set off from the airport in the Merc.

Patrice got out of the vehicle behind and ushered us into the hotel lobby.

It was an incredible scene inside the reception area. Numerous sprays of fresh flowers decorated the round tables dotted around the sumptuous room. Roman column-like palisades rose up from the marble floor. Large oil paintings adorned the walls in between decorative curtains to the sides. There was an impressive staircase ahead that seemed to lead to the bar and restaurant area.

The very smartly dressed staff behind the reception counter smiled as we approached.

Patrice spoke quietly in French to them. Clearly, they were expecting us and knew exactly who we were. The reception staff handed some keys to Patrice.

He smiled as he gave the room keys to us:

We were shown to our room and let in by a porter. He put our bags in the space just inside the door. I gave him a dollar note, after which he beamed and said an effervescent:

'Thank you, sir!'

The room was spacious and well laid out with a desk and large double bed. There was a terrace with a spectacular view over towards the city in one direction and the water of the bay in the other.

I picked up the telephone and rang Nick Munns. I knew it was very late, but I felt it was important that he knew what had happened. I was still in a state of shock and bemused that the Nigerian Air Force were up and waiting for us on a Saturday night at six o'clock.

Nick answered the phone in a very quiet voice:

'I was just drifting off,' he said, 'but the wife is fast asleep. Just a moment, I will transfer to the downstairs phone.'

After a moment, he came back on. I then relayed all the events up until our arrival at the Hilton.

'God,' he stated breathlessly. 'I cannot understand what that is all about.'

We both paused on the phone for a moment trying to fathom out the answer, but it was impossible at this stage.

'I will give Shirlstar a call tomorrow informing them that I'm in Abidjan with the aeroplane and get them to release the first tranche of the fee. I will also ask them to send some funds to cover the incidental costs while we're here sorting out G-LORI's engine and hydraulic problems,' I said. 'I won't go into any more than that because I'm certain that they have not told us the *whole story*, Nick.' I hesitated and continued, 'It seems that Ben has been involved in illegal currency deals, and one may have gone wrong.'

'God, Mike, really? I suppose, having dealt with him, it's not a huge surprise!'

I emphasised the 'whole story' knowing full well that there had to be a bigger picture beyond what I already knew.

I then went through everything as briefly as possible to Nick so he might get his head around what had happened. I included what I had seen in Ben's notes: the comment about the 890,000 naira and the name Graham Bott. That Dave Fagan had confirmed Bott was a 'fixer' of 'ill repute' and was probably involved in shady dealings, how Dave had made enquiries and it appeared that Bott had disappeared from Lagos after financial problems, and based on the notes on his desk pad, it was not hard to deduce that Ben's fingerprints were all over this.

I explained all my thoughts on this to Nick, although the Nigerian Air Force's appearance and unsuccessful attempt to shoot me down was still a complete mystery.

'You do need to contact the British Embassy, Mike,' Nick said with lawyerly earnestness. 'Depending on how this is perceived by the Ivorian government, you may need some protection from the local Embassy.'

'It's already done, Nick. The guy from the Ivorian government has already arranged that. Someone called Jimmie Jamieson is coming over tomorrow.'

Nick and I agreed to speak the following day.

Having hung up, Catriona and I discussed all the events while in the room. We were both relieved at the help being provided by the Ivorians through Patrice, and also that the British Embassy were going to assist us, too.

Clearly, it was the case of 'what happens now' that concerned us. Catriona and I then fell into bed for an exhausted sleep, trying to ignore the unknowns that faced us the next day.

CHAPTER 21

The Nigerians Turn up 'Mob-Handed'

The next morning at 6 am the phone rang.

'Captain Howard, this is Patrice.' He sounded concerned. 'Apologies for calling so early, but I thought I ought to inform you that the Nigerians have turned up during the night at Abidjan airport in some force. You have clearly upset someone very much high up in their government!'

'Crikey, what have they turned up in?' I asked.

'There is a C-130 Hercules and two large Bell Helicopters,' he explained. 'From all accounts at the airport, there were a large number of special forces on board with other army personnel. We can only deduce that they want to collect you from here and take you back to Lagos.'

'Mmm… I do not like the sound of that, Patrice. I think the last place we want to go is Lagos!'

'Don't worry, we will *never* allow the Nigerians to dictate to us what happens in our county,' he replied emphatically, emphasising the word 'Never'.

I was very relieved. This further underlined my decision to come to Abidjan.

Patrice continued. 'I have discussed this with the president, and he has decided to put guards on your floor in the hotel and the whole floor has been cleared of other occupants.' He paused before adding, 'We have also put our special forces into the hotel in plain clothes; they are fully armed. The Nigerians will not get too far. We are also monitoring their movements.'

'Patrice, I cannot say how sorry I am to cause you all these problems. Thank you again for your help. Also, please can you pass on our sincerest thanks to your president for his help?'

I was absolutely shocked at this news. It was Sunday morning in West Africa, yet the Nigerians had managed to organise a major operation.

That would have been a surprise on a weekday, let alone on a Saturday night/Sunday morning. I had taken off at around six and landed in Abidjan just under three hours later. The Nigerians had found out where we were and had sent a fully crewed aircraft and helicopters within a few hours. Amazing.

Sorry to keep repeating this, but it reinforced the feeling that there was an awful lot more to the events of Saturday than I was aware of.

Catriona was listening intently to my side of the conversation. I filled her in on the details. She was as shocked as I was. We were both in a state of incredulity.

Once I mentioned breakfast to Catriona, we both immediately realised that we had not eaten since the previous lunchtime. We both became focused on getting showered (and me having a shave) to go to the restaurant as soon as possible.

After we left our room, we were confronted by a very large, beefy Ivorian military man in a camouflage jacket and sporting a M16 carbine. He bowed politely as we left the room.

I said, 'Bonjour,' in my atrocious French accent, bowing in return.

At each end of the corridor near the fire escapes were two more. Catriona and I walked to the lifts and there was another guard.

'Crikey, Coco, Patrice was not joking that they were taking the

Nigerian threat seriously.'

'Thank Christ we came here, Mike,' she replied. 'From what little knowledge I have of this part of the world, just the two weeks, I cannot imagine better protection elsewhere.'

'Remember Ghanaian air traffic inviting us to land there?'

'I sure do,' she replied. 'I guess we wouldn't have been in that country for long?'

'Probably no more than a few hours based on what has happened here this morning.'

We discussed the events further, as the lift descended to the ground floor. The doors eventually opened, and we stepped out into the reception. Again, there were military men near the exits. We went into the restaurant through the doors from reception.

The guards changed position, moving into the main reception area. I also noticed that two men in civilian clothes had moved into the restaurant from reception at the same time as us. I made eye contact with them, and there was a tiny acknowledgement from one of them. These would be the special forces guys.

There was a typical French-style breakfast. It was delicious. The croissants were good enough to die for. Yes, I know. Another bad joke!

Patrice arrived while we were enjoying a coffee after finishing breakfast. He strolled in, acknowledging the two men in civilian clothes with a slight nod. He moved with the confidence of physical fitness and someone in control. The evening clothes he wore the previous night had been replaced by a tailored, light wool suit and cream, silk shirt and matching tie. At nearly six foot, with square shoulders and a handsome black face, he caught the attention of all the guests in the restaurant – particularly the ladies.

'Good morning, Captain and Miss Spalding. I hope you were comfortable last night. I am sorry to have disturbed you so early with my call.'

'No problem, Patrice. Again, I apologise for the inconvenience we have caused you. Please, call us Mike and Catriona.'

It was noticeable that there was no antipathy from Patrice. I had deduced he was some sort of senior intelligence officer – probably military – and that this business was almost certainly interrupting his normal weekend with family or whatever. However, I felt that the story we told him in the airport after arriving, which was supported by the documents, had been believed. And because we had told the truth, there was a lot of sympathy for us from the Ivorian government's point of view.

The Nigerians turning up the way they had helped us, too. No country likes to be bullied, either diplomatically or militarily.

Patrice sat down with us. 'I have spoken to my friend Jimmie Jamieson at the British Consulate this morning and explained your circumstances,' Patrice continued. 'He will be joining us shortly.'

'Do you know what the Nigerians are actually doing, Patrice?' I asked.

It was difficult to guess what their plan might be, turning up in a foreign country like they had – I was baffled by this along with the other events.

'We are monitoring them. Most are still at the airport, but some have left in plain clothes. This is why we are not taking any chances with you two.' He paused and then continued, 'The ones who have left the airport are the Nigerian special forces, which is worrying us.'

'I have to say, that is worrying me, too. None of this makes sense… given all the circumstances.'

I had explained everything to Patrice the previous night, so the arrival of the Nigerians just added to the mystery.

During all my time in Africa, I had not seen such a degree of coordination and in such a short time. I was more and more baffled by it all. Then I remembered the Ghanaian air traffic control calling me to land in Accra. Again, this had been coordinated by the Nigerians in an incredibly short time.

'Must all have been organised at a very high level,' I mused out loud.

'I agree,' said Patrice. 'We believe that if the Nigerians manage to get hold of you and take you back to Lagos, your safety and security cannot be guaranteed. This is why we are taking steps to ensure you are kept safe.'

Patrice must have been a very busy man, but he seemed in no hurry to leave. We moved into a lounge, which was part of the bar area. We ordered some more coffee and continued to chat about the events until Jimmie Jamieson arrived.

Jimmie bustled into the lounge an hour later. He was a short and energetic man, with dark hair that was long in the fringe (probably overdue for a cut), so it flopped over his left eye. He was wearing a cream, tropical cotton suit that was crumpled from sitting in an office chair or vehicle for a long time. Under that was a white shirt with a brown, patterned silk tie, the shirt buttons straining a little due to too many diplomatic functions.

He first shook Patrice's hand and bid him good morning. Catriona and I had stood up in anticipation of being introduced.

'Captain Howard, good to meet you,' he started.

Like Patrice, Jimmie had a glint of mischievous humour in his eye, even though the manner was very serious.

'You have created something of a storm in an African teacup.'

Whilst it was a humorous phrase, Jimmie also pursed his lips in an expression of concern.

I held my hand out and shook his. It was a firm handshake. Jimmie's hand was small and slightly moist – probably due to the rush to get here.

'This is Catriona, my co-pilot.'

I held my hand in Catriona's direction by way of introduction. I watched as Jimmie held out his hand, glancing up and down her slim and neat figure in a floral cotton dress. We had travelled very light but Catriona had managed to pack some nice changes of clothes in her bag.

'Pleased to meet you,' he said with a slight, respectful nod.

'Pleased to meet you, too,' Catriona answered. 'And thank you so much for coming to our assistance.' Catriona shook Jimmie's outstretched hand.

'Please sit down, both of you, over here may be a little better,' Jimmie said. He gestured to a group of flower-patterned sofas in between the restaurant and bar area. These sofas offered more privacy than the ones we had originally sat in. 'We need to chat about the situation and see what can be done to extricate you... The Foreign Office is aware of the situation and has briefed me on the Nigerians' reaction.' With pursed lips, he added, 'The Nigerians are very, very upset.'

This was (what I guessed to be) a substantial, diplomatic understatement!

We all sat down, Catriona and I on one side, and Jimmie and Patrice on the other. I then went through the whole story again to bring Jimmie up to speed. I could say intentionally, but that would be a lie!

It also had the benefit of repeating the story that Patrice had heard the previous night. By repeating the story with no inconsistencies, it underlined to Patrice that we were telling the truth. This was to give us some extra credibility.

Our fates were in the hands of these guys. We were effectively in a kayak in rapids with no paddle. They were the ones with the lifebelts and ropes to get us out. We would have absolutely no chance at all if we were grabbed and taken – or sent – to Nigeria.

The four of us talked animatedly for a few hours. The time passed quickly, as we were all engrossed in this wildly unusual tale.

After a while, I could see that Catriona was beginning to fade; I, too, felt knackered. We had barely slept for two nights – including the Friday night, after the aborted take-off.

'Do you guys mind if we take a break?' I asked.

'Please do,' replied Patrice. 'Shall we meet you for supper? He glanced at Jimmie to confirm that he would like to join us.

'Yes, that would suit me. I shall hopefully get some further information from the Foreign Office West Africa desk,' said Jimmie.

'Okay.' Patrice nodded. 'See you at, say, seven p.m.?'

'That is fine with us,' I replied.

'And, just to confirm, our friends will be around to keep an eye on things.'

Patrice nodded to the men sitting strategically covering all the entrances and exits. There were uniformed army personnel at the hotel entrance, too, but the plain-clothed officers had the air of formidable and capable operators.

'Thanks again for your help. We are so grateful,' Catriona repeated.

We got up and left them. On reaching our room, we collapsed on the bed and fell into an exhausted sleep within a very short time.

After a few hours of much-needed sleep, we both had a shower and felt much better. I grabbed some clothes from my bag, pulled on a pair of trousers and buttoned up a clean shirt. Catriona was looking great in a different, cotton, slim-fitting, dark blue, patterned dress that came to just above the knee. It showed off her lovely slim legs. I knew Patrice and Jimmie would appreciate that!

We got ourselves ready in good time to go for supper and headed downstairs just before 7 pm.

In the lift, Catriona asked:

'What day is it, Mike? I have completely lost track of time.'

'It's still Sunday, but feels like Tuesday!' I answered.

The sofas became our meeting place over the next few days. They were comfortable with tables in between for papers (and drinks!), and they were far enough away from others not to be overheard. We were also easily visible from most angles by our 'minders'.

Catriona and I sat on one side, with Patrice and Jimmie on the other. There was not much to update us on after they had checked with their respective offices. We chatted generally about the situation and speculated about what was behind it.

As we were about to go into supper, I saw a figure coming through the main hotel entrance doors. He was tall, overweight, and with a slight stoop and round shoulders as if the world weighed heavily upon them. A shock of untidy blond hair was swept in a fringe across his forehead and down to the eyebrows.

It was a bit strange because the figure looked just like Nick Munns. After a slight pause, I realised it was, indeed, Nick. It seemed very strange to see my lawyer mate in the reception of the Abidjan Hilton. It just did not seem right.

Nick was grinning, as he walked up to us. He held out his hand as the grin expanded.

'Hello, mate, surprise!' He clearly thought this was great fun.

I shook his hand. 'Nick, what the fuck are you doing here?' I replied.

'Well, I just couldn't stay at home wondering what was happening. I had to come out and see first-hand. I grabbed the BCal flight early this morning.' He paused and continued, 'Thought you could do with some help.'

He gave Catriona a kiss on each cheek and then looked at the other two men. Patrice and Jimmie had both risen from their seats in anticipation of an introduction.

'Nick Munns, this is Patrice Koro. Patrice is representing the president of the Ivory Coast. Nick is our friend and lawyer from the UK,' I explained.

'Very pleased to meet you.' Nick and Patrice shook hands.

I then turned towards Jimmie:

'And this is Jimmie Jamieson. Nick Munns,' I formally introduced them. 'Jimmie is from the consulate here in Abidjan. He is also helping us.'

They shook hands and smiled at one another.

'Two questions, Nick. One, what would you like to drink? And two, what are you doing here?' I asked.

'Gin and tonic, and honestly, I just could not sit at home after what you said. I've organised some funds for you but thought you could do with some extra grey matter here,' Nick said. 'I just decided to jump on the BCal plane and come straight out,' he continued. 'My wife was not too impressed.' He said this last part with a sheepish, naughty schoolboy look.

But it was true. Nick was a very bright cookie, and I could do with some brain matter to bounce ideas off.

Nick Munns and Patrice Koro in the Hilton, Abidjan

Catriona was great, and we had a good relationship with good discussions on all matters, but it was also a little restricted because we were both immersed in the same situation. Nick was outside and I trusted his opinion, so it was really great that he had decided to come out here. Some out-of-the-box analysis was required.

'You are so right, Nick,' I said. 'The more the merrier!' I signalled to the waiter, who then came over and took a drinks order.

We all had a meal together, and then Patrice and Jimmie left, having arranged to see them in the morning. It was interesting to note that all of us got on very well, and we became friends in this short time. There was a superb affinity that developed between us.

Jimmie Jamieson and his wife join us for drinks in the Hilton, Abidjan

Nick, Catriona and I then had the opportunity to go through all the events. Nick actually took some notes.

'It will help us to make some sense of what has happened and why,' he stated matter-of-factly. 'There must be a reason for the Nigerians having that jet up ready for you, Mike – just must be.'

Like the rest of us, Nick was musing out loud, but none of us could, at that stage, have guessed just what the Nigerians were up to.

We were not to know at that very moment the team of Mohammed Yusuf, a retired senior officer in the Nigerian army, and Alexander Barak and Felix Abithol of Mossad were in London. They were already in the process of finding and carrying out the kidnapping of Umaru Dikko.

The next morning, another completely unexpected bombshell hit.

Jimmie Jamieson rang me at around 8 am.

'Mike, it's Jimmie. Bad news, I'm afraid. The Nigerians have arrested your friends, the two Bristow Helicopter engineers. The consulate has been informed, and they've advised me...' Jimmie paused. From the tone of his voice, the seriousness was apparent.

'They arrived at work at six this morning. The Nigerian police were waiting for them.' Again, he paused before adding, 'The West Africa desk are aware of this, and I have spoken to them, but they say they do not understand why the Nigerians have done this. It just makes everything so much more complicated. The West Africa desk will try to find out more during the day.'

Of course, later, as events unfolded in London, this would make some kind of sense but at that moment I was reeling from the shock of this news.

This completely unexpected and dreadful news would turn out to have a long-term effect on me.

I would later describe it as:

'it was not my fault, but it was my responsibility.'

In other words, I did not intend, through what I did, to get Ken and Angus into any trouble – none of us thought there would be any serious consequences for them. But the fact remained that if I had not taken on the Shirlstar job and asked for Ken's and Angus's help, they simply would not have been arrested. Therefore, I had a deep sense of responsibility for what happened to them.

This was to form a crucial part of the PTSD, from which I was to suffer long-term effects.

'I will be down a bit later at around eleven,' Jimmie continued. 'I will talk to Patrice to let him know what has happened.'

Catriona was watching me while I was talking to Jimmie. Her face had a fixed, serious expression trying to work out what had happened. When I explained to her that Ken and Angus had been arrested, she burst into floods of uncontrolled tears.

I did not cry, but I envied Catriona's free expression of emotion. We had grown very close to Ken and Angus whilst in Lagos.

I simply did not believe we would still be alive if they had not helped us.

CHAPTER 22

Ken and Angus are Arrested

For Ken and Angus, it was a normal Monday morning. There were five Twin Otter aircraft to check out and despatch to their various destinations. They were sitting together as usual in the Bristow Helicopters shuttle bus which took staff to and from the residential compound and hangar at the airport.

They chatted as the bus went along. Part of that conversation was about the flight out of Lagos on Saturday night and the speculation between them as to what had happened. At that stage, they had no idea at all about the interceptor or events in Abidjan. There were no mobile phones at that time to make communication easy. In fact, they had no idea where we were.

When they arrived at the Bristows hangar, they piled out with the other staff who were going into work at the same time, picking up their bags of bits and pieces for the day ahead. No one took any notice of the large, dark blue police wagon parked nearby.

Ken and Angus walked through the entrance door to the main hangar and headed for their lockers to store their bags for later.

The hangar was pristine and clean with a light grey painted floor. The Twin Otter aircraft sat just outside the wide hangar doors, awaiting their engineering checks before departure. All were polished ready for the new day. The chief engineer, Barry Glover, was a stickler for a clean hangar and polished aircraft – it was part of an overall impression of attention to detail.

As they went about their routine, a commotion started in the far side of the hangar. Both Ken and Angus turned around to see what was going on.

Half a dozen blue-clad police were going through the hangar grabbing people and manhandling them roughly, while a senior officer compared photographs to the unfortunate and confused person being held. A cursory look at a photo and the man followed with a shake of his head signalling the release of the individual.

'What the fuck is going on?' growled Angus.

'No idea,' replied Ken. 'Some kind of mistake, I'm sure. It's Lagos,' he concluded, as if this explained everything.

They continued to watch, trying to make some sense of what was going on. The police gradually moved through in their direction.

A feeling of foreboding began to envelop Ken and Angus, as they stood beside their lockers in the corner of the hangar. They watched the group of police eventually reach them.

Both were grabbed, unceremoniously by the arms, and held while the officer looked at the photographs and then at the two engineers. He then rechecked again, twice, and nodded to the officers holding them, indicating towards the door.

At that moment, when the two engineers realised something dreadful was going to happen, they tried to struggle.

'What do you want?' Angus growled louder, but with a hint of unease.

Barry Glover had come out of his office as the commotion started and was watching the goings-on taken aback, almost stunned into inaction by the scene playing out in front of him. He gathered himself and moved from his office into the main hangar towards the police. He intercepted the group of police as they reached Ken and Angus.

'What do you want?' he asked the senior officer.

The officer was on his second inspection of the photographs and the men held in front of him.

'These men,' he stated flatly, after a nod and tilt of his head towards the door out of the hangar to the officers holding them.

'Why?' Barry's voice held an edge of authority that showed he was used to being listened to.

'They are criminals,' the officer stated, sneering at the two engineers. 'They aided and abetted the theft of an aircraft,' he spat in disgust.

A terrible realisation took hold in all three men, not just Ken and Angus, but also Barry Glover. They all realised that this was the beginning of a desperate situation.

The Nigerians were very unpredictable, but this was out of all proportion to anything that these 'African hands' had experienced in what was, between them, 60 years of working in West Africa.

'You've got no right,' said Barry.

It was the only thing he could think of to say, but he felt impotent in the face of the senior officer's determination and expressionless manner.

'I have every right,' stated the officer flatly.

He was following the group who were almost carrying Ken and Angus between them.

Barry followed the group out of the front of the hangar building, continuing to argue with the officer even though it was clearly futile.

'I'll get you help! Don't worry,' Barry shouted to Ken and Angus, as they were bundled into the back of the large prisoner van.

The two men continued to look shocked and confused about the complete change to the Monday morning they were expecting.

Barry moved quickly back to his office and called the boss of Bristows Nigeria to advise him of the events.

Ken and Angus were going to need the best legal support to get them out of this situation. He also mused on the fact that it could have been him in the dark blue 'meat wagon' if things had been slightly different.

Inside the van, Ken and Angus were now in a small, airless compartment with barred and darkened windows. It was foul smelling – a mixture of urine and body odour. It was also very dirty and dusty, with some very suspicious dark brown stains on the floor and lower parts of the wall panels.

'Christ, mate, this is a disaster,' grumbled Ken quietly. 'I cannot believe this is happening.'

As he said this, the diesel engine on the van was gunned and lurched forward as the driver shoved it through the gears. With the transmission whining, it began to make its way onto the main road towards its destination.

In the back of the wagon, the two engineers had to grab the bars on the windows to steady themselves. They both watched as the familiar area of the Ikeja part of the airport began to disappear from view. For how long? And where were they being taken?

The last question was answered after a tortuous two-hour journey into Lagos city centre.

Eventually, the van jerked to a halt and the back door was thrown open. After the time in the back of the van with blacked-out windows, the bright African sunlight caused them to squint and cover their eyes.

'Out! Out!' a command was barked. 'Now!'

They slowly climbed down the few steps from the back of the van whilst looking around trying to gauge their surroundings.

The van had come to a halt in a compound and was then surrounded by a large number of police vehicles. It was clear that they were in a police compound in the centre of Lagos city.

They were again manhandled by two officers each, who guided them towards a doorway into the main building.

Ahead of them was a desk occupied by a short officer.

'Bring them here,' he barked. He clearly knew exactly who they were and was expecting them.

Ken and Angus both noted this; it made them more worried.

Normally in Africa things happened sort of randomly, there was seldom any real planning; situations kind of evolved. This was obviously not the case here. There was a clear definition in the process that was happening. They were on a conveyor belt of events.

For me as the writer and you as the reader, we have the benefit of hindsight. But for Ken and Angus, just as for me when the radar controller directed an interceptor towards me with the words 'Your target is taking off from Runway One Nine Left', they had absolutely no idea what was behind these events.

And they had little chance to gather any information. Very quickly, they were charged and unceremoniously locked in a police cell.

It had happened extremely fast. At first, they were shocked and then angry, then frustrated at not being able to challenge this incarceration.

Unfortunately, things were only going to get worse.

CHAPTER 23

The Plot to Kidnap Umaru Dikko Continues

As explained earlier, the plot to find and kidnap Umaru Dikko was well underway, but so far the Mossad team, despite using all their resources, had not been able to find him.

The arrangement between Tel Aviv and Lagos was a strange situation diplomatically speaking, but both sides had advantages to gain from the arrangement. Unfortunately, here, it created a series of events that spiralled out of control.

Mossad boss Nahum Admoni felt that London was the most likely hideaway for Dikko. London was a favourite haunt of Nigerian fugitives from justice. They were typically Anglophile and had retreats in the affluent areas of London. This was their best place to start looking, as it was the most likely destination for Dikko. Anyway, you had to start somewhere.

Mossad have many, many sources of intelligence worldwide. There had already been months of intelligence gathering, surveillance and a great deal of bravado to carry out this operation.

All these were Mossad specialties.

A little-known intelligence resource of Mossad is an extensive network of 'Sayanim'.

The Sayanim are non-Israeli Jews living outside Israel who assist

Mossad. To work for Mossad, a Sayanim must be 110% Jewish.

These Sayanim assist Mossad in many ways, clearly with the carrying out of covert operations and to circumvent red tape. For example, they may help Mossad to rent a car or apartment without having to fulfil the usual documentary and qualification procedures – therefore, leaving no paper trail. Or maybe offer treatment for a bullet wound without reporting it to the police. The Sayanim are an enormous resource that provides Mossad with a constantly available and loyal network of assistance not on its official payroll.

To this end, all Dikko's personal preferences and physical characteristics were to be exploited in order to find him.

Sayanim across Europe were put on alert and memorised Dikko's image and physical description. Doctors were even told to look out in case Dikko came in for plastic surgery to change his appearance.

Lookouts were posted at his favourite hotels. Clerks at car rental companies and airlines were on alert in case he rented a car or bought a plane ticket. Tailors were given his measurements, and shoemakers were given his shoe size and details of his customised shoes.

Even the publishing tycoon Robert Maxwell was tapped and asked to explore his high-level contacts for news of Dikko's whereabouts.

Dikko was up against formidable intelligence machinery. The team in London were carrying out the main focus of intelligence gathering.

In May, when I was negotiating with Ben Slade and travelling to Lagos to start the process of bringing the aircraft home, the whole Mossad/Nigerian operation was in full swing.

A few Mossad agents had set up base in London along with Major (retired) Mohammed Yusuf.

Yusuf was a 40-year-old former Nigerian army officer. After the military coup that overthrew Shagari, he was transferred to the Nigerian Ministry of External Affairs and posted to Nigeria's High Commission in the UK in May 1984.

Although Yusuf entered the UK on a diplomatic passport, the Foreign and Commonwealth Office was not notified that he was a member of the Nigerian diplomatic mission. Clearly, he had been planted for the specific purpose of taking part in the Dikko operation. Two separate groups of undercover agents worked underground amongst London's Nigerian community.

The search was narrowed to West London where many Nigerian officials had opulent residences purchased with embezzled Nigerian state funds.

The coup took place because unacceptable (even for Nigerian standards) amounts of criminal financial misappropriation were being carried out by members of the civilian government led by President Shagari.

There is a sort of unwritten rule in Nigeria that you keep your 'aquiring' of money within reason. That is okay but when you go too far, the military will chuck you out and take over running the country.

It is quite an efficient safety valve in the management of a basically corrupt country.

To say that Major General Muhammadu Buhari was a 'no-nonsense' military leader is a massive understatement. He was determined to make sure that, as he saw them, the 'criminals' who had been in Shagari's government were 'going to pay'.

Major General Buhari ordered every effort to find Dikko but even the concentrated hard work of the teams in London could not find him. There was no sign of Dikko; he seemed to have completely disappeared.

Buhari was very, very frustrated.

However, Dikko was actually in London having set up home there.

They actually located him by accident on 30 June.

CHAPTER 24

Back to Abidjan and Our Fate is Also in the Balance

Following the news about Ken and Angus, we all remained in a haze of shock. Because of my experience in Nigeria, their arrest was just completely unexpected.

I was distracted by thoughts of what was happening to them – I knew how unpredictable things could be and wanted to know where they were and if they were safe. But that information was not easy to come by. Bristows was a powerful company, so I was certain that they would be making every effort to make sure Ken and Angus were safe.

I could not imagine that the Nigerians would actually harm them. But then again, why had they been grabbed? It simply did not make sense.

I rang Nick to let him know the news.

After he came to our room, we sat around on the sofas talking at length about the situation, but this did not help. These were somewhat fruitless discussions; we were powerless to do anything about it. The only minor benefit was that we were able to offload some internal struggles with our guilty feelings. Nick, of course, was a sensible source of reassuring words.

I also had the practical problem of funds. The Ivorian government had provided the hotel room, but the food, drinks, phone calls, etc. were all mounting up. I also wanted to cover the cost of Nick's stay.

Shirlstar had said they would release the £12,500 from their solicitor's account where the total amount of the fee had been placed in escrow. They had also agreed to pay an additional £2,000 to cover incidental costs.

I rang Charles Gaskill, my NatWest bank manager. Charles was one of the last 'proper' bank managers. One of those old-fashioned ones who knew their customers and their situations – and could make decisions!

Charles was brilliant. Although he was the epitome of what a bank manager should look like, a smart suit, short, dark hair with dark eyebrows above dark brown eyes, he was utterly professional but with a fantastic sense of humour and a very practical approach to his responsibilities.

He helped people. In return, they respected that help and did not let him down. Unfortunately, this 'old-style' bank manager has been pensioned off by all the banks – a huge mistake in my opinion – just to save costs. We got on famously well and were friends as well as manager/customer. In actual fact, Charles was to save my bacon later in this story. Right now, I needed to know if that cash was in the bank. Charles, too, because my overdraft was testing even his goodwill!

'Charles, it's Mike. I'm in Abidjan, and Shirlstar are supposed to have released the first part of the payment.' Charles was aware of the whole repossession proposition. 'Can you check my account balance to see if it has come in for me?'

'Hello, Mike. Good to hear from you. Hang on, I will check for you. Are you both okay?'

I could hear Charles tapping on his keyboard.

'Yes, we are fine, but the whole thing has turned into an enormous drama. I will tell you about it when I see you,' I replied.

'There has been a lot of news about your situation here, on television and in the newspapers'. Charles said as he continued to tap. 'Bingo! Mike, you have had £14,500 paid into the account, so you are now £8,248.22 in credit. You are now back on an even keel!' he said.

'Now that *is* a great feeling, Charles,' I said. 'Again, thank you so much for your patience, help and support. I will buy you a meal when I return and tell you the story; you will find it very interesting,' I promised.

'I will look forward to that. Take care, Mike. Cheerio.'

After we closed the conversation, I felt a little of the weight removed from my shoulders following that news.

Nick, Catriona and I went down to the restaurant at 11am. Reassuringly, the guards were all still in place and looking very alert.

Jimmie was already there. We joined him on 'our sofas' and spent a great deal of time discussing the situation more thoroughly. There was no more particular news from Lagos, but he was encouraging in that the president of the Ivory Coast was paying particular attention to our case. Apparently, the president was very much a no-nonsense character and fiercely protective of his country's independence.

The next few days were more routine. We saw Jimmie and Patrice each day in the late afternoon to be updated on any news.

The high-level diplomatic negotiations were ongoing, but we had been assured that the outcome would be okay (for us, at least).

I learnt around this time that there was a massive amount of media interest in the story, and I was definitely not the hero! The newspapers in Nigeria compared me to a modern-day pirate, like historic British pirates such as John Hawkins (1560).

Hawkins was the first British captain to profit from the 'triangular trade'. This originated in Liverpool to West Africa, with various products but mainly iron ore. These products were then bartered for slaves. The slaves were transported to the Americas to work in the cotton fields and tobacco plantations. These crops were then brought back to Liverpool. It was a massively profitable trade and helped to build some of those huge stately homes.

I was also painted in very uncomplimentary terms in the British press. It was not surprising really. The media had painted me as someone 'who abandoned his friends who are now paying the price for the theft of an aeroplane'.

Ben Slade was initially very happy with the removal of G-LORI from Lagos and agreed to release the first tranche of £12,500. Also, the additional £2,000 was a great help for us while stuck in Abidjan.

I had let Shirlstar know that there were some significant system failures on the aircraft and that they would need to organise an HS125 engineer to have a look at it before it could go anywhere.

This was where the drawing up of the contract by Nick would come into play: 'In the event that the aeroplane was unable to be returned to the UK, the second tranche of £12,500 would be released 21 days after leaving Nigerian territorial airspace'.

There was, of course, the small matter of getting ourselves out of Abidjan, which was of a more pressing nature!

Nick had to go home after five days – he was effectively a one-man band solicitor and the pressure of work at home was piling up, so he jumped on a BCal flight back to Gatwick.

The goodbyes were very emotional, but his presence had been a massive boost to our morale and provided sage opinion during all the discussions between Patrice, Jimmie, Catriona and me.

Our original story had been tested during the whole of this period by the authorities, fronted by Patrice and Jimmie. Nick, as a 'neutral' and professional individual, was also able to confirm all the details that I had provided during my initial interview with Patrice. This also continued during subsequent discussions between Patrice, Jimmie, Nick and me.

Effectively, the story was being continuously tested. I was very pleased that all along I had simply told the truth. I suspect that had a fault line appeared in our story, especially with the intellectual strength of Patrice and his background in intelligence, he would have jumped on it.

Had that been the case, we would not have had such strong support from all concerned.

It took several more days to reach a resolution. Eventually, the president of the Ivory Coast made a decision to end the matter. He pronounced that the Nigerians could take G-LORI back to Lagos, and Catriona and I could go back to London.

We had been in the Ivory Coast for around 14 days.

The day we climbed up the steps of that British Caledonian DC-10 was a relief, but it was not a triumph by any means.

I saw G-LORI from the top of the steps as I boarded the DC-10 and took this picture. She was where I had parked her two weeks before. There was a lot of activity around the aeroplane to get her ready to be flown back to Lagos.

G-LORI (left) at Abidjan Airport – about to be taken back to Lagos. Photo taken as we board the BCal Flight home.

Very sadly, this was her last ever flight. I learned that G-LORI never flew again after the flight back to Nigeria. She eventually just rotted away in the bush at the side of the apron in Ikeja.

CHAPTER 25

Our Return to the UK and 'Normality'?

It was a strange feeling walking back into your home you left just a few weeks ago. It all looks the same, just exactly how you left it, except your whole world has been turned upside down and inside out by intervening events.

It is something that I had never experienced before; it was exceptionally unsettling.

These events began to undermine the relationship between Catriona and me.

I began to sleep in the spare room and it was in there that the first symptoms of PTSD began with sleepwalking. There were frequent episodes of extreme anxiety attacks; sweats that sent my body temperature up above a 100°F that would suddenly start out of the blue, rather like severe 'flu symtoms. All this was accompanied by long episodes of sleepwalking during the night. Sometimes I would wake up ten to twelve times; groping around the walls of the bedroom with my hands, appearing to be looking for a way out. It was the beginning of a period of years when I didn't ever get a proper night's sleep. It was truly awful.

Of course, the press camping outside our cottage in Oxted, Surrey, also showed that things had substantially changed for us.

The story of my departure from Lagos and the arrest of Ken and

Angus had created a storm of publicity with a hunger by newspapers for information and background.

I had obtained the contact details of the West Africa desk at the Foreign Office and had spoken to them frequently during my time in Abidjan. A good working relationship had been formed between us.

We were all focused on bringing about a resolution to the dire situation that Ken and Angus faced in Nigeria. I had also spoken to Bristows managing director and had arranged to see him when I arrived back in the UK. Bristows headquarters was at Redhill Aerodrome 20 minutes away from home.

At this time, my attitude was that I really didn't care if everyone threw metaphorical rocks at me, I just wanted to get Ken and Angus out of Nigeria safely and as soon as possible.

The difference between the events in Lagos and the threats we had been subjected to was that in Lagos I could actually take action. Now, back in the UK, there was very little within my control; nothing that I could actually do. It was a truly frustrating time for a person who is used to forming a plan of action and carrying it out.

So, now I was focused on the question 'What can I do?'. I was in almost daily contact with the West Africa desk, but the situation in Lagos remained status quo.

I also visited Bristows on several occasions and had meetings with their CEO and legal department. We went through all the documents and background details passed to me at the Shirlstar offices in Swallow Street, as well as what had actually happened in Lagos and the warnings from Hyacinth Odigwe; basically, all the same information that had been provided in Abidjan.

The press was a problem. I knew that any statement was a difficult thing to control. Call me cynical, but the press can 'interpret' any statement to assist it in supporting the 'editorial' line.

I had spoken to the West Africa desk about this. They were extremely helpful and reflected my view about the press.

It was very difficult to say nothing. There were journalists and photographers permanently camped outside our cottage. So, with the agreement of the West Africa desk, I formed a perspective that would support (or at least not jeopardise) the situation that Ken and Angus were in.

I had made some inane comments to the press (and, of course, provided tea) and a short appearance on *TV-am*. This prompted a couple of articles.

I was contacted by *TV-am* producers and asked to do an interview with Anne Diamond. I considered this and decided it was the most likely situation where I would, to some extent, be able to control the dialogue. So I agreed.

It did go okay. I had emphasised with the producers that the only reason I would consider an interview was to provide information that would assist Ken and Angus. They were good to their word. Anne Diamond interviewed me, and the questions were answered clearly and honestly.

The worst situation was a centre spread, two-page article in reputable Sunday newspaper by a journalist (I will use his initials here for various reasons), PD. I had never met or spoken to PD, yet he quoted me extensively in this article. Basically, he painted me as a rogue and criminal who didn't give a shit and was also mentally unstable. I was of course, furious, but there was nothing I could do about it at the time. However, revenge is a dish best served cold and karma tends to catch us out when we do bad things. *Oh yes*, I definitely did get my own back!

It was around this time, at the end of June, that the 21-day point in the contract had been reached. Nick had applied to Shirlstar for the release of the second tranche of £12,500. They refused.

This refusal prompted what became a legendary conversation with Ben Slade.

I rang him to discuss the release of the £12,500.

'Ben, it's Mike Howard here,' I began. 'I understand you're refusing to release the second payment of twelve thousand five hundred pounds. It is due under the terms of our contract.'

'I didn't get my bloody jet back,' Ben almost blubbed. 'You can't expect to get paid if you didn't get the jet back.' His voice went up an octave as he finished the sentence.

'But, Ben, we have an agreement which clearly specifies that the contract is completed when the aircraft is removed from Nigerian territorial airspace. Which it was,' I stated.

'But then it went back,' he replied. 'I did not get my jet back.' I could almost feel him thinking, *sue him, Stan!*

This conversation went back and forth in roughly the same manner and was going nowhere. It eventually finished with the ultimate threat of legal action.

I was still furious with him for getting Victor Vanni into his office, putting us in danger, and not telling us about the Graham Bott situation with the missing 890,000 naira. More importantly, there was not a mention of the situation surrounding Ken and Angus during the whole conversation, for which he bore at least some responsibility.

'The contract was completed by the aircraft being removed from Nigerian Territorial Airspace. It was removed from Nigerian Territorial Airspace. The contact was completed. I repeated. If you do not pay, Ben, I will take you to court,' I stated matter-of-factly.

'Have you ever played poker with a millionaire?' he asked.

'I really do not see what that has to do with the situation.' He was annoying me now.

'Well, Mike, when you play poker with a millionaire, it doesn't matter how good a hand you have got, he will bid the hand so high you won't be able to stay in the game.'

Now I could see where he was going.

'Well, Ben, I fully understand the threat you are making. However,

I am prepared to take the risk, and we will just have to see how the mop flops.' I replied.

So that was it. Ben would not pay what was due, and I would have to sue him. I was not too concerned about this. In a strange way, I was pleased; all the skulduggery that he had been up to could be brought out into the open in court room. He never mentioned Ken and Angus and I didn't suppose the matter had crossed his mind.

The conversation basically ended there, but the 'mop flops' phrase (not sure exactly where that came from) has been one which I've always felt summed up the karma of the situation. However, my advice to anyone considering a major legal action is expect any legal fees estimate to be at least double in the end – in other words, don't do it!

During the frequent conversations with the Foreign Office, it became clear that we were not making any progress with the Nigerians. Ken and Angus were still being held in the police cell they had been originally taken to and the situation continued to be at an impasse.

This, however, was going to change for the worse very shortly.

The Africa desk and I had discussed many aspects of the situation, including the media attention. In the end, we decided it would be helpful if I was to disappear off the radar for a while. We thought this would remove the 'oxygen' of publicity from the story, with the idea that it might assist in the negotiations with the Nigerians.

I was not exactly sure how to do this but would give it some thought.

As it happened, like the proverbial bad penny (and, clearly, I had not learnt my lesson the first time), Owen O'Mahoney rang me.

'Mike, what are you up to at the moment?'

Silly question. *Having a wonderful time... living the dream!* Tempting as it was, I did not say it.

'Just dealing with the fallout, Owen,' I replied.

'How would you like to go to South Africa?' he asked.

'As it happens, that may be a good idea. The Foreign Office would like me to *go dark* for a bit. So I would consider it. What's the deal?' I asked.

'It's a South African businessman in Johannesburg who has an HS125 400 series. Needs a captain for a short spell, and then ferry it back to the UK for maintenance. The last bit is why I thought of you – not many guys I know can do that.'

I had flown these aeroplanes all over the world. Many pilots just flew 'local' European operations and did not have the required experience to tackle a trip like that, especially one with a limited range like a 400 series.

Owen continued, 'Also, the aircraft operates into Zimbabwe with senior government officials and over to Namibia. Again, this is challenging flying that also requires a calm approach to difficult passengers.' This was 'Owen-speak' for the whole thing was a pain in the arse!

'Perhaps we can get together and go through the details,' I replied. 'Who is the first officer?' This was also a major question. I did not want to spend hours with another Jeremy Palmer!

'It will be me for part of the trip, and then another guy for the trip back to the UK, but I'll make sure that they have the right experience,' he replied.

I wasn't convinced, but I did need to get out of the UK for a while – beggars cannot be choosers.

We arranged to meet in London in a few days' time to sort out the details.

This took us, timewise, to the end of June/early July, when there were developments in the Mossad operation to find and kidnap Umaru Dikko.

CHAPTER 26

Umaru Dikko Gets Kidnapped, but All Does Not Go to Plan

Yusuf and the Mossad agents had narrowed things down to West London, but the Dikko trail seemed to be running cold. That was until a chance encounter during late June 1984.

On June 30, 1984, one of the Mossad team members spotted a man fitting Dikko's description in London's wealthy Bayswater neighbourhood.

The agent surreptitiously followed Dikko on foot to a house at 49 Porchester Terrace. When Mossad Director General Nahum Admoni was informed of the development, he ordered surveillance of the address.

For several days, the house was continuously watched by the agents. Routine and unusual movements were noted.

So, the plans for Dikko's capture were put into action. Dikko had to be captured, anaesthetised, boxed and then transported out of the UK to Nigeria to face that 'fair' trial and then the public hanging on Bar Beach.

For the administration of anaesthetic, a Dr Levi-Arie Shapiro, who was a consultant and director of the intensive care unit at Hasharon Hospital in Tel Aviv, was brought into London. A 43-year-old Israeli national, 'Lou' Shapiro was to act as the doctor responsible for administering this anaesthetic to Dikko and keeping him alive in the box.

You may ask yourself, 'Why is a senior consultant working in one of the top hospitals in Israel volunteering to basically lie in a box with a kidnap victim?' Great question. And the answer is that Lou Shapiro was also a reserve major in the Israeli army!

Shapiro was recruited by Alexander Barak, and Barak gave Shapiro cash to purchase the anaesthetics which would be used to drug Dikko.

Barak and Abithol had been in the Russell Square hotel and running the teams looking for Dikko. They organised Major Yusuf to hire a van to 'grab' Dikko in Knightsbridge, which was then eventually used to convey Dikko once he had been put in the box and anaesthetised.

For some strange reason, Yusuf's men opted to hire a bright and very conspicuous yellow van.

At around this time, in fact on July 4, a Nigerian Airways Boeing 707 Freighter Aircraft flew into Stansted Airport from Lagos with no cargo on board. The UK authorities were informed that the plane had come in to collect 'diplomatic baggage' from the Nigerian High Commission in London. Several security officers were on board the aircraft and had orders not to leave the airport.

The next day, Major Yusuf drove the van he had rented from Notting Hill Gate in West London and parked outside Dikko's house on Porchester Terrace. In the van with Yusuf was Shapiro, Barak and Abithol.

Meanwhile, back at Stansted Airport, the captain of the Nigerian Airways aircraft filed a flight plan to depart at 3 pm. He claimed that on its way back to Nigeria, the aircraft would be carrying 'documentation' for the Nigerian Ministry of External Affairs. Diplomatic immunity was claimed for the documentation.

Meanwhile, back at Porchester Terrace just before midday, Dikko emerged from the house for an interview with a Ghanaian journalist, Elizabeth Akua Ohene.

As Dikko left his home, the men burst out from the yellow van, grabbed him and forced him into the back.

Within seconds, the van doors had closed, and it sped off at breakneck speed. Quick, surgical and precise; it was a typical Mossad operation. Inside the van, Dikko was dumped on his back and his hands bound with cable ties.

The van eventually came to a halt. Initially, Dikko was relieved and thought his kidnappers had been stopped by the police. Unfortunately, he was wrong. They had simply stopped to refuel. (Doh, not such good surgical planning – Yusuf had forgotten to fill the bloody tank with fuel!)

Dikko was threatened and told to keep quiet, as his captors refuelled.

At a predetermined rendezvous point near Regent's Park, Dikko was transferred to a waiting lorry. Dr Shapiro went to work and injected Dikko in the arm and buttock with the powerful anaesthetic. Dikko fell unconscious.

However, there was another hitch to the plan.

Through a window of Dikko's office, his secretary, Elizabeth Hayes, witnessed Dikko being bundled into the van.

The astonished secretary managed to compose herself quickly enough to dial 999 and alert the authorities of the incredible incident she had just observed.

Given Dikko's profile as a former government minister, the call was quickly escalated. Within minutes, police had arrived at the scene, closely followed by officers from Scotland Yard's anti-terrorist squad. The Foreign Office and even Prime Minister Margaret Thatcher were alerted.

A massive, well-oiled police and security procedure went into action. All customs officials at airports, ports and border crossings were told to be extra vigilant, particularly with regards to any Nigerian passport holders or Nigeria-bound vessels.

Meanwhile, back to Stansted Airport…

By mid-afternoon, Dikko had been anaesthetised into unconsciousness by Dr Shapiro, locked into a crate and taken to Stansted Airport in the back of the lorry.

The authorities were being extra vigilant at Stansted looking for Dikko and his kidnappers. Particularly interesting to them was the Nigerian Airways 707 freighter with a flight plan filed for Lagos that afternoon.

Shortly before 3 pm, the lorry containing the two crates turned up at the airport. It was escorted by two black Mercedes-Benz cars bearing Nigerian diplomatic number plates.

The authorities were looking, but there was no sign of Dikko. This was mainly because he was unconscious in the crate with Shapiro, in the back of the truck, alongside the other crate containing the Mossad agents, Abithol and Barak.

The two crates labelled 'Diplomatic Baggage' and addressed to the Nigerian Ministry of External Affairs in Lagos were being loaded onto the Nigerian Airways plane.

These crates, carefully constructed by Johnson Odahlu in his workshop some weeks before, were the required 1.2 metres in height, 1.2 metres in depth and 1.8 metres in width, and were accompanied by Major Yusuf and a member of the Nigerian High Commission in London named Okon Edet.

The customs officers at Stansted were being unusually inquisitive and vigilant, having been warned to be wary by the UK security forces.

Charles Morrow, a senior customs officer, who was watching the vehicles approaching the Nigerian Airways 707 from the windows of his office in the terminal, decided to go downstairs to see who they were and what was happening. It struck him that there was something odd about this aircraft's plans. Morrow met a guy who turned out to be a Nigerian diplomat called Mr Edet. Edet was asked to show Morrow his passport; he told Morrow it was 'diplomatic cargo'.

Being ignorant of such matters, Morrow asked him what it was. Edet told Morrow it was 'just documents and things'.

Strangely, no one on duty at Stansted had dealt with a diplomatic bag before, so Morrow went to check the procedure.

Just then, one of the other customs men returned from the passenger terminal with startling news. There was an all ports warning from Scotland Yard saying that a Nigerian had been kidnapped, and it was suspected there would be an attempt to smuggle the man out of the country.

Customs note at Stansted Airport alerting them to the kidnap of Dikko

Hearing the news, Mr Morrow realised that he had a big problem on his hands. 'I just put two and two together. There is a classic customs approach: do not look for the goods, you look for the space,' he later said. 'So, I am looking out of the window and I can see the space, which is these two crates, clearly big enough to get a man inside. We've got a Nigerian Airways 707 freight aircraft, which we don't normally see, and they don't want the crates manifested. That would mean there would be no record of them having gone through. There was very little other cargo going on board the aircraft,' he said. 'If you want to hide a tree, you hide it in the forest. You don't stick it out in the middle of Stansted Airport in Essex!'

I thought the last part of Morrow's statement, which he made after the events, was quite amusing.

The marking of the crates as 'Diplomatic Baggage' did not comply with the Geneva Convention of diplomatic baggage marking. Considering all the planning that had gone into this plot, it was a major cock-up.

The absence of the correct diplomatic documents was about to come back to haunt the kidnappers. On the pretext that the crates did not have the correct official seal and accompanying documents, Morrow insisted on having a closer look at what was inside them.

Although the 707 was minutes away from take-off, it gave Morrow an excuse to use red tape to get a closer look at the crates. Major Yusuf protested furiously that the crates were protected by diplomatic immunity and could not be searched. His vehement protests were dismissed by Morrow.

Morrow also noticed an unusual medical smell, probably the powerful medical anaesthetic sodium pentothal, and also a noise emanating from one of the crates.

When Morrow made the decision to open the crates, it would have to be done by the book. This required the presence of a Nigerian diplomat – but, as Mr Morrow later pointed out, one was already on hand, Mr. Okon Edet.

By now, the crates were on special trolleys ready to be loaded onto the plane. This was part of Morrow's statement:

'Peter, the cargo manager, hit the underneath of the lid and lifted it. As he did, the Nigerian diplomat, who was standing next to me, took off like a startled rabbit across the tarmac. You have to remember we were on an airfield which is square miles of nothing. He ran about five yards (4.5 m), realised no one was chasing him and then stopped.'

Peter looked into the crate and said to Morrow:

'There are bodies inside!'

He then parked a forklift truck so its tines lay across the top of the crate so it couldn't be opened.

Morrow dialled the emergency number 999 and asked to speak to the anti - terrorist police.

'My name's Morrow, from customs at Stansted. We've got some bodies in a crate. Do you think you can send someone over immediately?' he asked.

'Are they alive or dead?' came the reply at the other end of the line.

'That's a very good point. I don't know,' Morrow replied.

'We'd better send an ambulance as well,' was the response from the police operator.

Following the call to anti-terrorist police, they cordoned off the area and evacuated the airport staff.

Morrow and his team of customs colleagues, some of the special branch officers and armed police all watched whilst the crates were prepared to be opened. The customs officers now opened them fully with a crowbar.

What they found inside was shocking. In the first crate was a bound and unconscious Dikko with his torso bare. Beside him was Dr Shapiro brandishing syringes and a supply of additional anaesthetics with which to administer replenishments so Dikko did not die during transit.

The armed police then surrounded the Nigerian cargo plane on the freight aircraft parking area, arrested its crew and refused to allow the plane to take off. They also arrested the Nigerian officials and Israelis who drove the crates to Stansted, and several members of Nigeria's High Commission in London a short time later.

Dikko's captors had shoved an endotracheal tube in his throat to prevent him from choking on his own vomit when he was out cold, but he was still alive. They wanted him brought to Nigeria alive rather than dead. It was important that Dikko made it to Bar Beach for his hanging after the fair trial.

The quote of the day went to Dr Shapiro. He had asked Charles Morrow and his colleagues when they opened the crate, exposing the two men inside: '*Well, gentlemen, what do we do now?*'

Abithol and Barak were discovered in the second crate.

Dikko was rushed to Herts and Essex Hospital in Bishop's Stortford by the ambulance that was standing by. He regained consciousness at midday the following day having been unconscious for 36 hours. Dikko awoke, totally oblivious to the ensuing drama and his very dramatic rescue.

The treatment he received in the hospital was carried out under heavy police guard.

President Buhari would have correctly guessed that Britain was very angry at the kidnap attempt on its soil; sending foreign security agents from a friendly country to commit a crime on its shores was a hostile act.

It was a long time later, after much research, that I made the connection between the conspiracy to kidnap Dikko, the recommendation from Hyacinth Odigwe for us to take off and why the Nigerian Air Force jet was waiting for us. There is a certain logical excuse when the diplomatic shit hits the fan:

'Well, your people come to our country and break our laws, so we have just done the same here in your country'

Barak later blamed a Nigerian Air Force officer for the plan's failure. When subsequently interviewed by Israel's bestselling newspaper *Yedioth Ahronoth*, Alexander Barak said: *In retrospect, I found out that the main culprit had been Group Captain Banfa, formerly head of the Nigerian Air Force and now CEO of Air Nigeria. This guy was supposed, according to the plan, to meet at 9:00 am with Yusuf and Dr Shapiro at the apartment in London and give them the right documents and join us, to supervise the loading of the diplomatic crates at Stansted Airport. But, at the last minute, Banfa got cold feet.*

As expected, the Nigerian government denied any involvement in the affair. Nigeria's High Commissioner in London, Major General Haladu Anthony Hananiya, claimed that the incident was the work of *some patriotic friends of Nigeria*. Hananiya was formerly Nigeria's military attaché at the Nigerian High Commission in London.

A total of 17 men were arrested. Shapiro, Barak, Abithol and Yusuf were convicted within a few weeks – very quickly, due to the diplomatic nature of the offence and the breaching of various Geneva Conventions on diplomatic baggage and kidnapping. They were sentenced to prison terms of 10 to 14 years.

All four were released after serving between six and eight and a half years and then quietly deported.

The Nigerian and Israeli governments never admitted any connection to the incident. Nonetheless, the British government immediately expelled two members of the Nigerian High Commission in London, including the high commissioner.

Diplomatic relations with Nigeria were broken off for two years. The CEO of Nigeria Airways was at one point almost arrested by British police. In the aftermath of the affair, Nigeria filed a formal extradition request for Dikko, but it was refused.

The Nigerian government's war against the previous government's corruption was also weakened, as the British government also rejected Nigerian requests to extradite other politicians wanted in Nigeria on corruption charges and living in exile in Britain.

It was a complete shambles. It would have been a comical situation if the consequences of all this did not dramatically and negatively affect Ken and Angus's situation.

I was in the process of heading off to South Africa (for the next chapter of my personal dramas of 1984) when all this was happening. As I said, it was later that when considering the events surrounding Dikko and the attempted shooting down of G-LORI that it was logical that these two events were associated. There simply was no other rational explanation.

Prior to this, Ken and Angus were still in the police cell in Lagos, but the practical circumstances were not too bad – it was clean and they had food.

However, when the kidnappers were sentenced after their appearance at the Old Bailey, Ken and Angus were then taken to the equivalent court in Lagos.

Despite a good defence team provided by Bristows and no real evidence that there was any intention on their part to commit any crime, they were also sentenced to 14 years in jail. They were sent to Kirikiri jail; definitely *not* a nice place. This was absolutely devastating news.

CHAPTER 27

June 1984
Heading Off to Johannesburg

Eventually, an agreement was reached with Owen and Jack Sacks (his boss) in South Africa regarding pay and a timetable, so Catriona and I headed off to Joburg on a British Airways flight.

Whilst the relationship between Catriona and I had been under strain by the events of the last few months, conversely there was still a strong link between us *because* of these events. So, she came along with me. It was also the Foreign Office's recommendation that both of us should be out of the media's sight for the time being, especially in the light of recent events at Stansted.

Owen had gone out to South Africa a few days earlier and met us at the airport on our arrival. While he drove us to our accommodation, he briefed me on the plans for the next few weeks and what Jack Sacks was like as a boss.

'He lives in Sandton, an *upmarket* part of Joburg,' Owen explained. 'He has a nice house, but the strange thing is that the carpets are all threadbare. I get the impression he's very tight.'

'Well, the name is a bit of a giveaway,' I replied. 'Perhaps he's an archetypal Jewish person,' I joked.

As it turned out, that was very accurate. Jack was someone who seemed to have a lot of actual cash but was very protective over it.

Obviously, I did meet Jack, and the description of his home was very accurate. It didn't quite make sense.

We arrived at our accommodation. It was in a district of Joburg near the centre of town called Hillbrow. Hillbrow (pronounced 'Heelbrew' in a guttural Afrikaner-style) was a pretty (er, very) rough part of the city, but I was not to know that.

During the months of the stay, I got in the habit of walking through parts of Hillbrow on the way to Joburg's equivalent of KFC. I would say a confident 'Hi' to the groups of black guys who were hanging around the streets, waiting to rob and kill some loner white guy.

Maybe they thought I was an armed martial arts expert if I had the balls to stroll through that part of town…

I never had a hint of a problem. However, I casually mentioned to friends I had made in Joburg about my 'Joburger' trips through Hillbrow. They were completely shocked.

'You cud 'ave beean keeled!!' they remarked in that guttural South African accent.

The accommodation was in the form of an aparthotel, so it was possible to produce basic meals and there was a fridge. Having said that, it was very basic… And probably *very* cheap! I cannot remember the name of the hotel, but it might as well have been called the 'Gloria Hotel', like the one in Borneo – around the same standard, but hopefully with less cockroaches. It did have an underground car park, which was useful in the centre of town, but this had to be paid for (not a large amount, though).

We got ourselves into the rooms and unpacked. It had been a long journey from the UK, and we arranged to meet Owen later.

Apparently we were going to the Carlton Hotel after a drink in the 1505 Bar in Hillbrow. None of this meant anything to me, as it was the first time I had been to Joburg.

The Carlton was at that stage one of the larger buildings in South Africa and a very nice hotel. The 1505 Bar, however, was rough as shit, full of old miners and stank of stale cigarette smoke, but the booze was cheap – which was why Owen had found it! 1505 did have a certain charm once you got used to it, though.

So, we had a couple of drinks in 1505 and then went down to the Carlton.

I loved the Carlton. It had a large function room and regular entertainment in the evenings. We sat in on the show that evening which was being performed by a guy called Paul Melba.

The show was absolutely brilliant. Paul was essentially an impressionist in both voice and song. All this was wrapped up with great humour that had its foundations in his Liverpudlian origins. Paul had performed in Royal Command Performances and was also a regular performer on an ITV show called *The Comedians* with Lenny Henry and Russ Abbot. He had also done a lot of work with Freddie Starr (famous for eating hamsters). Somehow or other, they had all fallen out and Paul, who was probably the most talented, had been sort of left behind in terms of major fame. But he was successful in his own way and very respected.

The show comprised impressions of Prince Charles and the Duke of Edinburgh, Eric Morecambe, Ken Dodd, Billy Connolly, Tommy Cooper and Sir Robin Day. His singing impressions were superb, with renditions of Frank Sinatra, Dean Martin, Tony Bennett, Sammy Davis Jnr and many more.

I, of course, being shy and retiring and for a bit of fun, began heckling him from the audience. Paul, of course, shot me down in flames every time, far more effectively than the Nigerian Air Force!

We all met after the show and had a great laugh at my expense. Paul and I became great friends.

I did try to make contact with him recently. Paul had moved to the Algarve and was making a living performing there. Unfortunately, a couple of years ago, he suffered a stroke which caused severe brain damage. I was very upset when I found out.

We were regular visitors to the Carlton during the months in

South Africa. Paul and I had a great double act organised. I was a professional 'unfortunate' heckler, but we had a sort of script that we worked to. It was all great fun and a lot of light relief.

There was a lot of 'nothing much happening' with the aeroplane, but this was not unusual. Executive jet flying was a lot of nothing and then, rather like buses, a lot of trips would come along in a short period of time.

The first flight with the aircraft G-JSAX was interesting. It was to Port Elizabeth, which was on the east coast halfway between Durban and Cape Town. Owen was determined that I was to act as captain – mainly because, although he had operated between West Africa and UK/Europe, he did not seem too confident in this environment. He did, however, maintain control of the client and negotiations about the operation.

The main problem was that he turned up at Lanseria Airport and informed me that Jack Sacks had only given him enough cash for 6,000 litres of fuel.

'There is no fuel in Port Elizabeth, so that is enough for round-trip fuel,' he confidently Informed me.

'Fuck off, Owen,' I replied. 'We need *at least* eight thousand litres to be comfortable,' I said in a firm, uncompromising tone, highlighting the 'at least' in the sentence.

I had done a quick calculation in my head (no fag packet to do it on) and worked out that the taxi, climb, cruise (as high as possible), descent, approach and landing, taxi in and double that to come back from Port Elizabeth to Lanseria gave me a figure of about 7,000 litres, and then I added some for my lovely mother…

We argued about this for a while until eventually, after having looked at what was in the tanks before refuelling, I made my final offer:

'The absolute minimum I will accept for uplift of fuel is seven thousand litres. That will give us fifty per cent of fuck all when we get back to Lanseria, so that does not allow for any unexpected contingencies,' I stated firmly. 'Any less than this and you can find another captain.'

As far as I was concerned that was the end of the matter. Sure enough, the aircraft was refuelled with 7,000 litres and off we went.

When we arrived in Port Elizabeth and Jack buggered off to do whatever he was doing, Owen got back into the co-pilot's seat and seemed preoccupied. He was looking at the fuel gauges that were showing around just under 3,500 lbs per side.

'That doesn't look like very much fuel, Mike,' he said, frowning deeply.

'No shit Sherlock' I replied.

Of course, for me, it showed exactly what I expected. They say in the flight instruction world that you should not make a point with a student by doing something illegal or 'not recommended'; quite rightly, it's regarded as 'negative training'. As I explained earlier, I had a lot of instructional experience, but in this situation, I was determined to make a point.

We set off back with me flying it (Owen had flown it out). I climbed to 41,000 feet, which was very high for a trip of just over an hour, but it was the only way to use the least amount of fuel (remember the flights from Zarzaitine to Kano?). I then calculated when to descend – the best point for the least use of fuel for the approach. Basically, once I'd closed the thrust levers to descend, I was not planning to touch those levers again until the wheels were on the runway.

Normally, you would use a bit of thrust when you lower the landing gear and flaps. Here, however, I needed to use as little as possible, because at the top of the descent we had, as I forecast to Owen, 50% of fuck all fuel!

'Owen, call Lanseria and tell them we cannot delay our approach, and we cannot perform a go-around as we are low on fuel,' I instructed.

There were little training aeroplanes in Lanseria, and I did not want one of them to get in the way and delay us. It would be very embarrassing not to make the field by running out of fuel – remember the three rules of flying?

As we began the descent, Owen was completely fixated on the fuel gauges that were now beginning to drop into the red section.

'For fuck's sake, Owen, staring at the gauges will not create any more gas,' I said. 'Now, have I made the point about fuel that I was talking about before we set off this morning?' I asked.

'Yes, yes, Mike,' he said in a shaky voice. 'I will never argue with you about fuel ever again.'

'Good,' I said flatly. As I said this, I reached behind my left ear and pulled the circuit breaker for the fuel gauges. They both now dropped obediently to read zero. 'Now,' I said, 'with the breaker pulled, they are reading zero, so you can now concentrate on monitoring and doing the checklists,' I barked.

We did land at Lanseria after a *very* short final approach and, as I selected the parking brake on, the engines wound down without me touching any of the fuel cut-off levers.

In other words, my fag packet fuel calculation had been spot on. We had run out of fuel as I parked the aircraft. I looked at Owen, who was white as a sheet and sweating profusely.

The next flight was to Harare in Zimbabwe to pick up the Botswanan foreign minister and take him to Lüderitz Airport in Namibia on the edge of the Namib Desert.

It seemed Jack was selling our services or getting some kind of business advantage from the use of the aeroplane, but I did not give a shit. We were going to have a night stop in Lüderitz and depart midday the next day to Gaborone in Botswana, drop him off and then back to Lanseria; job done.

It was the first time I had been to Zimbabwe. Arriving at the airport, we had to wait for a few hours for the client to arrive. I had parked G-JSAX outside the terminal building and, surprisingly, a red carpet was rolled up to the front door of the aircraft.

'Mmm, I guess this guy is important, Owen,' I observed.

As we had to hang around, I took the chance to get a taxi tour of the city. It was quite shocking. Mugabe had been effectively 'ethnically cleansing' anyone who was not in his tribe. The devastation was clear and shocking.

There were long queues outside bread sellers. In fact, Mugabe had manufactured an artificial shortage of flour. Although there was plenty of flour given to the government by the charities to help feed large parts of the population, this flour was held in warehouses and controlled by Mugabe. Because it was stored for a very long time there, a lot of it was rendered useless by weevils.

The latest wheeze that I had heard about was the cutting of fresh water supplies. This was a clever move as cholera then started to permeate the community over a relatively short period of time. What a vile man.

The strangest thing in world politics, despite there being a Europe-wide travel ban in force, Mugabe turned up at the Vatican for the inauguration of the Pope. When challenged, he apparently said:

'This is not Europe!'

And why the Catholic Church saw fit to invite such a murderous monster to an event like that was completely beyond me.

I returned to the airport after an hour or so and was very depressed. How can one human do this to other human beings? Even in Africa, it was exceptional.

The client turned up after a couple more hours. There was much ceremony and a band to say farewell. It actually felt rather like a very cheap royal flight.

The client was a decent chap. I chatted to him on the way to Lüderitz about timing for the following day and he was very pleasant. You never know in executive jet work whether or not the person paying for the flight is going to be an arsehole or not!

It was quite late when we landed – around 7 pm. There was the usual plethora of black Mercedes to sweep the client off away from the aeroplane, leaving the area completely quiet.

As Lüderitz was just on the edge of the Namib, the views of the airport surroundings were dramatic and beautiful.

Owen and I had to refuel G-JSAX before travelling the 9 km into town to find somewhere to stay. I went into the control tower to pay the landing fees and organise transport.

'No telephone,' was the short answer by the air traffic controller. 'It no worko.'

'Can we get a ride into town?' I asked.

This was also a negative. 'All gone,' was the explanatory reply.

Owen and me in Joburg International Airport with G-JSAX

It took me back to the early days of flying around Europe in small, piston twin, 'air charter' aircraft for Fairflight at Biggin Hill. My friend Ian Faggatter (now a captain on 777 aircraft for British Airways) and I had a challenge for a month of who could get around the week's programme spending the least money. This involved finding transport to and from the hotels without paying.

Owen was getting into a bit of a panic, worrying that we would be stuck at the airport all night. So, in this situation, I was going to apply the same skills learnt in those early days of flying.

I told Owen, 'Get your bag. We are off!'

After we locked up the aircraft, I led us out of the airport to the main road into town and walked into the middle of the road in front of an approaching truck.

Obviously it stopped, because I am here writing the story.

'Hi, matey, is there any chance you can give us a lift into town?' I asked the driver.

The driver was more than happy to help. We chatted happily in the front of the truck during the short drive. The driver had never met a pilot before. He asked lots of very intelligent questions about flying and actually recommended a decent hotel, dropping us outside the door. Excellent!

Owen was astounded at my organisational skills:

'I cannot believe you just did that!' he exclaimed.

We checked in and had a couple of very cold Namibian lagers to celebrate a good day.

The flight back to Lanseria via Gaborone was uneventful. I said goodbye to the Botswanan foreign minister. He said he would see me again in a few weeks for another trip.

The 'Jack Sacks Unofficial Charter Company' was doing okay.

We went to the Carlton that evening. Catriona had been visiting some of the shopping malls and the Carlton Hotel, where she had met some of the regulars, while Owen and I were off on the Harare trip.

There had been some new arrivals. These were American businessmen who were in South Africa for a few months on business.

We had tea with Paul before his show and, as usual, had a great evening. During the time in Joburg, I kept in contact with the Foreign Office and Bristows to keep updated on the situation with Ken and Angus.

Generally, the situation was very, very bad indeed.

The photograph shows the conditions in Kiri Kiri Jail that Ken and Angus were having to suffer.

*Kirikiri Maximum
Securuity Prison*

When I spoke to Bristows, they explained that one of the problems with being in a Nigerian jail was that there was no food provided by the authorities. The only way you could get food was for it to be thrown over the prison walls in bags. If you did not get bags of food thrown over the wall, you did not eat.

If you look closely at the photo, you can see bags hanging from the ceiling. These are the food bags for the inmates. The reason that they were hanging from the ceiling was to keep them out of the way of the rats and cockroaches that were present in hordes.

When I spoke to the Foreign Office, I asked if there had been any opportunity to get consular access. The FO explained that this had become a problem because of the ramifications of the Dikko kidnapping affair.

I had been following this bizarre situation and reading into the background of the story as it was being taken through the Old Bailey.

As I became aware of the nature of the planning and execution of the kidnapping of Omaru Dikko, the obvious diplomatic consequences that clearly would have occurred for Nigeria following it, may explain why that Nigerian Air Force jet was up waiting for me. Taking everything into account, that it is my belief. A 'tit for tat' plan by the Nigerian Military Government did make some sense.

241

It was the worst diplomatic incident for a very long time. Diplomatic relations had been completely broken off. Many Nigerian embassy staff had been arrested in relation to the Dikko kidnapping and the Nigerian Consul had been expelled.

It was a major diplomatic storm and, as I said previously, one which would have been easily anticipated in Lagos.

The discussions with the Foreign Office helped with some pieces of the jigsaw.

The FO had been able to gain access to Ken and Angus by using the Swedish High Commission in Lagos. The feedback was that Ken was okay and mentally quite together, but Angus had been seriously adversely affected. I was not surprised at this, because most of us would be suffering mentally in such circumstances.

It was around this time that I decided to try to swap myself for them when I got back to the UK.

I also spoke to Nick Munns frequently during my South African trip. And we discussed, amongst other things, the way forward with Shirlstar.

He advised me that taking them to court would cost somewhere in the region of £30,000 (£60,000 in today's money). Nick did have a mate, Nicholas Yell, who had just been called to the Bar. Nick had talked to Nicholas about the case and had said that he was very interested. He also said that he would take it on without charging too much. Nick also had another mate who he had trained with in law school who had more experience of Civil/Commercial actions. Martin Barrett was persuaded to join our small and highly motivated team.

We agreed to get Nick Yell to do a 'Counsel's Opinion' on the matter as a starting point.

Apart from the cottage that I bought with Catriona; I also owned a small terraced house. I had bought the house while I was (temporarily) well off. This had been while I was working for Fairflight at Biggin Hill. It paid good money and I had very few expenses – just the odd beer.

The property was rented out to a couple, Mike and Catherine Curtiss. Mike was a driving instructor and they were friends of mine. They had talked about buying the property for around £70,000. So after clearing the £20,000 mortgage, I would have the funds to pay the legal fees.

I told Nick that I was going to sell the property to finance the legal action. 'Staking the house' is a phrase that comes to mind. It was a legal gamble. But as I said earlier, for me this was a major point of principle – to expose Ben Slade for what he had done. Along with the Nigerians, Slade was behind the situation in which Ken and Angus had been innocently caught up.

Owen seemed to be very well informed about the matters surrounding Ben Slade's activities. He inadvertently dropped information into conversations that indicated he must have been in frequent contact with Shirlstar.

I think Owen fancied himself as a bit of an MI6 agent. He probably thought he could have also got G-LORI out of Lagos. My God, though, he would have been the last person I'd have wanted with me – he would have freaked – a little low fuel on the way back from Port Elizabeth was a good indication of Owen's reaction to stress!

I did subtly pump him on various aspects of the history of Ben's activities in Lagos. Putting that together with the information provided by Ben's PA and David Fagan, this gave me a very good background picture to Slade's financial activities. When you added the kidnapping of Umaru Dikko, I had a pretty good idea of why the whole story had panned out this way.

Owen had an old-fashioned typewriter that printed from a roll of polymer tape. I used to hear him thumping away on it at night. I joked with Catriona that I was going to pinch the ribbon and unwind it to find out what he was actually up to.

It wasn't too much longer before Owen had to go back to the UK. He had arranged a 'Jeremy Palmer II' for me to have as a first officer to replace him. I guessed that Owen was not at all comfortable with the idea of flying G-JSAX back to the UK.

To be frank, though, it was a very challenging route back. Apart from avoiding various war zones, Jack Sacks had told me that he and his wife were to accompany me on the aeroplane.

Bollocks, I thought, *this will make it much more complicated in the planning of the route.* With South African passport holders on board, it severely restricted the countries over which we could fly or stop for fuel. So, for this reason, I had to organise special overflight clearances allowing for this.

White South Africans were not the most popular individuals on the African continent, and I reckoned that he was just saving the cost of a couple of airline tickets! Speaking of which, he had not paid me the whole amount due for my stay. As described earlier, getting the money out of the boss was sometimes a challenge. It was something I was getting increasingly concerned about as Sacks was clearly a tight bastard.

We spent the evening at the Carlton and watched Paul's show. The Americans had become part of our group in the hotel. Owen said that he wanted to go on a mini safari before returning home, Paul Melba came along too. Catriona did not want to go, but I did. She encouraged me to go along with Owen.

We had a great day. It was a long trip to get there, around four hours each way, but the opportunity to cuddle lion cubs was a once in a lifetime opportunity. We stayed the night in a safari camp 'hotel' which was basic but okay, and better than some places in other areas in Africa.

* * *

We arrived back in Joburg in the late afternoon. I wanted to pop over to Lanseria Airport to check G-JSAX out for a trip the next day and fuel her up. I went to the apartment and said hi to Catriona.

'Hi, Coco, what have you been up to?' I asked.

'I went to Sandton yesterday, but just stayed here in the apartment all day today,' she replied.

I briefly told her about the cubs and explained that I needed to sort out the aeroplane for the trip; Owen's last.

After that, I went down to the car park and rolled up to pay the fee to get the car out. The fee was only two rand.

Mmm, that's strange, I thought. *It should have been twelve for overnight parking.*

This bugged me during the drive to Lanseria. I looked at the parking ticket when I got there. The vehicle had been checked into the car park at 4 pm. I searched around the car and found another ticket on the floor showing the car leaving the car park at 11 am the previous day.

I thought of this together with other events, including when one of the American businessmen, Eddie Tracy, had been very generous buying rounds of drinks and food in the Carlton.

Paul Melba had mentioned that Tracy was focused on Catriona, and he smelt a rat. I, of course, being a dim male, had not noticed. I didn't particularly like Tracy. As far as I was concerned, he was a greasy salesman.

Putting this together with the car park tickets and her stating that she had been in the apartment all day, I came up with an overall picture of deceitfulness.

I was back at the apartment quite late; Catriona was asleep. I stood at the end of the bed and waited. She sensed my presence and woke up.

'What's the matter, Mike?' she asked.

'My problem is this,' I said and tossed the parking ticket in her direction.

She looked at the parking slip completely confused as to the significance of the parking ticket and what exactly the 'problem' was.

'What do you mean?' she asked.

'You said you were here all day today. If that is so, how do you explain the parking ticket showing you arriving back in the car park at four pm? And, apparently, you left here at eleven the previous day!' I growled, darkly.

Catriona started to cry. This was a default position of someone who had been caught out and did not know what to do or say.

'What you want to do is entirely up to you,' I said quietly. 'You are entitled to decide on what you want to do with your life.' I paused for effect and continued to lecture her. 'But *DO NOT* lie to me. Do not offend me with lies. You will always get found out anyway.'

She carried on sobbing.

'We will talk about this later. I must get some sleep before the trip tomorrow.'

I finished speaking. I shut down any further comment. As far as I was concerned, that was the end of the matter for the time being.

When I came back from the trip, another Zimbabwe/Gaborone shuttle, I went over to the Carlton after a few lagers in the 1505 and met Paul for tea before his show. I explained what had happened the previous evening. He told me that they had been at the Carlton and were 'very close' while I had been away.

It was a bit sad; Catriona and I were good friends. I was sure that would not change, but, as far as I was concerned, the relationship was over.

Owen left shortly after that trip, and the new first officer that Owen had organised turned up. I can't remember his name, so we will call him JP II, 'Jeremy Palmer Mark II'. To be fair, he was okay, not very experienced, but competent.

CHAPTER 28

July 1984
Ferrying G-JSAX to the UK from Johannesburg

The next trip I began to get very ill. I made it back to Lanseria, but I was really 'properly' ill, sweating profusely with a very high temperature. I went straight to Joburg main hospital.

They took my temperature, which was 105, giving them a shock.

The doctors asked me where I had been during the last few months. When I told them, it gave them another shock! As a result, they decided the best thing to do was shove me into isolation.

Joburg hospital is a centre for tropical disease expertise in Africa. They started by taking a couple of armfuls of blood to ascertain what was causing my fever.

My temperature was varying plus or minus six degrees over one to two hours and, apart from finding malaria present in my blood, they could not identify the virus causing the fever. It was a severe liver infection. I looked jaundiced and generally like shit.

I was very well looked after, and they controlled the temperature changes very efficiently. When I was stabilised and back to normal, the doctors explained that my liver had taken a huge hit with this virus and that I needed to look after it. I had been in the hospital for nine days, most of that with a massive fever.

'Best you leave alcohol alone for the time being, Mike. It puts the liver under a lot of strain, and your liver has been put through the mill,' said the doctor who had been looking after me.

I took this advice to heart. So, from then onwards, apart from an occasional glass of champagne at special events, I left off alcohol and felt a lot healthier for it, funnily enough.

Catriona informed me that she was going to San Antonio in America with Eddie Tracy. We had this conversation on one of the occasions she had visited me in hospital. I genuinely wished her the best of luck for her future. It was a sad goodbye.

My focus became the trip back to the UK with G-JSAX. Jack was insistent that he was coming with me, so I had to work out the route.

In the end, I chose Lanseria to Moroni airport in the Comoros Islands, then on to Djibouti, Cairo and then Corfu in Greece. Finally, on to the UK, but Jack was a little vague about the final destination.

G-JSAX was going for maintenance, which would normally be in Bournemouth or Luton – these were the main maintenance centres for HS125s in the UK.

That first part of the trip was a very long day. It was the only route back that I could plan with Jack and his wife on board as they had South African passports. We could 'tech stop' at all these airports but could not stop overnight with them on board.

There was also my concern that Jack still had not paid me the outstanding £1,500 due under our agreement.

When I landed in Moroni to refuel, there was one of those bizarre moments. I had parked G-JSAX at the edge of the apron. While I was waiting for the fuel bowser, I stood beside a huge sign saying 'NO SMOKING'. The Comoros Islands are volcanic islands and the area behind the sign was smoking from one of the many active volcanic fissures. I wished I'd brought a camera to record this, as I could not stop laughing about it.

On arrival at Corfu airport, we went to a hotel next to the airport. This was when I began to be suspicious about what Jack was up to.

He still would not commit to a final destination, and he must have known by this time where the aeroplane would be having maintenance. He was also not committing to a departure date from Corfu.

This, combined with his penchant for 'cash' deals in South Africa that I had witnessed, made me feel very uncomfortable.

There was a responsibility on the commander of an aircraft to know what was going on in his aircraft. If Jack was smuggling something and it was found, I would be responsible, not him. So, I did two things: firstly, I called the boss of HM Customs and Excise in London and informed him of my concerns. I explained that I did not, as yet, know our final destination. This covered me on the 'commander's responsibility' front. *Customs can take it from here*, I thought. Secondly, I went to the aeroplane and took the aircraft logbooks. Without these, an aircraft is basically unflyable. No maintenance could be signed off, so it would effectively be grounded. I carefully packed these logbooks and then called DHL in Corfu.

DHL collected the large package and off it went in a van. I had sent them to my home address. Yes, you have probably worked out what I was up to… It's called leverage!

After lots of faffing about, we finally set off for the UK to 'either Bournemouth or Luton'. Eventually, Jack decreed that we would land in Bournemouth, Hurn Airport. It was all very, very strange.

After landing, I asked Jack and his wife to wait on the aeroplane while I went into the customs office.

'Are you aware of the contact I made to your head office?' I asked the customs officer.

As I was saying that, I noticed a note on the pad on his desk. Reading upside down, it said 'G-JSAX – hold, do not disembark'. The officer nodded at me. *Good*, I thought, *I will find out soon what the bugger is up to!*

At this moment, Sacks came into the office and growled:

'What is going on?' in his strong Afrikaner accent. 'Why are we being kept on the aircraft?'

'Sir, you are required to remain on the aircraft until I say you can disembark,' the customs officer said with the undeniable authority of his position.

Jack Sacks boarded G-JSAX again muttering in frustration.

A few minutes later, a large, dark blue transit van arrived at the aircraft with blue lights flashing. This was referred to as a 'rummage crew'. They were a team of experts who would search ships, lorries or containers that were suspected to contain contraband. They had come at great speed from Southampton with a 'blue light' police escort to meet us.

A female officer climbed out and approached Jack's wife who had placed a bowl of fruit on the aircraft top step, ready for removal, and presumably for disposal. The officer was dressed in black, tight work overalls with various tools and torches dangling from her belt. Another couple of similar officers had also climbed out of the van.

'Get rid of the fruit,' she barked at Jack Sack's wife.

'Why?' replied an indignant Mrs Sacks.

'Because it will upset the scent for the dog,' was the curt reply from the female officer.

Well, I could hardly contain my mirth. The dog! Upset the scent of the dog! Priceless, absolutely priceless! I had to feign walking away to conceal my tears of laughter.

While Jack and his wife looked on, the team stripped out the soft furnishings and then proceeded to look in every nook and cranny of the aircraft. Torches inspected inside the fuel tanks and up in the rear equipment bay. Doggie sniffed at anything they brought out – including all the baggage.

I was totally surprised. Customs did not find a bloody thing. To this day, I am still mystified by the behaviour of Jack on that trip back. He was up to something, of that I am absolutely certain.

We were eventually released by customs. I then taxied G-JSAX around to the maintenance organisation's parking area, where we were met by the chief engineer of the maintenance company. There was a short discussion about the annual maintenance that was due on G-JSAX between Sacks and the engineer, while I stood beside them. At this stage, I decided it was a perfect moment to interrupt the proceedings.

'Oh, Jack,' I started innocently. 'I meant to ask what arrangements you were making to settle the outstanding amount that you owe me for the time in Joburg and bringing the aircraft back to the UK?'

'I will get around to sending you a cheque in due course, Mike,' he replied in that curt Afrikaans accent.

Obviously, having worked for various African chiefs, I was very aware of the importance of being paid for the work carried out.

'Okay, Jack, fine and thank you,' I continued. 'When I receive your cheque and it has cleared into my bank account, I will send the aircraft logbooks down to these guys so they can carry out the scheduled maintenance.'

Jack looked a little confused: 'You have got the logbooks? You have taken them?' he replied. 'You can't do that – they should stay with the aircraft.' He turned to the chief engineer. 'Is that true? You cannot do any maintenance without the logbooks?'

The chief engineer shook his head. Jack was getting the idea.

'The logbooks are in safe hands, Jack.' I now talked down to him in a tone like a schoolteacher. 'You know my address and telephone number. So, sort the cash out when you're ready, and then I will send the logbooks,' I replied.

Funnily enough, Jack was able to give me a cheque there and then – magic!

'How do I know you will send them?' he asked grumpily.

'The logbooks are of no value to me, Jack. I simply wanted to be sure of being paid,' I replied curtly.

The chief engineer knew me and was surreptitiously smiling behind Jack's back. I folded the cheque into my wallet and grabbed my flight bag and overnight bag and said: 'Thank you, Jack. The logbooks will be here in three days.'

I went through to the reception of the maintenance company and organised some transport home.

CHAPTER 29

November 1984
Swapping Myself for Ken and Angus

It did seem strange to be in the cottage on my own. Catriona and I had been together for a few years and had even talked about marriage. Following the events in Nigeria, as I started sleepwalking, Catriona had shown significant signs of anorexia and bulimia. Due to the environment of her early life, these were her go-to signs of psychological distress.

I was philosophical about the relationship ending, but I did feel a responsibility towards her and her little sister Simone who had come to stay with us at the cottage. They were both messed up by the actions of their mother.

Having said that, now I was back, it was time to take action to sort out the circumstances surrounding Ken and Angus in Lagos.

I called the Foreign Office and had a long talk with them, floating the idea of arranging a 'swap' of Ken and Angus for me. We all knew that Ken and Angus had, in all probability, been grabbed in a moment of frustration after the unsuccessful attempt to shoot me down. This had then been exaggerated massively by the Nigerians being caught red-handed with Dikko in a box at Stansted. When the Nigerians and Mossad agents were banged up in the UK, the only lever for the Nigerians was Ken and Angus, so they pulled it.

I left them to think about this and arranged to speak with them later.

The idea was not warmly received by the West Africa desk. It just replaced one problem with another for them and potentially a more difficult problem.

We spoke a short time later.

'The trouble is, Mike, we have made enquires through third parties. The Nigerians have got themselves boxed into a corner. It is our opinion that you would simply be another problem for both countries,' my friend on the Africa desk told me. 'So no, we will not try to officially discuss a swap.'

So, that got me nowhere. However, around the same time, I received a call from a *Private Eye* journalist called Paul O'Halloran. Paul said that he was very interested in the activities of a certain Ben Slade. He asked if I was prepared to meet him:

'I'd like to buy you lunch, Mike,' he offered.

I had become very wary of reporters but decided to go along for a free lunch, courtesy of *Private Eye*, with Paul.

We met in the Grosvenor Hotel. Paul was a stocky, slightly overweight man, around 40 with early greying hair. He told me that he loved the Grosvener in a soft Irish accent.

'If you look around this room, Mike, you will see all sorts of deals being done,' he said. 'Any dirty deal that you have ever heard of was almost certainly carried out in this room.'

The dining room at the Grosvenor is a beautiful old English-style, with white tablecloths on round tables neatly laid out, grey wallpaper dotted with fine art paintings, and high ceilings in subtle blues. The tables were all occupied with mainly grey-haired men dressed in similar suits, very formal suits. It seemed a contradiction looking at these well-dressed 'gentlemen' that dirty deeds were organised in this plush dining room.

'It doesn't matter whether it's politics, big business or big crime, it all goes on here,' he finished in a quiet voice.

Obviously, if Paul was correct, and some of these were criminals, they went to the same tailor as businessmen and politicians!

We had a great lunch and discussed all the events of the last six months or so. Our first meeting was 'off the record' until I got a handle on Paul and some sort of trust. But *Private Eye* does not go by normal rules – they are not after the 'big' headline or 'exclusive' story like normal newspapers. After this meeting I grew to trust Paul O'Halloran and his opinions.

Paul and I met a few times. It was very useful, particularly as I was about to take Shirlstar to court. Paul and I swapped lots of information about Shirlstar and Ben Slade. We also spoke in some depth about 'swapping' me for Ken and Angus.

Paul had a number of contacts in the Lagos establishment. He sent messages to them to sound out the desire for a swap.

These all came back negatively with the same sort of message as that from the Foreign Office. The Nigerians had got themselves into a diplomatic cul-de-sac of their own making, and Ken and Angus were paying a very high price for it.

So, I was stuck in this mire of responsibility, and it seemed there was absolutely nothing I could do about it.

Flying-wise, there were very few options; there was very little work around.

My flying 'friends' of many years made it clear that I was not going to be helped. I found out years later that this was based on jealousy. This was not just because I had not taken a 'pilot' with me to Lagos, but also because I was flying jets and they were not. How sad is that?

I did fly regularly for the Ancient Monuments Research Department in a tiny four-seat Cessna 172 aircraft. This involved flying low over various areas with an archaeologist directing a photographer taking photos of fields with and without crops in different stages of the seasons and growth.

They built up a catalogue of pictures of each site. The reason was that Roman and other ancient ruins and roads showed up at different times. It was very interesting. I had never noticed these extensive signs until I flew with these guys. It paid quite well too.

A few months later, I was offered a chief pilot position for a small air charter company in Lydd Airport on the south coast. I would be chief pilot, senior to two other pilots and mainly involved in night mail contracts.

Before that, Nick Munns and I started working with Martin Barrett and Nicholas Yell properly on the case against Shirlstar. We then issued proceedings commencing the legal action in the high court to recover the outstanding £12,500 owed to me by Slade.

As I mentioned earlier, Nick Munns was, at that time, opening a new office in Redhill, Surrey, in addition to his office in Godstone. He was on a budget with that opening. As he had helped so much in Abidjan (voluntarily and unpaid), I offered to help with the work in Redhill. This involved painting and decorating and a bit of wiring and carpentry.

As I had plenty of spare time, I was signing on as 'unemployed' for months before the Lydd job, I did a lot of work there; it was a pleasure to help him out.

CHAPTER 30

February 1985
Revenge is a Dish Best Served Cold!

At this time, when they were *very* stuck, I had been doing some ad hoc work on Bandeirante aircraft with Fairflight at Biggin Hill, but they were messing me around on trips. The other pilots were ensuring that I got to do as little as possible.

This was very disappointing because I had worked for Fairflight Charters on and off for nine years. This prompted my decision to take the job with 'Business Air Travel' at Lydd Airport in Kent.

Whilst the name was pretty impressive, in actual fact, it was a very small company run by a couple of very enthusiastic guys.

The main contract was out of Lydd to Southend, pick up the mail and then off to East Midlands to drop the mail, wait an hour or so and load the mail for Brize Norton, and then back to Lydd. This went on for five nights a week.

This suited me, because I could do the trip and drive home and be in bed for 5 am, which gave me an afternoon to deal with legal matters. Occasionally, there were also some 'ad hoc' charters.

It also meant that the reporter – 'P.D.' from that *Sunday Paper* dropped into my clutches. Ah Ha!! – karma!!

'Mike, we've got a charter to Vigo in Spain. Can you get down here for ten?' asked David, the managing director.

'Sure, I can get there before that,' I replied. 'What is the deal?'

'It's a charter by *[a reputable Sunday Newspaper]* to go to a pickup of a chap who was rescued by the Vigo fishing fleet. He had been on the upturned hull of his yacht that had capsized in the Bay of Biscay,' he explained. 'His wife died; she was washed off the hull. They have bought his exclusive story.'

My ears pricked up at this, 'what are the passengers' names out of Lydd?' I asked.

'Err, hang on. I'll check… It's a photographer called James Simpson and a reporter called PD.'

Bingo. This was manna from heaven in the world of Karma! I was *so* looking forward to this trip.

'I'm on my way in five minutes,' I said to David.

I went to find my copy of the newspaper containing the article and put it in my flight bag. You are going to like this.

On arrival at Lydd, I prepared the aircraft for the flight, fuelled it up and completed the pre-flight checks before the passengers arrived. A single pair of seats had been fitted in the front of the cabin to accommodate the passengers. This aeroplane did not have seats for the night mail flights. The Bandeirante is a large(ish) turboprop aircraft, quite powerful and fast with a cruising speed of around 220 mph.

When the passengers turned up, I introduced myself in a very specific way: 'Hello, I'm your pilot for today, Mike,' and shook each of their hands. I omitted to mention my surname.

'Hello, I'm PD, I'm the journalist, and this is James Simpson. James is a photographer.'

I looked at the reporter carefully. 'PD? Mmm… I don't think we have met before, have we?' I asked. Bear trap warning!

'No,' he replied, 'I don't think we have.' Slam dunk.

'No, we haven't,' I confirmed. The journalist looked slightly unsettled but dismissed the exchange.

We climbed into the aircraft. I put the photographer into the passenger seat in the cabin and P.D. into the co-pilot's seat next to me. I gave him some headphones so I could speak to him.

We set off on the three-hour trip to Vigo. Once we were level at 9,000 feet in cruise flight with the autopilot flying the aeroplane, I set my plan into motion.

I started, 'This newspaper business can be quite nasty, I understand...' I paused, as if thinking about it. 'I've heard that some newspapers can make up stories, quote people without talking to them and print the story without a care.' I paused again.

There was no rush; he was stuck up here for another few hours. P.D. seemed attentive, thinking this was the musings of an interested pilot. He clearly had absolutely no idea who I was.

'I don't know much about the newspaper business, but I guess your newspaper does not do that sort of thing?' Another long pause... 'I guess that would be the *News of the World*?'

I was chatting in a relaxed way, just a conversation, asking questions as if seeking to understand the newspaper business.

'Oh God, no! We are a reputable newspaper. We certainly would not indulge in any such behaviour,' he replied. 'You are right, the *News of the World* is a rag. I cannot imagine why anyone would want to buy it,' he concluded.

'So, you can't imagine quoting someone you had never met, or anything like that?' I was now drawing him in for the kill...

He looked a bit baffled at the way the converstion was going now.

'No, definitely not. And I couldn't work for a news organisation that would.'

I reached into my flight bag and pulled out the newspaper: 'When we met at Lydd, we both agreed that we had never met before. Yes?' I asked.

Now he began to look a bit confused with the direction of the conversation and slight change in my tone: 'Yes, that is correct,' he confirmed.

'If that is the case, how do you explain this?' I said, placing the newspaper in between us, open at the centre pages for him to look at. I pointed towards his name at the top of the article. 'This is *your* byline, isn't it?' I asked.

'Yes, it is, but I don't understand why this is important,' he said, now very uncomfortable.

'Well, it is quite simple really,' I said in a matter-of-fact way. 'We have never met. You have written this article about me. You have actually quoted me in the article, but you *have never met me.*' I paused to let the information sink in. 'What's more, in the article you painted me as a cowboy pilot *who had serious problems with mental stability.*' P.D. now began to look very pale indeed.

I continued, introducing the punishment.

'If I was the sort of person you have described in this article, I may be the sort of person who could do something like this.' My voice had now lost any sort of soft tone, turning loud, clear and firm.

I disconnected the autopilot and began hand flying. I looked at P.D. and pitched the nose high up and began to roll the aeroplane beyond 90 degrees so that it was becoming upside down. I then began to pull towards the Bay of Biscay 9,000 feet below and said:

'I might roll the aircraft upside down and pull until we hit the water!'

I then rolled the aircraft back to level flight and re-engaged the autopilot. Everything returned to normal after a very extreme manoeuvre. I looked behind me to the photographer. He was sitting up holding the sides of his seat.

'What's going on?' he shouted.

'It's okay, just a bit of fun for P.D.,' I replied. 'Don't worry, it's all under control.'

I looked at P.D. He was white as a sheet with a tinge of green. After a few minutes, I did a similar manoeuvre, though not as severe. He went even greener. I handed him a sick bag. The photographer was looking white, too.

I did not need carry out the extreme rolling manoeuvre again, but I did occasionally disconnect the autopilot. Doing this kept P.D.'s attention. As parents, we know that the anticipation of punishment is far more frightening than the punishment itself.

'I will tell you something, P.D. I am *not* the person you described in your article. So, for the rest of this flight, which is approximately another hour and a half, you won't be sure if I am going to actually do what I've said I will do.' Again, I paused for effect. 'But while I have your attention, I'm going to tell you a story. It's one that highlights your responsibility as a reporter.'

I then told him about a young actor, around 17 years old, who was in one of the soaps on telly. This young man lived in Tatsfield in Kent, a couple of doors from where I lived with Catriona, before buying the cottage in Limpsfield.

The newspapers hounded him on a particular story (I cannot remember the context), camping continuously outside his house. Untrue articles were written about him and they quoted the poor lad. This went on for some time. It was probably a 'slow news' period.

In the end, this young man hung himself in his garage. It was an awful tragedy, not just for the lad but for his family, too. At the inquest, the media was blamed. The coroner said that the saddest part was that the story was not true.

'You see, P.D. I *am a very strong* individual and can sustain the sort of nonsense you wrote about me, but there are a lot of people who are not that strong,' I said very firmly. 'And as that coroner in the lad's case said, you have a huge responsibility. You need to bear that in mind.'

We landed in Vigo, so my part of the charter was finished. The newspaper had chartered a jet (an HS125 as it happens) to fly the man back to the UK. They were keeping their options open about the destination in the UK, so no other bastard journalists could get their hands on him.

I shook hands with P.D. in a very friendly way. I said I hoped he had got something out of the flight. I think he did. He actually apologised.

I did hear the photographer asking P.D. as they walked away: 'What the fuck was that all about?' P.D. put his hand out in a blocking gesture and shook his head at the photographer indicating not to pursue the matter any further.

I flew back to Lydd feeling very happy – yes, revenge is definitely a dish best served cold.

CHAPTER 31

Taking Ben Slade to the High Court

Nick Munns, Nicholas Yell and I had worked through all the evidence against Ben, and Nicholas Yell had carried out a Counsel's Opinion on the case.

Taking everything into account, we had an 80% to 20% chance of winning. I had gleaned a lot of information from Paul Halloran and also David Fagan in Lagos.

David Fagan had actually found me a contact for Graham Bott. Bott had fucked off to Florida when the 890,000 naira went missing. He must have known that he was done for if he stayed in Lagos.

Bott provided a statement for us that was admissible in court as it was sworn in Florida in front of the equivalent of a Notary public. He was happy to do this as Ben had stitched him up sometime before this particular episode. Bott also confirmed the information that I had gathered from the documents given to me by Ben's PA, Jenny, as facts.

There was a serious amount of organising required to get ready for this court case. I spent every spare moment sorting it out. I took over the dining room table in the cottage and covered it with documents.

Sitting at the table, I was on the phone to my friend Lorna, who was working in the Scilly Isles at this time. We were chatting about a plan for me to visit her, to get a break for a few days, when Catriona appeared at the window.

I was shocked. In my mind, Catriona had gone forever to set up home in San Antonio in Texas with her boyfriend, Eddie Tracy. When I had headed off from South Africa back to the UK, she had gone off to Texas with him. I thought that was the last I had seen of her. She had let me down in a big way.

Opening the door, I asked: 'What are you doing back?' I was genuinely surprised.

'I had to come back,' came the weak reply.

There was never a proper explanation for her return, but I suspect that Eddie Tracy became tired of her anorexia/bulimia once the novelty of a new sexual partner had passed.

I did not go to the Scillies. This is something I regret.

I have been asked about this since then, and my answer had a number of aspects. I had to explain to Catriona the up-to-date situation with Ken and Angus and the position with suing Ben Slade. Also, I felt a responsibility for her state of mind. Although a lot of the harm was done to her and her sisters by her parents, the events in Nigeria had exacerbated this.

I joke nowadays in my professional life, where psychology is referenced in the training of professional pilots, that my knowledge of psychology came from some very bad decisions in relationships. Indeed, I did study the subject in great depth to assist Catriona and me in these excepionally traumatic events.

It would be inappropriate to go into too much detail here, but, on a number of occasions, Catriona threatened suicide. This was a serious threat.

I did have to accept the possibility that she may succeed. I did not want to feel responsible for this and sought the very welcome help and advice from great professional psychotherapists and a very special bereavement counsellor (for what I referred to as pre-emptive bereavement counselling).

I applied all the lessons learnt from these very knowledgeable ladies.

I believe that, without this being applied, Catriona may not have survived. The driving school had been running during these events with the the help of Mike Curtiss and his wife, Catherine, who had been renting my house.

Bentleys Driving School worked quite well and employed Catriona and Simone in the office with 12 cars out on the road.

It had been set up on the premise that the instructors got paid before the school got its money. This was a reverse of the norm. There is a reason why it's done the other way around! But that, as they say, is another story.

Catriona, I think, was hoping we would renew and continue our relationship, but that was not going to happen. What I did do was support and help her and Simone, which I did to the best of my ability.

While all this was occurring, progress towards the high court was slowly taking place. We had issued proceedings and a date for a hearing was expected soon but the process was very, very slow. I had received the cash from the sale of the house, and I had sold it to Mike and Catherine Curtiss. As they had been renting it, the sale went through very easily. I had to give Nick Munns funds to run the case.

Sorry to go off subject (no I'm not!), but that house sale being easy reminds me of one a couple of years later that did not go so well. The buyers were absolute bastards. They tried to get a nice garden shed, curtains, light fittings and a posh loft ladder within what was already a very good price by prevaricating about the small price I was asking for these things.

I was so pissed off at this, that on the day of completion I got some mates with a van and literally pulled the shed apart with claw hammers and a big crowbar.

In the house, I went into the loft and took the loft ladder down having put a single bulb up there – switched on!

I removed the loft ladder and then arranged the loft door so it would drop open suddenly as soon as it was touched.

I took out all the curtains and light fittings (I was required under the contract to leave at least one light fitting – which was up there in the loft), but I was still very cross.

I really should be embarrassed about this bit , but I feel this should be shared with you..... You see, after all that exertion, I felt a very strong desire to go to the toilet; you know, number twos! Well, I did a huge one in the downstairs loo. It was like some kind of huge sea serpent poking its head around the bend... I did not want to spoil this dramatic effect, so I finished the 'personal cleaning' part in the upstairs loo.

I do not know what they thought when they arrived in their new house, but I am pretty sure I made my point!

Sorry about that. Now, where were we...?

Oh yes, starting the court case with Ben. He did ring me up and threaten all sorts of stuff, but, as you have probably gathered, I am not easily scared.

After a very long time, we eventually went to the high court in London. The judge, Justice John Gower, was actually a senior judge from Lewes who had been seconded to the high court.

I was very impressed with Judge Gower. He was very sharp and grasped this esoteric subject without any doubts. According to Nicholas Yell, this was not unusual. To become a judge, you have to be put through the mill as a barrister for many years and then, eventually, have to be selected to become a judge.

We were also very lucky that John Gower had started out as a journalist and had a natural instinct for grasping the intricacies of this story.

The high court in London was a very impressive building, with a huge arched entrance at the top of a set of stone steps – you will have seen these pictures on the television.

We were in a smaller side courtroom, which was nonetheless very impressive, with polished wood all the way around the room. The seats where the judges sat were well above the floor level of the rest of the court occupants. Actually, there were three seats up there in the event of three judges being needed. Down below the judges' seats were the clerk's and court secretary's seats.

With a space in the centre, there are then the seats for the two sets of barristers representing the two sides of the argument. These were arranged in two rows, one for the barrister and his assistant and behind them the instructing solicitors. The public seats were at the back of the court. These are set above on a balcony in the larger courtrooms.

On our side was Nick Munns, Martin Barrett, Nicholas Yell and me. Over on the other side was a barrister with silk – Longmore. He had a junior barrister to assist and two solicitors sitting in the benches behind them. Longmore and Nicholas Yell were both dressed in a wig and gown. The court clerk and secretary were also dressed in gowns.

'Fuck me, guys. We are outnumbered here!' I said. We all laughed.

The high court is an extremely majestic place; it is designed to be very intimidating. It is also a venue where you need to be very well prepared. And there is only one rule for us ordinary beings who seldom have to face this sort of setting: always tell the truth. If you don't, you will get caught out!

As it happened, Nicholas Yell was a brilliant barrister, and we were very confident that we were as well prepared as possible.

My Dad Roy next to his favourite car – his Rover!

The nicest thing that happened when we started on the first day was my dad, Roy, turning up. I looked back towards the entrance door behind us and saw his smiling face (I do miss him!).

Roy had a huge traditional RAF, handlebar moustache and swept-back, dark hair; he was a very distinguished and handsome man (I only say that because, obviously, I take after him!). I signalled to Roy to come in. He sat in the public seats just behind us.

Roy came from a British generation where if you hugged a man, it was a sign of homosexuality. I had decided when I was around 18 that I was going to change that.

> 'Roy,' I told him at the time, 'I'm going to give you a hug now, but before I do, I want to make the point that a hug between father and son is an indication of affection and respect. There is absolutely no homosexual connotation involved at all in this sort of behaviour.'

I then gave him a hug. After that, he got used to it and it became a normal part of life for us when we had not seen each other for a while.

The proceedings had not begun, so I gave him a hug and introduced him to Nick, Martin and Nicholas Yell. He could not stay for the whole court hearing, but it was great to have him there. Roy had travelled down from Norwich on the train to support me. My mum and dad had followed this whole tale and were very supportive during the years the repercussions continued.

Although the case was planned for five days, it actually lasted a total of nine days with various people giving evidence, including Ben Slade; Stanley 'Sue 'em Stan' Beller; Mark Tolner, the MD of Shirlstar; and, of course, me!

The contract was completed on the aircraft leaving Nigerian territorial airspace, which I had done. The Shirlstar defence was that the contract was not valid because the flight out of Lagos was technically illegal and you could not have a contract for an illegal act.

Our argument to this was that there were mitigating circumstances that contributed to the decision to depart and that Shirlstar had contributed to those circumstances in various ways.

We managed to cover all the various documents and the missing Naira. Because the subject of the missing naira was covered, we were then also able to cross-examine Slade on the validity of obtaining judgement for repossessing the aircraft in the first place. Also, during Slade's cross-examination, Nicholas Yell was also able to get him to drop into the evidence that he had brought Vanni into his office during my initial time in Lagos.

It was an exhausting experience. Whilst the hearings started at 10, you had to be there at around nine to have a pre-hearing conference. Catriona was there in the public seats behind us and was very helpful in picking up on details we had not noticed. Our pre-hearing conferences took place in a small café near the high court. We finished at four each day. My appearance on the stand was due to take place towards the end of the week.

When the presenting of evidence was taking place, concentration was absolute. Nick Munns and I would be listening very carefully, making notes, and searching and highlighting documents for Nicholas Yell to assist him, as he was cross-examining a witness. It was so impressive to see such intellectual capacity in action. Nicholas would be asking questions and reading our notes, or identifying documents, without losing track of his questioning of the witness.

Although Longmore, Ben's barrister, had 'Silk', in other words was a senior barrister, he did not have the same skills. Fortunately for us, he was particularly unimpressive when questioning or cross-examining a witness.

It came around to my turn in the witness box. Longmore set about questioning me with glee. Clearly, he thought I would be easy meat. I was actually in the witness box for a day and a half. This was a truly gruelling experience.

Trouble was, as I said earlier, I stuck to the truth. There were no embellishing facts to assist my evidence. So, whenever Longmore tried to trap me into admitting that I deliberately took the aircraft out of Nigeria without any real reason, he was not successful.

There was a continuous stream of questions that, on face value, asked one thing, but the underlying point was to uncover any inconsistency. Once an inconsistency was discovered, the barrister would then, unmercifully, pursue that inconsistency to uncover the 'truth'. But, because I simply stuck to the truth, this didn't work.

There was also an underlying inference that I had financed the court action by selling the story.

We reached a high point of this belief towards the end of my time in the witness box. It was almost the last question at the end of my cross-examination, when Longmore could not help himself, probably because Ben was clearly frustrated that this case had not gone the way he had wanted or expected.

'Captain Howard, how did you finance this legal action?' he asked in an imperious tone.

Ken and Angus remained in Kiri kiri jail in Lagos. Diplomatic relations were still frozen between Nigeria and the United Kingdom. There was still a lot of publicity relating to the whole events in Nigeria and the attempted kidnapping of Umaru Dikko. *Private Eye* had been writing frequent pieces on Ben Slade's activities, which had been picked up by more mainstream media. Obviously, there had been a massive amount of publicity into the events in the first place. To be honest, in these circumstances, I could have easily sold the story. But it would have been wholly inappropriate to sell the story with Ken and Angus in Kiri kiri jail in Lagos.

'I do not see the relevance of that question in relation to the action here,' I replied bluntly.

'It is not for you to decide the relevance of my questions, Captain Howard, it is your obligation to answer them,' Longmore stated before he pursued his line of questioning.

He looked more confident with my refusal to answer: 'I repeat, how did you finance this legal action against my clients?'

'That question simply does not have any value in my evidence, and I will not answer.' I stubbornly continued my line of response.

We batted this back and forward for a few minutes with me refusing, in different ways, until Judge Gower intervened.

'Captain Howard, I insist that you answer Mr Longmore's question. If you do not answer the question, I will find you in contempt,' he stated with finality.

'Yes, Your Honour, I do understand.'

Having addressed this response to Judge Gower, I turned towards Longmore and his crew. He wasn't there through every day of the hearing, but even Ben had turned up for my interrogation. I gave a long pause and finally answered:

'I sold my home.' I said this firmly and with a strong voice. It was a short answer but of devastating effect.

Nicholas Yell, sitting in his barrister's seat in front of me, was grinning like a Cheshire cat who had had some of the very best cream. He told me later,

'Mike, there is one rule that is drummed into you when you are training to become a barrister. That rule is never ask a question to which you do not know the answer!' He was still smiling. 'That was an absolute bombshell for them and gave a great footnote to your evidence.'

Longmore was lost for words.

'Mr Longmore, do you have any further questions for the witness?' Judge Gower asked.

Still looking lost for words, Longmore answered, 'No, Your Honour.' Longmore had sat down.

'Mr Yell, do you have any further questions?' asked Judge Gower.

Nick stood up and addressed the judge: 'No further questions, Your Honour.'

'Captain Howard, you may leave the witness box.' Judge Gower paused and then addressed the court. 'We will adjourn proceedings for today. As discussed before, this hearing has long overrun its expected time, and there is another case due to start in this court. So, the final submissions from Mr Longmore and Mr Yell and their summing-up shall have to take place in my own court in Lewes next week. After that, I will be considering my verdict. Are there any objections to that?'

Both barristers stood and confirmed that there were no objections. Judge Gower then stood up.

The clerk also stood. 'All rise,' he called out.

Judge Gower bowed.

We all stood and bowed respectfully in response to the judge.

Judge Gower turned and left by the side door to his chambers. As he left the court, we all let out a subconscious sigh.

The tension had now been relieved. The three of us were smiling on the front bench with Catriona also smiling in the public seats just behind us.

We started collecting all our documents to pack back into the boxes. The day had gone very well for us.

I find it very strange that barristers can immediately be friendly with each other the moment a court rises. However, in this case, Ben's team were not particularly happy. That last question had been a huge own goal for Longmore. Ben looked particularly pissed off.

We now had to get down to Lewes in Sussex for the last couple of days. Then hopefully, with a judgement in our favour, it would be over. Thank goodness, these things are called a trial for good reason.

We arrived in Lewes in good time on Monday the following week and met in a coffee bar near the court. Nicholas Yell had come down from London on the train; Nick Munns and I had come down from Surrey by car.

The last few days in court were wrapping up some of the witnesses' testimonies and then the summing-up by Nicholas and Longmore. Longmore tried to introduce various strategies to divert attention away from the fundamental issues, but he was stopped by Judge

Gower. He said that these were irrelevant, making an indirect reference to my objections to Longmore's question about my funding. It was all highly amusing.

The last day was just the summing-up.

'Thank you, gentlemen, I am now going to retire and consider my verdict.' Judge Gower rose.

'All rise,' demanded the clerk.

We all stood. Judge Gower bowed to the court and we returned his bow. He then left the court.

All we could do now was wait for Judge Gower's decision.

We all left the court and returned to the coffee bar and spent a few hours chatting. We were all distracted, though. Nicholas Yell had spoken to the clerk who said he would call us 10 minutes before Judge Gower was ready to deliver his verdict.

This took four hours. One of the longest four hours of my life!

When we got the call and walked back to the court, it was a very long (short) walk. We sat down in the seats alongside the group sitting on the other side and awaited the arrival of the judge.

When he arrived into the court, we rose and bowed respectfully as he took his seat.

'This has been a very unusual case...' he began.

Having not been involved in a court case before this one, I had expected Judge Gower to deliver a verdict. What I had not anticipated was the judge's summing-up, which took a long time, somewhere around two hours. He then described the pros and cons of the case that contributed to the judgement that he had arrived at.

I had been sitting on the edge of my seat for almost five hours before he finally gave the verdict.

'Taking all this into account, I find for the plaintiff,' he finished.

Judge Gower then provided the detail of the decision. He awarded the original £12,500 outstanding under the contract. Interest was also due on the amount from the time that I had crossed the boundary of Nigerian airspace. On top of that, he awarded costs against them, so the eye-watering £30,000 I had spent would be repaid to me. I was struck dumb for a moment.

Nicholas Yell turned to me, nodded enthusiastically and quietly said, 'YES… YES!'

The three of us shook hands, smiling.

Longmore then stood up and addressed the judge, 'Your Honour, thank you for your decision. My client would like leave to appeal,' he finished.

'Mr Longmore, your leave to appeal is granted,' replied the judge.

I turned to Nicholas and asked what exactly that meant.

'It means they have twenty-one days to decide whether or not to take this to the Appeal Court in London,' replied Nicholas. 'We will have to wait until after that time to see if they are going to appeal.'

'God, I thought we had won!' I said. 'If they do appeal, how long will it take to get into the Court of Appeal?' I asked.

'Mmm, maybe another year,' Nicholas said thoughtfully. 'I am not sure how long cases take to get to court.'

'Oh God,' I said. 'So we won't know whether they will appeal and after that, if they do appeal, it won't get to court until around a year later?'

'That's about the score, Mike. Sorry,' he finished.

We left the court in Lewes happy, nevertheless. It had been a complex and difficult case to construct and present with very limited resources – basically with just the three of us. So, we were pleased with ourselves at the achievement.

Slade was not there at the court in Lewes. I would not have envied Longmore when he had to call Ben and break the news of the loss. I wondered whether to ring him and discuss the vagaries of 'flopping mops'!

CHAPTER 32

Summer 1985
Visiting the Families of Ken and Angus in Aberdeen

The whole process of taking Ben to Court took many years and during this process, there was a continued dialogue in the media about Ken and Angus. Most of it was incorrect, and they were blamed for getting involved – mostly citing monetary gain as the speculated reason. Also, that I had left them to their fate without caring.

All this type of incorrect media/editorial emphasis was incredibly frustrating.

Catriona and I spoke about this frequently. In the end, she suggested that I see Ken's and Angus's families in Scotland, hopefully to give the correct account of what had actually taken place.

'After all,' Catriona stated firmly, 'it is only *us* who actually know what was said between us. Ken and Angus cannot tell the truth to their families.'

She was, as is often the case (with the much derided 'female logic'), completely correct. It was in some ways an easy decision – at least I would be doing *something*!

I had absolutely no intention of defending my actions in Lagos. It was more important to give the families a clear face-to-face account of what had happened and precisely why Ken and Angus had helped us.

'Trouble is, whilst I agree with you, Coco, I'm not sure how well I would be received,' I replied. 'I will speak to the bosses at Bristows and see what they say. They are in contact with the families on a regular basis,' I continued. 'They can sound them out. I will go if the families agree to meet me.'

So, I did go over to Bristows and had a discussion about the proposal. The ball was set in motion.

At around that time, I had also been talking to the bosses at Fairflight in Biggin Hill to set up an executive jet, air ambulance department. They were persuaded to buy an HS125 (600 series). This was a later model of the Rolls-Royce-powered HS125s.

I actually made a bit of commission from selling the aircraft to them. This is incredibly difficult to achieve, and highly unusual. It was £12,500. This cash was very welcome to feed my 'wolves', keeping them from the door for a bit. The cost of the legal action had exceeded my available cash.

The aeroplane interior was remodelled so it could be converted from 'executive' mode into 'air ambulance' mode relatively easily.

We had to carry out various flight-testing at Biggin Hill to prove that it conformed to their noise requirements. Rolls-Royce Viper engines were very noisy, but I managed to construct a 'low noise departure' procedure that kept the noise to a decent level.

I did fly a trip with the directors of Fairflight to Malaga for a week in the new aircraft before it entered service properly. They accommodated me in Puerto Banús in Marbella for a week. It was basic accommodation but okay.

Gordon and Reg were both ex-British Airways pilots as well as running Fairflight, but they did not fly very much, so one of them sat in the co-pilot's seat each way. This was fine with me – as you know, I can fly the aeroplane on my own!

Some other news arrived around this time. It was not long after the end of the hearing in Lewes, and within the 21 days, Nick Munns called to tell me that Shirlstar were going to appeal.

This was very bad news. Apparently, Nicholas Yell had said it was going to cost £13,000. Ouch! I had spent all my available cash on the first hearing, so now I did not have a bean.

The commission on the HS125 was just enough to feed those pesky wolves. Anyway, it would not get into the Court of Appeal for at least another year, so that problem was for another day. That fucking 'mop' might get me in the end!

After a week or so, I got an answer back that the families in Aberdeen would meet me. It had taken some time to reach agreement because Angus's family, in particular, were in two minds as to whether they wanted to. In the end, it was agreed.

Getting there was the only problem.

My dad, Roy, was still working for Air Anglia out of Norwich Airport. I spoke to him about my plans and drove up to stay with Mum and Dad for a couple of days. Roy was travelling up to Aberdeen taking the early morning schedule from Norwich to Aberdeen on the day that I had arranged to meet the families.

It was difficult to see my parents due to work commitments, but it was good to see them. I spoke to them most days on the phone, though. They liked to keep in touch with the developments – both the ups and downs in my life. It was never dull being Mike's parent!

We went down to the White Lodge restaurant. It was just a short drive from The Willows, the home where they had lived since 1969 when Roy left the RAF.

The White Lodge do a wonderful roast buffet. It was a family tradition to make a beeline there for lunch when I visited. It was a great opportunity to update them on the latest situation and what I was expecting from the visit to Aberdeen. We discussed the news from Lagos and how Ken and Angus were doing – which was still not good.

I also told them about the flight to Vigo and the 'revenge'. Hopefully a lesson learnt by P.D. Both Mum and Dad were highly amused at the description of the flight, and we were all amazed at the 'coincidence'.

(As you know, I do not believe in such coincidences!) And as Ben Slade/Shirlstar had appealed the decision, there was now the question of funding the appeal.

'I can give you the money for the appeal, Mike,' Roy said.

Roy had always been very supportive. As you know, he had originally paid for my instructor's rating, the commercial pilot licence course and after that the instrument rating; all very expensive training undertakings.

The instrument rating is another of those hurdles that a prospective pilot has to cross over. It is a flying exam which my wife describes as 'having to drive down the centre lane of a busy motorway blindfolded, juggling six oranges and reciting the times tables whilst having a conversation on your mobile phone' – apart from that, it is easy.

'No thanks, Roy, that is very kind, but I will sort it out myself,' I explained. 'Thing is, if it all goes wrong, you will not get your money back. At the present time, if it goes wrong for me, it will be the difference between falling off the World Trade Centre or the Empire State Building, so best you keep your cash, but thank you very much for the offer, it is much appreciated.'

We all laughed at my analogy – you see, I *am* funny, Victoria is wrong! Mind you, this analogy would not work now, post 9/11.

I then told them that, in fact, Charles Gaskill, my ever-patient NatWest bank manager, had offered to help me.

Charles had asked for an update on the court case and was very pleased to hear that I had won. When I explained to Charles about the appeal, he offered to stand the (bank's) money to finance it.

I relayed the conversation that I'd had with Charles to Mum and Dad.

'But, Charles,' I said, 'if I lose, there is no way I can pay the money back. It will bankrupt me!' I was emphatic about the possible outcome.

'Don't worry, Mike,' he replied. 'NatWest is getting rid of proper managers like me. They have offered me a pay-off for early retirement. I can lend you the thirteen thousand pounds; it is within my branch limit. If it all goes wrong, I will field the shit that results from it.' He grinned. 'So, there is not much they can do about it if I am leaving, and I'm sure you are going to win anyway.'

I was very lucky that I had fantastic support from family and friends during this whole episode in my life.

We continued our lunch, chatting about various aspects of my life at that point, including the situation with Catriona.

The next day, very early, Roy and I set off for Norwich Airport. The departure for the Edinburgh to Aberdeen schedule was 07:00. As captain, Roy had to be there at least an hour before. I knew all the cabin crew at Air Anglia having worked at Norwich for those early years. It was great to catch up with the girls on the flight.

When we arrived at Aberdeen, I said goodbye to Roy and that I'd see him later (if I survived the day).

It was a strange feeling getting into a taxi and giving Ken's address. There was trepidation, but I was not nervous as such. My inner feelings were that no matter how I felt, it did not in any way compare to Ken and Angus's situation. However, as we got closer to the address, the adrenaline began to flow; I had no idea what to expect, but I did know it would probably not be warm reception. I had to focus on breathing slowly and deeply to control the resulting 'fight or flight' instinct.

The taxi stopped outside the detached house in a residential road. I paid the driver and kept his card to call when I wanted to return to the airport. I had an open ticket back to Norwich, as I did not want to set a limit on the time spent with the families.

I had been seriously advised not to go and do this by many friends, but, in the end, Catriona was right. They needed to hear what had happened directly from me.

I walked up the drive and went to ring the bell, but the door opened in anticipation of my arrival.

'I am Cathy, Ken's wife, please come in.' She spoke with a soft voice, but her face looked like the granite stone of the surrounding mountains.

'Thank you,' I replied and stepped in through the door.

'This way.' She indicated with her hand to a doorway.

I stepped into the large living room which was packed full, with about twenty people, some seated and some standing. There were mostly men but a few women as well as Ken's wife.

She pointed to a seat opposite the throng. They were sitting in various chairs and seating, some clearly brought in to accommodate the numbers. Many of Angus's family had come up from Glasgow for the meeting with me.

It was an incredibly intimidating situation. You've probably heard the stories about the rough parts of Glasgow and the type of people who live there. Well, what I was confronted with was the epitome of those types characterised by the old joke quoted earlier in the book: 'Aay, *can ye sue? Sssshhhe!* (Sound of a razor being slashed!) Well, steeeetch thaaaat!' (Please read with a broad, deep Glaswegian accent.)

As I sat down in the seat, the antagonism in the room was palpable and threatening.

One of the older men sitting opposite started:

'You fuckin' just left them there to be picked up after you went,' he snarled in a strong Glaswegian accent. 'You deserve a beating for what you did.' He looked *very* capable of delivering such a beating very efficiently.

The other guy next to him chipped in with a similar vein,

'Aye, you didna geeve a sheet,' he said, sneering at me.

Expecting this kind of reception, I had carefully prepared my first words. These came from the heart.

'I am here to talk to you about what happened in Lagos,' I started. I looked around at the room, making sure I made eye contact with the entire assembled group.

'You can throw rocks at me, beat the shit out of me, do what you like. I do not care... but that is what I am here to do.'

I spoke slowly and deliberately, maintaining a calm exterior. The same could not be said for the interior.

This appeared to disarm some of the anger in the room, as it became apparent that it was not an easy thing for me to do. I had to be very brave and convinced of my ground to do it.

'Apart from the appearance on *TV-am*, I have not given any interviews with any news organisation. Anything that has been printed has been made up. On the advice of the Foreign Office, I have not defended any incorrect information that has been published because it *may* have had a detrimental effect on the behind the scenes negotiations with the Nigerians to get Ken and Angus released.' I let this sink in and waited for the assembled group to respond.

'So, why did they help you at all if you were just going to take off, causing such a stir?' Ken's wife asked softly. 'I just do not understand.' She ended sounding very sad.

'I am truly very sorry. Very sorry to you all,' I responded earnestly. 'From the bottom of my heart, I am truly sorry for what has happened.' I paused again to let the apology sink in. 'This must be the most awful situation for you all, particularly you wives, not knowing how or when this can come to an end and bring Ken and Angus home.'

I then started to explain some of the things that had happened in Lagos before I took off. Of course, they were not aware of our negotiations with Hyacinth Odigwe and my attempts to negotiate through him with the new military government.

They, of course, had no idea about this and had all assumed, due to the publicity, that I had just turned up and conned Ken and Angus into helping me, and then that I'd just buggered off leaving them to take whatever flack occurred after I had gone.

Addressing Ken's wife directly, I said, 'Ken and I worked together in Miri (Borneo) for nine months and he looked after the Bristows HS125 out there. We were all good friends. You met me there and knew me pretty well from that time in Borneo. That may help you to judge my character.'

I then turned to Angus's wife, 'Angus is very close friends with Ken. He just wanted to help,' I said. 'Catriona and I were in danger. Basically, they just wanted to help. There was no money involved,' I explained.

I then explained the background to the contract with Shirlstar and Prince Olori's money that had gone missing in Lagos when Graham Bott handed it over to the bunkering company. Also, Vanni's meeting in London and the offer to be let off the debt to Slade to obtain release of Olori's jet, and that these factors led to Catriona's life, as well as my own, being threatened. Finally, I told them about the warning by Hyacinth Odigwe, head of the CAA in Lagos.

'Ken, Angus and I discussed the warning by Hyacinth Odigwe and what it meant,' I explained. 'We discussed this at great length. The option for Catriona and me was to leave by scheduled airline, but there was a very high risk that we would be abducted – it has happened before. The real problem regarding the airport is that Vanni had a lot of contacts there. This was the risk. We did not know how close Vanni and Olori were to locating us.'

I paused to see if there were any questions from the families, but they were listening intently. I noted that Angus's family were also listening and had downgraded the very aggressive look to just aggressive.

'When we discussed the options, we all decided that, taking everything into consideration, taking off without permission was the best.' I then explained that I had told Ken and Angus how worried I was about the consequences for them if I took off. 'I asked, what will happen to you guys when the shit hits the fan and you've been seen with me sorting out the aircraft?'

I paused before continuing to explain that both Ken and Angus had been emphatic that we were in danger and they would have to help:

'Och, they will kick up a fuss, but it will die down over a few days. You know what it's like here!' I said, repeating what Angus had said. I added, 'Ken had agreed wholeheartedly, as he said, "Yes, there is no debate about this, Mike, you need to get out of here quick. We will be okay."'

I then explained about the Nigerian military jet waiting for us on a Saturday evening and his attempt to shoot us down:

'I did not understand this at all,' I explained. 'But with the attempted kidnapping of Dikko in London by the Nigerians, it began to make a little sense,' I said. 'Clearly, the fact that the kidnapping plot was foiled and the diplomatic tsunami occurring has made everything a hundred times worse for Ken and Angus.'

Again, I paused to take in the reactions of the families. There were no real questions; they were still listening intently to all that I was saying.

'I feel a huge responsibility for what has happened,' I stated flatly. 'There were a lot of external events taking place that were not in my control which have had a major effect on what has happened.' Again, I paused; I did not want to rush what I was saying. 'So, to describe how I feel, it would be a *huge responsibility* but not directly my fault, if that makes sense… If I had not been there, this would not have happened, but external influences have made this situation dreadful.'

I went on to explain my contacts with the Foreign Office and Bristows, as well as my attempts to swap myself with Ken and Angus, both through official and unofficial channels.

'All these have been refused. When the kidnappers were caught, I think the Nigerians reacted by jailing Ken and Angus. When I tried to swap myself for them, the feedback from both directions was that the Nigerian government had got itself into a situation which it could not see a way out of whilst maintaining some sort of dignity,' I concluded, my voice shaking.

At this point, my composure fell apart. I was very tearful and could not contain myself. All the deep feelings of responsibility surfaced. I cried. It took me a few minutes to pull myself together.

'There was never at any time a question of money in exchange for what Ken and Angus did. They helped because they knew we were in danger. That danger was real, and I stand by what we felt was the right thing to do,' I continued. 'The reports that there was money involved are completely and utterly false.'

I did add that Barry Glover tried to get involved with a payment when I first arrived in Lagos, but that I had turned him down. This did get a giggle from Ken's and Angus's wives. Barry had that reputation.

We all then had a general discussion that related to the information I had given. My description of my efforts to swap myself for Ken and Angus had helped them all understand how I felt and what I was prepared to do to help.

We also discussed the events in London and Stansted. Some of the family members had completely missed the significance of catching the kidnappers at Stansted. When the jail terms in Lagos matched those in London, they began to see the link. This link was obvious when you saw how the two events mirrored each other.

I had been there for about four hours and was eventually given a cup of tea. That meant the antagonistic atmosphere had more or less subsided.

'Ken and Angus will confirm what I have said today when they get home,' I said towards the end of my visit. 'I will continue to keep in touch with the Foreign Office and Bristows. If I hear anything of any significance, I will get in touch immediately.'

I did not want any of them to think that this was the end of the matter having been up to see them. Whilst we did not all leave as firm friends; I did not get the shit kicked out of me. I did feel that although it was a very difficult thing to do, Catriona had been right. It was the right thing to do.

I got a taxi back to Aberdeen Airport and was able to catch the last Air Anglia flight back to Norwich. I arrived back late to my parents' house in Attleborough. They were waiting up for me – it was very touching. I gave them a summary of what had happened during the day.

Eventually, long after midnight, I collapsed exhausted into my bed. An hour later, I awoke to find myself 'hand walking' around the walls of the bedroom.

'For fuck's sake!' I said out loud. I had to do something about this!

CHAPTER 33

Autumn 1985
Air Ambulance Flying and More Sleepwalking

So, eventually G-FFLT was all ready for its new role as an air ambulance aircraft. It was very successful. There was a healthy market for this type of aircraft, and we were very busy.

I was the only captain initially, as the other pilots in Fairflight had to be trained on the plane type. A couple had been flying Bernie Ecclestone's Lear 35 jet – but this, as they say, is another story. They had jet experience but needed to be qualified on the HS125.

My only problem was my first officer. Peter Coster was not a 'Jeremy Palmer III'. Peter had started flying later in life and had been my first officer on the Shorts 330. He was a short, rotund chap with quite grey hair. His shirts tended to be under a lot of pressure as his stomach tried to escape. The one huge problem that he did have was intensely unpleasant body odour. I had to deal with this very early on in our flying together. I was not going to dress it up.

'Peter,' I began, 'we are going to be flying some VIP passengers as well as the air ambulance flights,' I said. 'There is no easy way to say this, but you have a horrendous body odour problem. If I go back to the far end of the cabin, I can still smell it. That means all the passengers can smell it, and that is no good.'

Peter looked shocked and a bit dismayed. I do not believe he knew that he smelt that bad. Clearly nobody, neither friends nor family, had ever mentioned it to him. I do admit to having been very brutal, though.

'I do not know why you have the problem, Peter, but you will not be continuing to act as first officer unless something is done about it.'

Peter continued to look shocked, but he could now see his first 'jet job' in his aviation career disappearing before his very eyes!

'If you want to stay on this aeroplane, Peter, firstly you need to have a shower *every* morning. Next, I am going to give you a piece of advice that was given to me when I was eighteen by a very experienced pilot. Buy a very good deodorant, an expensive one, not a cheap one. Cheap ones smell like cat's pee after a few hours! You get what you pay for where deodorants are concerned,' I finished.

Peter did what I had suggested.

Whilst the HS125 was a terrific shock for him, the speed that everything happens and the wide variation of challenges that faced us, particularly on the air ambulance flights, Peter became a competent and diligent first officer, and we became a very good team.

He was with me on *another* epic flight when I had both engines fail at four in the morning on the way into Gatwick, which I am sure you are interested to hear about.

This started out of Biggin Hill to Thessaloniki in Greece to pick up an injured girl who had fallen (probably pissed) down some stairs and broken her leg very badly. She had been patched up by the local Greek hospital and then cleared by the insurance company to get her home.

Couple of tips here: firstly, get really good holiday insurance. Secondly, never ride scooters on holiday, especially after drinking.

I had to pick up some terribly badly injured people during these air ambulance flights, as was the case after Thessaloniki. The next stop was the island of Kos in Greece to pick up two patients, one a young girl who had been on the back of a scooter and come off.

Her boyfriend had persuaded her it was 'cool' not to use a helmet. This was a massive mistake. When she came off the scooter, she

287

suffered severe head injuries. The hospital had done what they could, but it was really outside their range of abilities. Again, the insurance company decided her best chance was to get her back to the UK to a specialist hospital.

One of the two doctors went to the hospital in Kos to supervise her transport to the airport with one of the two nurses.

While they were away, I set about getting G-FFLT refuelled. This turned into a drama. The fuel bowser broke down. Bollocks!

I knew that the patient coming was in a very bad way, so ideally I wanted to get her back to Gatwick as soon as possible. Getting from Kos to Gatwick without stopping for a refuel was a challenge. My main concern was getting away as soon as possible and doing so with the maximum possible amount of fuel on board.

The refuellers offered to hand pump fuel for me from a standby fuel bowser. I eagerly agreed. This had a couple of advantages. As they were hand pumping into one wing, I could use the aircraft fuel pumps to transfer this to the other wing and into the tail fuel tanks.

I will not bore you with lots of esoteric aviation language, but every nook and cranny in G-FFLT was full of 'motion lotion' by the time we had finished.

I also popped up to the tower where we got permission from the Turkish radar controller in Izmir, just down the road from Kos, to give us immediate climb to 41,000 feet. Normally, they would stick you at under 30,000 feet until well into Turkish airspace when flying out of Greek airspace. (The Greeks and the Turks do not get on particularly well after all that trouble in Cyprus!) But tonight, with a bit of sweet-talking, the Turks gave us some welcome help.

I got back to the aircraft just as the ambulance arrived. The doctor jumped out of the ambulance looking very concerned. I knew these guys very well; they were very experienced in what was a very specialised area of medicine.

'Mike, we have got a serious problem here,' he said as he approached me. 'The patient was on a ventilator and in a bad way when we picked her up from the hospital, but she has died in the ambulance on the way here.'

The poor girl had lost a significant part of her skull in the accident as well as sustaining other serious injuries.

'I'm not sure what to do, Mike,' he continued. 'Her mother is in the ambulance with her. I have not informed her yet; the ventilator makes her look like she is still alive.' He paused for a moment. 'Trouble is, if we declare her dead here, it will take months and months to get her home. I wanted to see how you feel about taking her back to the UK, still on the ventilator, and declaring her death in the UK?'

'Mmm, have you done this before?' I asked.

'Yes, once. It was in a similar situation. It is a grey area,' he concluded with a slight tilt of the head.

After a moment's thought, I made a decision: 'I do not have a problem with it, but we will have to tell the girl's mother,' I said. 'Shall I tell her? She will have to be a passenger with her daughter on my aeroplane, so I will have to explain that – I am happy to do this.'

'If you are happy to, Mike,' he answered. 'Normally, I would inform the next of kin.'

'I will,' I replied. 'I'd be happier if I spoke to her. Can you get her out of the ambulance, and I will have a chat with her now.'

So, the doctor brought over the girl's mother, and I then explained the situation:

'This is very difficult. I am so sorry to tell you, but the doctor has informed me that your daughter has died as a result of her injuries in the ambulance on the way from the hospital to the airport,' I said in a soft voice.

She started crying.

The poor lady must have been going through hell since the injury, probably sitting with her daughter in the hospital. She would have known the extent of her injuries. Being told this in a chilly parking area of a deserted Greek airport at midnight must have been awful.

'The problem is that I am not allowed to carry a person on board my aeroplane who has passed away. What the doctor has said to me is that if he does declare your daughter as passed away here in Greece, it will take you months and a lot of expense to get her back to England,' I continued. 'We have an option here, as your daughter is on the ventilator, if the doctor does not take her off it, she can remain effectively "alive" until we reach Gatwick.' Again, I stopped talking to let the whole thing sink in.

It was a very difficult situation. The poor lady would have to sit next to her daughter on a long flight back to Gatwick, knowing her beautiful daughter was lying dead beside her. Having said that, once she had composed herself, we discussed the options and the reasons for offering her the decision. The doctor was standing beside me while I spoke to her. He put an arm around the lady's shoulder to comfort her.

She decided to go with the option to take her daughter home.

After we loaded the stretcher onto the aeroplane, I got Peter to call for permission to start the engines.

Once everything was secure, I jumped into the captain's seat and started the engines. I made sure it was a short taxi out onto the runway so as not to waste any fuel on the ground. We took off and headed almost straight away into Turkish airspace having thanked the Kos air traffic controller for all his help.

Three hours or so later, at around four in the morning, we were passing over Calais. It was the most breathtakingly beautiful night. They say 'gin-clear', but this morning it was an understatement. I could see Gatwick's runway from France.

The French air traffic controller handed me over to London Control, who cleared me direct to Gatwick for a 'straight in approach with no delay'. Bueno! Just what I wanted to hear.

I had been at very high altitude and in very cold air to get the best range out of G-FFLT, and this had worked. My planned fuel on landing covered all the legal minimums laid down by the glorious Civil Aviation Authority.

Unfortunately, things now started to go wrong...

I could see Gatwick's terminal lights in the far distance and asked air traffic control for descent clearance. We carried out the checks required before descent and Peter, who was 'pilot flying' on the way back, reduced the thrust of the engines. G-FFLT then began to lose altitude from our final cruising altitude of 41,000 feet.

When you reduce the thrust on an engine, the fuel flow also reduces; if there are any water droplets in the fuel, they can crystallise on the fuel filters. On the HS125, there is a system that automatically pumps a bit of methanol (alcohol) into the fuel filter area, which melts the ice very efficiently.

Before descending, we manually select the pump to send some methanol into the filter area before selecting automatic. This ensures that the filters are clear of ice at the beginning of descent. I *always* used to stick my finger into the methanol tank up in the tail before each flight to ensure that it was full – there was no indication in the flight deck to show the methanol level.

A few minutes into the descent, the right-hand fuel filter light illuminated along with the bright amber CAGS – as mentioned earlier, the Central Attention Getting System.

I cancelled the CAGS and frowned. I'd never seen this light come on except momentarily after a long flight at very low temperatures. This had been a long flight at minus 67 degrees. Problem was that the bloody light did not go out when I pumped the methanol into the filters.

'Mmm, Peter, that is strange,' I said. 'I will select manual again and see if it goes out.'

I did this, but the light stubbornly still would not extinguish. In all the drama at Kos, I had still checked that the methanol tank was full, so there was definitely no doubt there.

While I was thinking about the indication, the CAGS started flashing again. I looked to the instrument panel and saw that the left-hand fuel filter light had now come on.

'Shit!' I said out loud. 'We have a problem, Peter.'

I repeated the selection of manual to no effect. I was guessing that there was some kind of water contamination in the fuel from the refuelling in Kos.

'If I am correct, we have got a load of water in the fuel, Peter, and that means our engines are not going to work properly,' I said seriously. 'You carry on flying it, and I'm just going to see how much power we have available.' I slowly advanced the thrust levers from idle to about half of maximum.

The engines responded by completely failing. This is called a 'flame out' in the business. A situation where both engines fail is very rare indeed (a very undesirable aircraft state) – that's why we have two!

I immediately selected 'idle' with the thrust levers. The ignition system in the engines relit the jet engines, so at 'idle thrust' the engines were operating normally – well, sort of.

'Peter, stating the obvious, we are in an emergency situation. As you saw, both engines failed if I increased power but are operating normally at idle power.'

I was reviewing the situation out loud for both of our benefits, 'We can see Gatwick, so I am thinking that we have to treat this as a deadstick landing.'

A deadstick landing is an old RAF term for 'no engines operating' that had been inherited by civil aviation from the RAF:

'What I am thinking is that you should carry on flying, and I will monitor and advise you with changes to speed and or flaps as we proceed. We will aim for the far end of the runway as a touchdown point. We can move that touchdown point nearer to the halfway point of the runway as we get closer. Are you happy with that, Peter?'

'Yes I am, Mike,' he replied.

Peter and I discussed the plan and reviewed any other possible options. He could not think of anything else to improve the situation. Although it was tempting for me to take control and fly the aeroplane, we both felt it gave me much better judgement of our approach if I was not occupied with actually handling the aeroplane. Actually, if I had started flying it, Peter would have effectively been 'along for the ride', as he was not very experienced on the jet. With him flying, both of us continued as a crew, communicating between us about the progress and decision-making.

'Okay, Peter, I will make a Mayday call to let ATC know. I do not propose to tell the passengers at this moment; I will talk to them a bit later.'

'Mayday, Mayday, Mayday. London… Golf Foxtrot Foxtrot Lima Tango, we have a double engine failure, possibly due to fuel contamination, and will be carrying out a no-engines approach to Gatwick. Request handover to Gatwick Radar as soon as possible to coordinate approach.'

'Golf Lima Tango, Mayday is copied at time zero four thirty-two hours. Contact Gatwick Radar on one two six decimal two five. Best of luck!'

I called Gatwick:

'Gatwick Radar, Mayday Golf Foxtrot Foxtrot Lima Tango is visual with Runway Two Six Left and carrying out a glide approach. Obviously, we do not have any capacity to make a go-around from this approach. And we cannot accept any delay.'

'Golf Lima Tango, the Mayday information has been passed to us from London. Emergency services have been advised. Do you need any further assistance?'

It is always difficult for air traffic controllers. They are in an air-conditioned room, remote from the drama at the end of a radio, so feel impotent and rather helpless. Having said that, when it all goes wrong, they are the usually the only ones left at the following board of enquiry!

'Negative. We have two doctors and two nurses on board with a load of medical equipment. If we don't make the runway, I'm sure we will be able to look after ourselves!'

There was a slight laugh as a reply. As a regular visitor to Gatwick, my voice was recognisable. In the past, I was in and out of Gatwick every night, so they had been subjected to my sense of humour. I am sure that the controller repeated that incident a few times afterwards.

Peter and I were discussing progress all the way down. The technique was to keep the far end of the runway in the centre of the windshield. As it moved down in the windscreen (meaning we were getting high), we could increase speed a bit to correct it. If it moved the other way, we could decrease speed a little.

As we got closer to Gatwick at a lower altitude, the judgement of maintaining the correct flight path became more difficult. The trouble is that you naturally tend to lean towards staying high rather than too low (remember the three rules?). Problem is, if you go too high, there is a chance you would finish up going off the far end of the runway, smashing into all those expensive runway approach lights and the hedge, missing the runway altogether. This would be rather embarrassing (and an undesirable aircraft state).

I started to use the wing flaps and undercarriage to control the approach path. The judgement about when to select the flap and gear was difficult, as once this was done, you are committed, and the aircraft will then come down at a much steeper angle.

It worked out well. (Obviously, as I didn't crash because I am still here!) Peter flew it well, and I cross-checked with him before selecting the flap/gear. The final stage of flap and the most effective stage was lowered more or less over the beginning of the runway. G-FFLT touched down in the centre of the runway.

The whole incident was conducted in a very calm atmosphere. As I taxied in to the apron, two ambulances were waiting to transport the two patients (one being the poor girl who had passed away), and I sort of wondered about the whole incident. It seemed to be a slight anti-climax. The question floating around in my head was: *Was that really a big drama?*

'I'm just going to start the APU, Peter,' I said. 'We'll see what the APU does.'

The APU started and ran for about 90 seconds, and then ran down as the contaminated fuel reached it. That confirmed any of my doubts.

The last patient was going up to Manchester to a hospital near her home, so G-FFLT was planned to be taken up to Manchester by another crew, captained by Keith Faulkner.

I said goodbye to the mother of the dead girl. She thanked me for being straightforward with her and for all the help. I also said goodbye to the doctors and nurses. None of them were aware of the additional drama of the night. I had decided that it was not worth worrying them as all it would have achieved is some very scared passengers without it altering the outcome.

Keith Faulkner was waiting at the edge of the apron, not wanting to get in the way. Keith was waiting to take the aircraft off to Manchester on the next trip.

I went over to explain what had happened, assuming that G-FFLT would be grounded to drain all the tanks and the fuel pumps checked for damage.

'No, bollocks to that,' he said. 'Gordon (the managing director) would be furious. We'll get it looked at in Manchester.'

Of course, this was Fairflight, not known for the following of rules, especially if it meant losing money!

'I wouldn't do it, matey,' I replied. 'You have no idea how much water is in there.'

'Thing is, Mike, it will be filled with fuel now, and whatever is in there will be stirred up and mixed with neat fuel. It will be fine,' Keith replied happily. 'By the way, please do not file any Mandatory Occurrence Report for today,' he stated flatly.

I was cross at this very unprofessional behaviour; at that moment I decided that I'd had enough. It was time to move on and join an airline to get away from the 'general aviation' scene.

Shortly after this, I did join Britannia Airways (now Thomsonfly/TUI Airways) flying Boeing 737, 757 and 767s, who were professional, with an exceptionally high standard of pilot training and operation of the aeroplanes. It was great to be in this sort of environment. What a relief.

Not long after joining Britannia, I finished up in Kos again in the early hours, this time refuelling a 737 ready for the trip back to Gatwick. It was the same refuellers and they (obviously) remembered me.

'Ere, you buggers were trying to kill me that night!' I said, grinning all over my face. I went on to explain what had happened on the trip back to Gatwick.

'We are very sorry, Captain,' the lead refueller said (I was now a lowly first officer, of course). 'It must have been because the main bowser was broken. The normal bowser cuts the refuelling automatically if there is more than one part per million of water, and we check every day by doing tests.'

He was rather upset by my tale, but I reassured him that I was not bothered and knew it was 'one of those things'.

You may remember that a similar thing happened to a British Airways Boeing 777 in January 2008. It landed just short of the runway at Heathrow after being refuelled in Beijing. Mmm, embarrassing!

It was now 6am I went home exhausted and went to bed, falling asleep very quickly. Soon after that, I found myself walking the walls of my bedroom again and sweating profusely. It was 7:30.

'Bollocks! An hour and a half sleep!'

I got back into bed but again went to sleep only to find myself doing the same. It was 9 am.

'Bollocks, bollocks, bollocks. I am going to sort this out.'

Clearly, continuous subconscious preoccupation was behind this.

CHAPTER 34

Sorting out PTSD

As I mentioned earlier, because of Catriona's anorexia/bulimia and psychological distress, I had frequent contact with Linda, a bereavement counsellor. This had developed into a close friendship.

One of the main reasons for seeing Linda was Catriona's frequent threats of suicide and general destructive behaviour. If she had been successful in carrying out these threats, I did not want to feel responsible, having done everything I possibly could to help her.

The frequent interactions had prompted an interest in psychology, so I began studying the subject in some depth.

I explained to Linda what was happening and asked her advice about what to do.

'PTSD is a problem that frequently occurs after a traumatic event. Often, people do not realise that it is actually PTSD they are suffering from.' she explained. 'Your situation was so dramatic at the time and the preoccupation has been extended over a long period because of the situation with Ken and Angus. Along with your deep feelings of responsibility, your PTSD has become more exaggerated.'

'So, what can I do to help myself?' I asked.

Linda frowned and thought for a minute.

'I think you are going to have to undergo extensive hypnotherapy to sort this out, Mike. I do not get involved in hypnotherapy; it is a different specialisation.'

'God, how do I find the right person to do that?' I asked. 'Do you know anybody?'

'No, but I will make some enquiries for you. I am sure that I can find someone.'

A few days later, Linda rang me and gave me the number of a guy called Paul Cross:

'He comes very highly recommended, Mike. He's an ex-CID detective who has retired and gone into the area of hypnotherapy,' she explained.

'Great, thank you very much, Linda, I will call him straight away.'

I called Paul Cross and went to see him very shortly afterwards. He lived in Tunbridge Wells, which was a half-hour drive away.

Paul was a typical policeman type with that air of no-nonsense they often carried with them. He was quite tall with the easy and confident movement that came with a long career of 'containing scrotes', as he delicately put it.

Paul had light brown hair cut short with very dark brown eyes. He also had a few scars dotted around his face, no doubt injuries sustained while 'containing one of those scrotes'!

I will not give a blow-by-blow account of this because it will bore you to death. But it was a very interesting experience. And it worked – I cannot tell you the relief I felt about having a normal night's sleep!

I had some sixty plus sessions with Paul. To begin with, it was a rather strange experience. People tend to imagine that hypnosis is like that shown on stage and you can be made to do something you do not want to do. Nothing could be further from the truth. Hypnosis is a state of extreme relaxation.

The best way of explaining hypnosis is that it's the point just before you actually fall asleep. This is the state you're in when hypnotised. In this state, you are able to access your subconscious, so the therapist directs your contact with that subconscious.

Paul was great at this, as he said once during the therapy:

'It really helps to have a background in the CID to do this. As a hypnotherapist, a lot of the work I do in therapy requires in-depth detective work.' He joked, but it was true.

We gradually zeroed in on the centre of the problem. This was carried out with various 'creative visualisations. This was just a way of getting the subconscious to allow us to access hidden memories.

I encountered some very disturbing and upsetting things during this therapy. The sleepwalking did reduce, but it did not stop.

We concentrated on a particular memory buried deeply, hidden away deep down. This memory was so upsetting that I simply could not confront it, even under deep hypnosis. It became a joint effort to try to retrieve it. Paul and I were both fascinated and frustrated because the moment I got close, I started shaking and sweating and was clearly very distressed. On coming out of the hypnosis, it took a little while to recover.

Imagine being alone in a dimly lit corridor in a very old house with a door in front of you. Behind the door is the most frightening thing you can ever imagine. You know you need to open the door to confront whatever is on the other side, but you become petrified with fear.

This is what it was like, except I had absolutely no clue what was on the other side. It became a matter of intellectual interest for both Paul and I to find the answer. Eventually, Paul had a brainwave.

'Remote writing,' he announced in a triumphant tone.

'What the fuck is that?' I asked.

'I put you under hypnosis with your eyes open, and you have a pad and pen in your hand and we ask your subconscious to write what the memory is, but you do not come into direct contact with the memory,' he explained. 'It is an unusual way of communicating with the subconscious but has worked. I have been in contact with the professor who I trained with, and he suggested it.'

'Let's give it a go,' I replied. 'Should be interesting!'

After so many sessions of hypnosis, it did not take very long for me to reach the required state. The difference now was after becoming hypnotised, Paul asked me to open my eyes. Once I did so, it was very peculiar. Rather like looking through misty binoculars. You could see everything but at the same time were strangely detached.

'Mike, I am going to put a pen in your hand and a writing pad in your lap. Is that okay?' he asked.

'Yes,' I replied. I heard my voice as if it was in another room.

'When you are ready, I want you to write on the pad what it is that's upsetting you. While you are writing, you will not be aware of the words that you are writing,' he said.

Shortly afterwards, my hand began to move.

Now this really was fucking weird. I could see my hand moving but had no connection with it at all. It was like watching a robot hand moving, forming letters.

When Paul brought me out of the hypnosis, we both looked at the paper. The writing was tiny. The words were imperceptible. There was definitely 'the' and 'and' dotted about, but we could not make any sense of it.

'Mmm, clearly we need to ask for very large writing on the next attempt,' Paul said. 'But we definitely have something written down. Just can't make out what it says… We'll have another go and ask for the text in giant letters – that should give us legible writing. How do you feel?' he asked.

'It wasn't too bad. There was an element of anxiety, but it was nothing like before,' I replied.

So, we tried again. Once I was under hypnosis, Paul gave the instruction to write in giant letters. It worked. It was very laborious;

I watched through my 'dusty binoculars' with detached interest as the letters formed. The letters looked huge, but I could not read the words. I felt anxious as I watched.

Soon, my hand stopped moving and the writing came to an end.

Paul brought me out of the hypnotic state again.

We looked at the writing. It was still small and spidery in appearance but now legible. We both read it at the same time.

It went: *When I was little and I wet the bed, my nan locked me in the cupboard under the stairs. I did not mean to wet the bed. I was scared of the alligators under the bed and didn't want my leg to be bitten off. So I could not go to the toilet. It was very dark in the cupboard, and I wanted to find the door.*

'Aha,' said Paul, 'that explains a lot… I think this sleepwalking goes back to these events. Can you remember any of this, Mike?' he asked.

'Not a thing,' I replied. 'But it must have been traumatic.' I felt the effect of adrenaline.

'Aha!' said Paul triumphantly. 'Rufus!' He began searching back through the extensive notes of our sessions.

The 'detective' Paul then made a series of connections from this to being bullied in boarding school that we had discussed weeks before.

I was sent to Midhurst Grammar School, a boarding school, when I was 11 years old. It was a traumatic experience. How parents can send their children to boarding school at six or seven years old is beyond me!

In the first-year dormitory there were 12 boys who slept on small wrought-iron beds. This was *Lord of the Flies* territory. If you did not bully someone *with* the 'pack', then you got bullied yourself. So, I finished up the one being bullied.

What happened was, as soon as the lights went out, the other 11 boys would jump on my bed, drag me out and kick the shit out of me. Nice.

When I went home for half-term, I spent the whole time constructing a self-defence weapon. This was in the form of an alligator-shaped soft toy. It had a long nose and long tail all heavily sewn. The tail was stuffed towards the end with papier mâché and lead fishing weights in the very tip of the tail to give it a bit of extra weight.

I called him Rufus, and my mum actually made a collar for him with the name embroidered onto it.

The boys took the piss, of course:

'What's Howard got? A little toy? Softie!'

I said nothing, but when the lights went out and they started coming for me, I jumped up and whirled this thing around my head fighting off the assaults, chasing them as they hopped over the metal beds, like some human Grand National, stinging their legs and backsides. The bullying stopped that night.

Actually, I was a very mischievous boy at Midhurst Grammar School and got into lots of trouble (possibly the subject of another book). I almost had my own seat outside the headmaster's office.

For example: I *did* put phosphorus on the radiator in the classroom, causing that fire. I *did* put potassium crystals on the plate of the Bunsen burner, filling the chemistry lab with noxious fumes, and I also mixed it with glycerine to make a bomb. I *did* put iodine crystals in the swimming pool, turning it purple. And (with my partner in crime, Andrew Turner-Cross) I *did* bury calcium carbide crystals into a hole in the school football pitch, wetting it with urine to produce hydrogen, which we lit. It was very entertaining to see police and fire engines trying to work out where the flaming gas was coming from (North Sea Gas had just been found, producing some ideas). But I want to make something absolutely clear, *it was not me who blew up the groundsman's hut – that was David Marshal!*

'So, Rufus was the thing that you were scared of underneath the bed when you were little – you simply constructed what you feared to protect yourself. Mmm… interesting,' he mused.

Paul went quiet for a while and then read some of his notes. Then he beamed: 'Unfair accusations,' he stated. 'That's what this is all about.'

He went on to explain that the flight out of Nigeria caused all sorts of problems with friends being locked up and bad things being said about me, but the accusations were unfair. I had not set out to cause these problems. Things beyond my control had happened causing these consequences.

'It was not your *fault*, but it *was* your responsibility.'

Paul was clearly very excited to find the answer to my problems:

'Your subconscious has linked the events as a child being locked in a dark cupboard for wetting the bed to the events as an adult. You were probably hand walking around the cupboard when you were locked in there,' he finished.

We both considered this for some time. Paul continued with further therapy going back to those events. Under hypnosis, he put me as an adult with little Michael in the situation in my grandmother's house. Paul got me to open the door of the cupboard and 'hug' the little Michael. It was a highly emotional experience.

I never sleepwalked again.

CHAPTER 35

The Appeal Court Hearing

The whole process of taking Shirlstar to court and then to the appeal court took literally years. The Appeal Court was a very busy place. By this time, I was working for Britannia Airways.

Eventually, a date came through for the early summer of 1990. Nick rang me to say it was scheduled; Nick Yell had had the documents through.

'Strange thing is that it's being heard by the very top judges in England, Mike,' he said.

'Who is that?' I asked.

'Lord Justice Donaldson, Master of the Rolls. That is the title of the most senior judge. Masters of the Rolls do not normally hear cases unless they are of the most important nature. He is hearing this with Lord Justice Taylor, who was in charge of the Hillsborough Inquiry and Lord Justice Staughton, he is involved in some contentious matters in horse racing.'

'Perhaps they were intrigued about the case,' I replied.

It had taken a year to get to the Appeal Court after winning in the High Court, during which time I had been living in the cottage in Surrey with Catriona.

Catriona continued with her adopted attitude that 'we' were a couple again, but I never went along with this. I had been in the spare room since she returned from her jaunt with Eddie Tracy. It was impossible to move on with my life until all this legal action had been finished one way or another.

The driving school business (yes, I know – *why?*) was not going too well. Shock, horror and surprise! Self-employed driving instructors were basically inclined not to work if pay was not linked to work. It was beginning to lose money. I had to step in and wind it up.

This was not easy and involved meeting each of the 12 instructors and giving them the boot, taking the car back and selling it.

I let Mike Curtiss carry on in our town because he was motivated and had always worked hard. He needed a chance to continue earning for a while; Mike was applying to become a driving examiner. So, we agreed that he could do this until he was employed as a driving examiner. I have great affection for Mike and Catherine Curtiss. They were very supportive during this difficult time, and I also felt that I'd helped to get their lives on an even keel during the years I knew them.

Catriona took up a job as secretary to the manager of the Hilton Hotel at Gatwick, so this kept her occupied.

The Appeal Court is a magnificent building, both impressive and intimidating at the same time – which I guess was the intention.

Nick Munns, Nick Yell and I were all very anxious when walking into the courtroom, and I am not normally one who is prone to being anxious.

We took up our seats on the right-hand side of the benches in front of the judges' seats that were set way above us.

On the other side was the Shirlstar team. As before, there were loads of them! Longmore, Ben's barrister, was in the front with his assistant next to him and a clutch of solicitors behind.

We chatted about the preparations for the appeal. The three of us had worked together again, but Nick Yell had spent a substantial amount of time preparing, especially when he heard who was hearing the appeal. Hence the £13,000!

'It is not often a junior barrister presents a case in the Court of Appeal, Mike,' Nicholas said, 'let alone in front of the Master of the Rolls, and I do not want to fuck it up!'

Nick Munns and I laughed at that, but in truth the judges at this level are pretty well the ultimate in intellectual superiority. For Nick Yell, this was a test that could affect his career depending on how it went. For me, it was also a case of either I win and survive financially or lose and face bankruptcy.

High stakes, indeed.

When I talked about the events in the Appeal Court to friends, I always described it as incredible theatre and fascinating to experience, if it hadn't been for so much riding on the result.

This was the culmination of the whole 'have you ever played poker with a multimillionaire?' threat from Ben Slade, yet I had stayed with him all the way.

Shirlstar had lost pretty convincingly in the high court, but he wanted to try to scare me with the cost of going with him to the Appeal Court. Ben just had not bargained for my having a house I'd made a good profit from and dear Charles Gaskill of NatWest for standing me the money for this part.

So here we were, sitting in the Appeal Court with not a clue as to what would come to pass over the next three days.

I looked across to Ben (who had turned up) and Longmore and smiled a big smile. They just scowled. My main aim had been achieved. All Ben's skulduggery had been exposed through the court and was now in the public domain, so I felt I was holding the high moral ground.

Below the judges' seats, the clerk of the court and the ushers and assistants were all going through the pre-trial preparations. After some time (court rarely starts on time), the clerk left the court quietly through a side door. Clerks of the court seem to be able to communicate with the judges by telepathy. They seemed to know when the process of bringing the judges into court was to begin and, of course, this was of the judge's behest.

He returned a few minutes later, stood at the side of his seat and called:

'All rise!'

We all obediently stood. The three judges walked solemnly into the area behind their seats, moved in front of their seats, bowed and then sat. My heart rate increased markedly.

'Be seated,' barked the usher.

We all sat.

The three judges looked at the assembled mass of lawyers on Slade's side and then looked at Nick Yell, Nick Munns and I on the other side, with Catriona sitting in the public seats just behind. It must have seemed extremely unbalanced.

Donaldson had a small, very worn wig on his small, grey-haired head. He had brown-framed reading glasses which perched on the end of his nose. He peered over the glasses.

As one would expect, he projected an air of great authority. Taylor and Staughton, again with small wigs, were also taking in the view. Taylor especially had an air of mischievousness. He had bright eyes and a smile subtly around the edges of his mouth. Staughton was just very, very serious.

With no nonsense, Donaldson barked:

'Mr Longmore, as this is your appeal, please present your case.'

Longmore stood up, 'My Lords, my client has appealed this case due to the errors made in the trial which we believe culminated in a wrong decision,' he started.

And then the sparring began...

'So, you are saying that Judge Gower, with all his experience, made a mistake?' intervened Taylor. 'Please explain this error.'

God! I was so glad I was not Longmore. He was taken apart in the most humiliating way. The three Appeal Court judges passed him from one to the other, like a tag wrestling match.

Taylor liked to lean forward, imposing himself on Longmore from the great vantage point of the Appeal Court judge's seat – something which I guessed they used to intimidate crap barristers.

Longmore then started with the same defence that he had used with Judge Gower in the original trial.

As I had committed an illegal act by taking off without permission, the contract was invalid. You cannot have a legally enforceable contract for an illegal act.

In other words, if you hire Nigerian hitmen to bump off your annoying wife (tempting, I know) and they fail, you cannot sue them to get your money back. And, no, I have not done that! My first wife was very annoying, but I never considered Nigerian hitmen. Albanian hitmen are much more reliable... only kidding!

By the way, obviously, I did get married again, to Heather (and she is absolutely wonderful) – the rule is you only do it twice!

What I found out later is that the judges would have read the transcripts of the original trial. Nick Yell said you become very good at fast reading as you become a more experienced barrister. So these guys were super quick. They also grasped the fundamentals and intricacies of the details very efficiently.

Donaldson was particularly theatrical in his behaviour. As they listened, Donaldson would demonstrate frustration by pushing his old wig to the back of his head and his glasses up onto his forehead. He would then drop his head forward and the glasses would fall onto his nose as he fired an Exocet missile question at Longmore. When the answer was not sensible, Donaldson would, with elbows on the desk, pull the wig back down low over his forehead with both hands. It was an act that resembled the 'face in hands' or, in other words, 'for God's sake, man!' – very entertaining.

I looked over at Ben Slade sitting behind Longmore. He had a face of thunder as the three judges demolished his brief.

Longmore was becoming very flustered. Nick Munns, Nicholas Yell, Catriona and I were really just an audience at this stage.

Taylor then interrupted Longmore:

'Mr Longmore, if I go to a wildlife park to see the lions with my family and there is a twenty mph speed limit in the park and the lions start chasing the car, I may have to go above twenty mph to escape the lions.' He leant forward to emphasise his point. 'With respect, sir, nobody is going to prosecute me for exceeding the speed limit, are they?'

As Taylor ended with the question, Donaldson leant forward, his glasses dropping forward onto the tip of his nose. He fixed Mr Longmore with an intimidating stare over the top of his glasses.

'It was an illegal act to take off without permission...' squeaked Longmore, impotently.

As Longmore repeated the same point, Donaldson's wig came forward with his hands covering his face in exasperation, again.

'But, Mr Longmore, what about the lions?' Donaldson muttered into his hands like a frustrated parent.

Longmore tried dressing up the statement in a slightly different guise; it was as if this was the only ammunition in his armoury. (I'm glad he wasn't representing me in the divorce from my first wife!)

'But what about the lions?' piped up Staughton, continuing the line of questioning set up by Taylor.

Longmore did not change tack. Ben looked even redder.

'But what about the lions, Mr Longmore?' came the response.

It was rather like watching three cats playing with a mouse for fun before the inevitable end.

That inevitable end came, rather unexpectedly at about 11:45 that morning. There was a brief conversation on the bench between the three judges and then Donaldson spoke:

'We are going to rise now to reach our decision in this matter. Mr Yell,' Donaldson addressed Nick, 'we will not be requiring your assistance in reaching our decision.'

In those few eloquently delivered words, we had won.

The only reason for not wanting assistance from Nick Yell was that they were finding in our favour. Otherwise, they would have had to hear from us to counter Longmore's arguments.

'All rise,' commanded the chief usher.

We all obediently rose and bowed. The three judges rose, bowed and then filed out of the court.

At that moment, I did not fully understand what Donaldson's statement implied, but I had a fairly good idea. I turned to Nick Yell and saw that Cheshire cat expression on his face. This confirmed what I thought it meant.

The three of us began grinning and had a victory 'man hug'.

'Nick,' I said, addressing Nick Yell, 'you just earnt thirteen grand without uttering a single word.' Pausing for effect, I continued, 'And you deserve every penny.'

Catriona joined in the hug, there was an enormous sense of relief for us all. I felt my shoulders drop as the tension evaporated. It was a palpable relief; it was over.

We were informed by the clerk that their Lordships would return to court in approximately two hours to deliver their verdict. No doubt after a very nice lunch with some humour at Longmore's expense.

Ben's entourage evaporated out of the courtroom, leaving the four of us laughing at lions and enjoying the moment.

We eventually left the court and adjourned ourselves to a coffee bar near the court to await the final moment. We chatted happily about the morning's events.

Just before two o'clock, we were back in court awaiting the judgement.

Eventually, the three judges filed back in. We all bowed and they sat.

'Mr Longmore, thank you for assisting us in considering this case.'

Donaldson spoke very respectfully to Longmore. He then went on to give a lengthy summary of the issues surrounding the case before finally delivering the final blow to Ben Slade's enterprise.

'We find in favour of Captain Howard,' Donaldson continued. And with that, it was confirmed that we had won. 'Further to the finding, we award costs against the plaintiff and interest on the amount claimed.'

And that was the 'killer blow' for Ben. All my costs were to be paid. I'm quite sure I heard that 'mop' flopping in Ben's direction!

This meant that Shirlstar had been found against comprehensively. And I was not bankrupted! Nick Yell, Nick Munns and I said our farewells after a long chat outside the impressive arched front of the Appeal Court. We agreed to meet up at a very nice restaurant (on me) once the payment had been forthcoming from Shirlstar.

I now had to have a heart-to-heart conversation with Catriona about the future (or lack of it, where I was concerned).

As explained earlier, I had continued to live in the Oxted cottage in the spare room. It was simply impossible for me to do anything else whilst this case was ongoing. Just the financial commitment to the case meant that there was practically no elbow room to change my situation. There was no doubt that our relationship was over, but, as mentioned previously, it would have been very convenient for Catriona if I had continued to look after her. But the huge betrayal in South Africa could not be expunged.

I took her to the coffee bar over the road that we had been in earlier. It was quite large and very quiet at that time of the day, especially in the rear part where we sat.

'Now the case is over, it is time to discuss the future,' I began. 'I am going to leave the cottage and move to my own house once the money comes through,' I told her.

I was speaking quietly to control the emotional response that was bound to come.

'What I am going to propose is that I will leave you with the cottage and the contents with a few small exceptions,' I explained. I wanted to be very fair. 'I do not want to leave you without a decent foundation for both your and Simone's future.'

It was a very difficult situation. I did feel a great deal of responsibility. But, in the end, she had gone off and shagged Eddie Tracy. This was a betrayal.

But I did not want to be cruel. It was, however, now time for me to begin rebuilding my life.

As I expected, she reacted in a highly emotional way, crying and howling very loudly. This brought our discussion to the attention of the waiters and other customers.

Unfortunately, the assumption of the waiters was that I was the bad boy being horrid to this poor, poor little girl. One approached and asked her if she was okay. Catriona just replied incomprehensibly.

'Listen, mate,' he said, pointing his finger at me, 'you need to back off, or there will be trouble.'

I fixed the waiter with a hard, no-nonsense stare, 'You have no idea what is going on here, buster, so I will enlighten you. This woman went off and had an affair. Now I am leaving her, but giving her a house and all its contents. Now, I suggest you fuck off and get on with clearing tables before you get out of your depth,' I responded angrily. I continued to hold him with my stare.

Catriona continued to sob uncontrollably in the background.

The waiter went off back to his colleagues and had a discussion, no doubt explaining that 'appearances can be deceptive'.

There was no point in staying any longer. I told Catriona that I was going back to the cottage and that I would see her there when she had pulled herself together.

You are probably thinking, *Mike, that's a bit rough on her.* I agree. Yes, it was, but there was no easy way, even though I had thought about it carefully, to dress up the news.

Catriona had used me as a crutch for a long time. Her coming back to the cottage was an example of that. It was now time for her to take responsibility for her own life, and her own decisions, without being able to use me to run to if it went wrong.

Tough love, yes, but I did also need to look after myself, too.

CHAPTER 36

Summer 1986
Ken and Angus Come Home

I had continued contact with the Foreign Office during the whole time since returning to the UK from Abidjan and now knew the officials on the Africa desk by their first names.

Whilst they could not tell me any detail, they did hint that there was a lot of diplomatic activity where Ken and Angus were concerned.

I was also in regular contact with Paul Halloran of *Private Eye*. God knows where he had got his information from, but he did say that there were negotiations surrounding the Mossad agents and Nigerians in jail in the UK for the attempted kidnapping. Paul said that they were trying to keep it very quiet, but there was going to be some sort of 'swap'.

I did not hear anything about the actual release of the Mossad agents and Nigerians; they must have been put on a military flight out of Brize Norton or somewhere. What I did hear from Bristows firstly, but also from the Foreign Office, was that an appeal was to commence in Lagos.

When I heard this, I began to cross everything, touch wood, pray; whatever I thought I could draw on to get Ken and Angus back.

From the very beginning of their arrest, I was completely helpless in being able to do anything. From every living moment since they were grabbed in Ikeja, there was a preoccupation in the back of my mind that they were in Kiri kiri jail and this was my responsibility. As I said earlier, I do not suppose that Ben Slade gave them a second thought.

The appeal in Lagos did, indeed, go ahead. It lasted a few days with some very noisy and contentious behaviour in the Court of Appeal there.

Eventually, the Appeal Court reached a decision. Ken and Angus were released.

I remember the words in the summing-up of the senior judge:

'The jailing of these men was a travesty of Nigerian justice. This has brought Nigerian law into disrepute around the world. Mr Patterson and Mr Clark, I apologise to you on behalf of Nigeria. You are released from detention and free to leave Nigeria forthwith.'

Ken and Angus were on a flight home within a few hours of their release.

It was during the last days of living in the cottage when the Foreign Office rang to inform me that Ken and Angus were on a BCal flight home. To describe the relief hearing of their release is very difficult. To say 'it was a weight off my shoulders' was a grave understatement.

A few days later, the phone rang in the cottage. It was a bright, sunny day and the sunlight streamed through the window, illuminating the area between the kitchen and dining room where the phone sat.

'Hello,' I said.

'Mike?'

'Yes,' I confirmed. I sort of recognised the voice.

'It's Ken.'

I was completely taken aback, not expecting a call from him at all.

'I just wanted to say, it's okay.' He then just hung up.

It was just a few words, which, as I write them, bring me to tears.

EPILOGUE

It took some time for the money to come through from Shirlstar following the appeal, but it did eventually arrive. Until then, I could not practically or physically leave the cottage in Oxted.

As I said earlier, during the period of taking action against Shirlstar, I decided to move on from executive jet flying, where, as explained earlier, your career was at the mercy of the economic cycle. Cycle goes down, posh jet gets sold and you are on night mail runs or the dole…!

So, I made the decision to apply for a proper job, in other words, apply to the airlines. This should give me some protection from the vagaries of the world economic cycle!

British Airways needed experienced pilots at the time and had contacted me to attend an interview. I'm not sure how they found me, but at the time they were clearly desperate!

Amongst the pilots at Biggin Hill, we used to call British Airways the 'Hounslow Flying Club'. This was because, at the time (he says to cover himself from being sued!), they did not have the best of reputations and the airline was run for the benefit of the senior pilots. Probably, wrongly on reflection, I did not really want to work for them.

However, I did go through the interview process. At the same time, I had applied to Britannia Airways (now TUI). Britannia had a very high standard of training and a very good reputation for the operation of their aircraft.

It was a day of going through (then) new and modern interview techniques. Before this, we pilots used to get hired by going into a flight simulator and showing you could fly a bloody aeroplane. However, human resources (sometimes known as human remains) hijacked this process.

Along with me were around 20 to be put through this torture.

Firstly, there was a couple of hours undertaking psychometric assessments and other intelligence tests (God knows how I got through these).

If you managed to survive this, and some didn't, you were moved on to the 'group exercise' part of the process.

We were all organised into groups of four. I was put together with three ex-RAF 'Phantom' fast jet pilots.

The task was to build out of some Meccano-type material, and I quote, 'A structure on which you can place a jug of water and rotate it remotely through three hundred and sixty degrees.' As stated by our HR observer holding their 'very important' clipboard in their hand.

'You have five minutes to discuss your plan and then ten minutes to construct your structure without talking,' he added.

God, I thought, *this is such bullshit!* The expression on the faces of my fast jet pilot colleagues showed the same feelings.

We built the structure and duly placed the jug of water on the thing and began rotating it. The jug fell off. All four of us laughed.

As the day went on, the original 20 were reduced as people were chopped, but amazingly, somehow, I was still there. Slowly, during the day, any already thin enthusiasm for British Airways had deteriorated.

The last part of the process was 'the interview'.

I was pretty well the last victim of the survivors for interview, so I had a very long wait. It was about five in the afternoon by the stage

I was called in.

I was ushered into the interview room and confronted by a row of four people, three men and one woman. I sat down in the chair in the centre of the room.

They asked lots of 'trap' questions.

'We spend a lot of money on marketing and promotion. How do you think you can assist in promoting British Airways?' was an example.

'Being the best possible pilot and ensuring that British Airways aircraft are operated in the safest possible way,' is the (inane and bullshit) correct answer.

I'm afraid that after 20 or so minutes of this, I reached the limit of my tolerance.

The female interviewer, who seemed to be the representative from human resources, piped up for the first time. She was about 30, petite, with long, dark hair and a very, very pretty face.

'Michael, what sort of things do you talk about when you're out socialising with your friends?' she asked.

I'm afraid, by this time, the 'Naughty Mike' took over... I smiled broadly at her, looked at my watch and replied:

'Well, you cannot be doing this for too much longer; why don't you join me and find out for yourself?'

Clang went the 'you've just blown it, Mike' bell.

She had to suppress a smile, but the other three looked extremely stony-faced.

Funnily enough, I did not get the job. Can't think why!

At least I did not answer the question 'Where do you see yourself in five years?' with the answer 'On top of one of your hostesses' like one of my Biggin Hill mates – he didn't get the job either!

I did get the job at Britannia after an interview with the chief pilot and chief training captain followed by a simulator ride; much more my style. I finished up flying Boeing 737, 757 and 767 aeroplanes all around the world, which was hugely enjoyable.

Following the time with Britannia, I took early retirement and now train and examine corporate jet pilots in flight simulators.

P.S.

As an 'unknown' author, I would like to make a request. As I have said in the dedications at the beginning of this story, My wife, Heather, my sister Jenny and I have financed the publishing of this book. If you think it has been any good, please can you recommend it to your friends and put some feedback on my Amazon account.

I have two other books ready to write – "A Cold, Cold Dish and 'Tilley Lamps and Tunnels'; The first one is already half written (please see my website for details) and I need the 'leg up' from you readers to help me get these into print.

Thank you for your help!

Cheers,

Mike.

FOOTNOTE

All the events in this book are true to the best of my knowledge and belief. The matters that relate to Shirlstar Container Transport and Sir Benjamin Slade are a matter of public record having been produced in evidence in both the High Court and Appeal Court in London.

I still retain the transcripts of the Court and that of the Judges both here in the UK and Nigeria.

Printed in Great Britain
by Amazon

As we passed 20,000 feet, I turned further right onto a heading of north-north-west; towards Abidjan. Yay!! We had not been shot down.

I was pretty sure, by this stage, that the Alpha Jet had lost contact with us. He must have been running low on fuel by now, especially if he'd been holding in the air for a significant time waiting for his 'target' to take off. They would not have known exactly what time I was going to go.

So, this was a moment for the pressure to come off a little and for me to collect my thoughts – back to the routine of flying a jet aeroplane.

The HS125 was designed as a two-crew aeroplane, but as Catriona obviously was not a pilot – I was flying it effectively as single crew, i.e. operating G-LORI on my own. Having said that, I could reach all the controls from the captain's seat except the pilot oxygen controls and the standby cabin pressurisation system over on the co-pilots side. However, if either of these were needed on this particular flight, it *really* would not be our day!

The next problem was that when I tried to engage the autopilot to give me a free pair of hands, it wouldn't engage, so there was no alternative but to 'hand fly' the aeroplane. Fortunately, as I'd flown old jets quite often with no functioning autopilot, I was used to hand flying at high altitude.

'Bollocks!' I said out loud.

'What's the matter?' asked Catriona.

'Bloody autopilot isn't working,' I replied.

'What does that mean?' she asked.

'Effectively, I have to work a lot harder hand flying at high altitude and navigating at the same time. It's not a huge problem, as I've flown lots of stuff without one working,' I replied.

All pilots use something called a 'Jeppesen' navigation chart to navigate the 'airways'. Airways are like motorways in the sky, following lines between navigation beacons. I'd had one of these on my lap since take-off.